The
Stone
Pillow

The Life and Times of Jona Lerman

Arlene Kurtis and Jona Lerman

*To the Goldstein
Family
with my best wishes
Jona Lerman*

A Globus Book

This is a Globus Book

Published by Globus Books,
P.O. Box 203, Lake Worth, Florida 33460

Library of Congress Catalog Card Number: 99-64708

Typography/Design & Map by LDH Communications, Inc.

Printed in the United States

First Edition, Published July 1999
Second Printing, December 1999
Third Printing, April 2000

To order, contact Globus Books
P.O. Box 203, Lake Worth, Florida, 33460
U.S. $15.00, $3.00 Shipping & Handling
ISBN 0-9676869-0-3

1. Israel; 2. Haganah; 3. Poland; 4. Holocaust

Actual events are portrayed as they occurred. Some names have been changed to conform to American spellings.

Front cover, Jona Lerman protecting the settlements for the Haganah, 1936, Palestine

This memoir is lovingly dedicated to all the idealistic men and women of Eretz Yisroel who, with their minds, bodies and souls, made possible the State of Israel in our time.

ACKNOWLEDGMENTS

For more than four years we, Jona Lerman and Arlene Kurtis, have collaborated to create this memoir of Jona's life in Poland, in pre-state Israel and throughout the early years of the nation of Israel, as well as his experiences in the United States. Our mutual goal was to bring these happenings as close to factual as possible.

Jona contributed his store of personal memories while Arlene researched the periods in which the incidents of this memoir took place in order to set them in historical context. Finally, Arlene put the whole into narrative form.

Our task was made easier due to the patient and valuable assistance of Anny Lerman who read and re-read the manuscript and made important suggestions. She also shared with us her own youthful experiences in Austria and her escape to Palestine one step ahead of the Nazis.

Miles Lerman was most helpful in describing his memories of family life in Poland and later in World War II.

We are indebted to the Harold and Adeline Kramer Judaica Library of Temple Emanu-El, Palm Beach, Florida and its librarian, Irene Levin Wixman, for making available its vast store of research materials.Our thanks go also to Evelyn Singer of White Plains, New York for her encouragement in developing the manuscript and her valuable suggestions. Alan A. Kurtis, Arlene's husband, David Bittner, journalist, and friends and relatives also offered insightful comments for which we are most grateful.

Our purpose in undertaking this collaborative effort is to bear witness to the dramatic circumstances that lit the flame which brought the State of Israel into being. It is our fervent hope that future generations will cherish that nation, and that it will be a continued source of truth, justice and peace for all time.

Arlene Kurtis and Jona Lerman
Palm Beach, Florida, July, 1999

Table of Contents

DAVID BEN GURION
ON THE HAGANAH

David Ben Gurion issued this statement on May 31, 1948:

With the establishment of the State of Israel the Hagana was transformed from an underground organization into a regular army. The people of this country and Jews everywhere owe an enormous debt to the Hagana for its accomplishments over the years, from the period when it consisted of a few isolated individuals in Petah Tikva, Rishon LeZion, Gedera, Rosh Pina, Zikhron Yacov, and Metulla, through the days of Hashomer, the Jewish Legion, the First World War, the defense of Tel Hai, the period of constant growth between the two World Wars — including the establishment of the Jewish Auxiliary Police during the 1936–39 riots — the setting up of the Palmah and the Field Units, the mass volunteering for service in the Second World War and the establishment of the Jewish Brigade, up until the decisive struggle which began on November 30, 1947, and has continued until this very day.

Without the Hagana's experience, loyalty, and bravery, we could not have withstood the terrible and sanguine test of these last six months, and would not have survived to see the establishment of the State of Israel. The story of the Hagana will shine forth forever in the annals of Jewish history.

PART I

THE BOY WHO ASKED
TOO MANY QUESTIONS

Chapter 1

A STRANGE BURIAL

It is the year 1923. In a small city in Poland, a storm is raging. But it is midnight, and the people sleep. The Jewish section of town, where fervent Jews reside, has a small synagogue with a wooden bathhouse near it used for ritual cleansing.

The Jewish cemetery lies on the outskirts of town. Water is pooling in a part of the graveyard that slopes down toward a marsh. A tall pole planted there begins to totter. The wind swirls. The pole springs out of the ground.

The pole, a blackened log, begins to move through the wind toward the Jewish part of town. Thunder rumbles. Lightning illuminates the scene. The bathhouse glistens in the rain.

The pole is horizontal now. Like a battering ram, it smashes into the middle of the wooden bathhouse.

The rain subsides. The town sleeps. The destruction will be discovered at dawn.

．　．　．

The morning of the storm, a man named Asher had been buried in the bog in the cemetery. In a community of deeply religious Jews, Asher was an outcast because he was a non-believer.

Asher openly scoffed at the community's strict observance of rules that were made thousands of years ago, and added to again and again. One could remain a Jew, he said, only by struggling with the modern world.

The young men of the town were drawn to Asher and would visit his thatched-roof cottage to talk with him about the currents of modern thinking. A few toyed with the idea of leaving their town of Tomaszov. In that city most everyone was poor, and the Poles tormented the Jews and cursed at them. It was fascinating to hear about places where Jews had more opportunities, studied at the university, shaved their beards, and danced with women.

Asher made his own rules. He smoked on the Sabbath and dined on non-kosher food. The young men, who followed their parents' beliefs at home, dared to experiment with breaking the rules at Asher's house.

Since childhood Asher had been sickly. And one Saturday night the young men coming to his home discovered to their dismay that he had died. They found him lying in his bed looking peaceful, his covers neatly tucked around him.

The elders were summoned. They shook their heads.

"A sad life," one father brooded.

Now came the question of burial. What to do with a non-believer?

The leaders of the small synagogue were in conflict. One suggestion was to bury him in the cemetery for non-Jews. Another was to put him in the city grave, reserved for unknowns or travelers.

"Ay, how can we do that?" argued one elderly member. "His father was our Torah reader. He must be given a Jewish funeral and burial."

"He will defile our holy ground!" protested another, shaking his bearded face in warning.

"We'll leave it to the rabbi," they agreed.

The rabbi, a quiet, thoughtful man, steeped in Torah, meditated awhile and then said: "This man mocked us. He trampled on our laws. He was a sinner. He must be made an example of — else the young will continue to follow men like him. This is my decision. We will bury him within the cemetery gates, but not on sacred ground."

"Where is that?" one asked.

"The swamp," another replied. "A brilliant solution, Rabbi."

"Further," said the rabbi, holding up a slender finger, "we will take a pole, cover it with pitch and place it on his grave as a sign. The blackened log will be a reminder to all who disobey."

The body was prepared and interred in a corner of the cemetery too wet for use as a burial ground. A tall log, that had been a telegraph pole until wires were moved, was covered with tar and placed at the head of the plot.

The young men who came to the gravesite were horrified.

"You call yourselves holy men. How can you do this!" one of Asher's friends declared angrily. "From dust to dust, the Torah says, but this body will molder here — it's nothing but a travesty!"

"Shush," his mortified father exclaimed throughout the young man's outburst.

Grumbling, Asher's friends left the cemetery whispering together.

That night the heavens opened. Rain and wind slashed the town. At first light a drizzle was still falling as the shamos, the man who opened the small synagogue, made his way through the muddy streets.

As he approached the ritual bathhouse near the synagogue, he let out a wail.

The front of the bathhouse was bashed in and a huge log lay inside the wooden building, its blackened top resting in the bathing pool.

The shamos was terrified. The log was covered with pitch. He looked behind him. Was this the log from Asher's grave?

The shamos was quaking. How could the pole, twenty feet long, come out of the ground and into the mikvah? The cemetery was a mile away. Even the most terrible storm could not pin-point such damage. He slogged down the road to see if the cemetery pole was still there.

More congregants arrived to say their morning prayers. All stood open-mouthed — awaiting the arrival of the rabbi.

Guided by several worshipers, the rabbi hurried toward the mikvah. He stood aghast. He scanned the horizon where the cemetery lay.

"The pole is no longer in the bog," groaned the shamos, who returned breathless from the graveyard.

The rabbi covered his face with his thin white hands. He looked up to the leaden sky for a long moment. Then he spoke.

"I have sinned," he intoned. "God has sent us a message. This blackened pole was His messenger. God is telling us He loved Asher as his child. I have caused a desecration.

"Oh, woe," he moaned, and he began beating his chest as he recited the Shemah — "Hear, O Israel, the Lord our God, the Lord is One" words that are central to the Jewish faith.

"Because we buried Asher in the swamp, because we placed this hideous pole over his grave, we must make amends," the rabbi said slowly. "God has shown me His wrath, and I quake before it.

"This is what we must do. We must rebury Asher on sacred ground. Further, we must fast until the funeral and observe the seven days of mourning for him. The entire congregation must mourn. We must also clean the pitch off the log and have a funeral for it — because it came from God's hand into our mikvah. It was His messenger, and we must therefore honor it and bury it in our sacred ground with all rights. We will observe the seven days of mourning for it also.

"This is my absolute understanding," the rabbi declared. Looking from one man another. "Let's begin the task at once."

So the shamos and the pious men spread the word in the community. The pole was withdrawn from the damaged mikvah. Solvents were procured, and volunteers scraped and rubbed the pole, cleaning it as best they could. The following day, helped by the young men, they dug a twenty-foot-long trench across the cemetery field. Asher's body, wrapped in a new white shroud, was carefully laid in a dry and sacred plot. Then the pole was lifted into the trench. Each man took the shovel in turn to place the loose dirt over the pole until it was covered by the earth.

The congregants, men, women and children, walked away with heads bowed to begin a week of mourning. None of the elders noticed the young men, tears rimming their eyes, raising their fists at one another in salute.

But standing just behind his father and brother, dressed in black like the others, the curls of his earlocks dangling, stood thirteen year-old Jona Lerman, who was as solemn and fearful as the rest. As he turned, he watched the young men raise their fists and clap one another's shoulders.

Jona fully believed God's wrath had sent the log into the bathing pool of the mikvah and they were all guilty of a misdeed. So why, he wondered fearfully, were Asher's friends congratulating each other?

Chapter 2

THE RELUCTANT PUPIL

On a warm day in the summer of 1910, in the city of Tomaszov, province of Lubelski, Poland, a lusty baby boy was born, squalling loudly as he made his entrance into a very special world.

He was given the name Jona, the fourth child in the family of Yachad and Israel Lerman.

The Lermans had been brought together by a matchmaker when Yachad Feldzon was nineteen and Israel Lerman, twenty-one. Both were from poor families, but the matchmaker saw that they were able and bright as well as fervent believers in the Hasidic way of life.

Fortunately, Yachad and Israel were pleased with each other on the two occasions before their marriage when they were permitted to meet. After the wedding, Israel Lerman moved from his small town of Shrebrashim to Tomaszov to open a grocery store with Herz Feldzon, Yachad's brother.

The men were energetic, and soon they were buying for smaller stores, becoming wholesalers. Before Jona was born, a terrible fire raced through town, burning the roofs covered with straw, and consuming the wooden houses. The Lerman store went up in flames, but sometime after, the partners were able to build a sturdy three-story brick house with room for both families to live in, with a store below, and a warehouse in the rear.

Yachad ran the wholesale grocery business from the ground floor of their house and managed the books for the family business.

Because the Jewish custom is to name newborns for a beloved parent or grandparent who had died, cousins often had the same name. Confusion reigned unless some descriptive label was attached. Among the several Yachads in her family, Jona's mother was known as the "Blinde Yachad" because she used a reading glass when she had to examine a bill or a label. A soft smile nearly always graced Yachad's pleasant face, even when she overheard her exaggerated nickname.

Israel Lerman was affectionately known as Srulke-Lerman, the names linked together. A man of serious demeanor, he could see the humorous side of life as well, and often had a joking remark to make about someone who acted pompous or foolish in the small synagogue where the family worshiped.

Srulke was of medium height, with a fine straight nose and deep-set dark eyes. His curly black beard grew in irregular clumps, trimmed only by singeing the ends; He wore the traditional black coat and brimmed cap of the Hasidim even when he traveled to the cosmopolitan Ukranian city of Lemberg. Under this hat was still another hat, a small skull cap, so that even indoors his head remained covered.

The Lerman home and warehouse was on one of the main dirt roads leading to the center of the Jewish section. It was not far from their small synagogue, which backed up to a still larger one.

Their shul was unadorned, its bare interior lit by a few windows by day and by gas-light lamps after dark. The focus of attention was the sturdy oak ark along the eastern wall. In it were stored the several precious parchment scrolls on which a scribe had carefully inked the words of the first five books of the Scriptures.

Even though this was a community of hand-to-mouth tailors

and shopkeepers, the Torahs they owned were housed inside the ark richly lined with wine-colored velvet. The Torahs were protected by ivory silk covers, each embellished with golden thread spelling out in Hebrew letters symbolic words, and the names of the donors of the covers. A silver pointer hung from a chain around the scroll's wooden shaft.

Jona's eyes widened when the cover was removed and a scroll gently laid on the broad table covered by a silken cloth. He held his breath as the Torah was unwound and the reader began. What did this torrent of words mean? When would he understand?

Just past three years of age, he would begin the struggle for answers. The boys in the community started school early so that many could read the Scriptures by the time they were nine. Anticipating a quick unfolding of the secret words, Jona was downcast after his first days in the school. He sat on a hard bench wedged between two ragged boys. It was difficult to squirm, so Jona rubbed his thighs with his hands and bent back and forth in frustration. He wanted to get up and flee. Only the teacher's piercing black eyes kept him in his place.

It was the one-room home of the melamed whose job it was to teach these thirty or so boys their letters, big black symbols arranged on worn cards. He would do his best, for little pay, but it was no easy task to keep his young pupils' attention.

"Stop moving, Jona, or I'll take the ruler to you," commanded the gaunt black-robed man to the boy before him. Jona knew the sting of the ruler on his knuckles because he had been whacked once already, and this was only the first week of school.

"Melamed, Melamed!" called Jona. "I have to go outside!"

"Outside! Outside! What do you mean, outside?"

"To the out-house, out-house," Jona whined.

"Go already," said the disgusted teacher.

Once released, Jona looked around. Two peasant boys were riding bicycles down the road, laughing and screaming.

"Hey, Jyid," one hooted at Jona. "Why don't you cut your hair, Jyid?"

Jona stuck his tongue out at them.

"Dirty Jyid, dirty Jyid," they chorused, riding past. Jona shut himself in the out-house, stamping his feet in anger,

I should go to my mother, he thought. He could eat the sweet raisins in a barrel near the counter of her store. But she had placed her hands on his head when he left for heder that morning, and he knew she would be angry to see him home before the session ended. He trudged back to the schoolroom.

He would prefer sitting in the small synagogue next to his father, even though he had to keep still. There were interesting people to look at, and whispered conversations to listen to. He felt a surge of power hearing his father recite the blessing in front of the congregation before the Torah was read. It was as if his father's distinction flowed to him.

Peddlers and beggars working their way through the town would turn up at the synagogue in time for services. They brought news of towns through which they had passed and were usually invited for a meal by a friendly face. On Sabbath eve it was considered an obligation to see that each worshiper had a home to go to. The poorest Jew, who could not afford a whole chicken, who made do with the feet and gizzard to enrich his wife's soup pot, would offer to share bread with a stranger. Srulke-Lerman took pride in inviting the least fortunate visitors knowing he could well afford to feed ones in need.

Jona wrinkled his nose sitting next to a guest at supper who smelled like the horse barn where he had probably slept on his way to Tomaszov. Catching his mother's disapproving stare, Jona leaned over his roasted chicken and breathed in that delicious aroma instead.

The shul also sheltered the neighborhood's unfortunates. A kindly blind man often slept on the benches at night after roaming the town during the day. He knew everyone's lineage. After hearing Jona's voice, he'd whisper — "Ah, the Groisse Jona, your father is Srulke-Lerman, son of Shmuel. Your mother is Yachad, daughter of Aaron Feldzon..." and so on.

By the time he was four and his little cousin Jona was born, Jona had earned the title of "Groisse."

Although as a group, Jews were held in contempt by most of the non-Jews of Tomaszov, some Jewish men had risen to important posts in the town of 12,000, half of whom were Jews. One was a fire chief and another an assistant to the mayor of the city.

Jona's father and uncle were leading Jewish businessmen of the town. Eventually they owned six flour mills located near wheat farms in the countryside. As their business continued to grow, they won contracts to supply flour to the government storehouses. They also became wholesale liquor merchants, supplying some of the grain used in making spirits. Srulke traveled to Poland's major cities to both buy raw materials and sell their products.

The family also operated several large farms. Jews could not own land in Poland at one time, so land was registered in the name of a non-Jew who was on the payroll simply for lending his name. The farms supplied some vegetables and dairy products to Yachad's grocery, but their main crop was wheat for the flour mills.

Yachad opened her doors each day at five a.m. When he woke, Jona could see from his window the line of horses and wagons outside, their drivers waiting for their turn to load up on supplies and produce of all kinds. The warehouse men would wheel their purchases to the wagons while his mother noted each sale in her large ledger, thanking the merchants by name, and recording their payments carefully.

However, business was only a means to an end for the Hasids. Their goal was to follow the teachings of the Rebbe of Belz, the revered Issachar Dov, who came from a two hundred-year-old dynasty of charismatic leaders whose center was in Belz, a city in the province of Galicia, 40 miles from Tomaszov.

The honorific "Rebbe" was reserved for the esteemed leaders of the several Hasidic streams who passed down their legacy from father to son.

Orthodox Jews who did not follow one of the leaders of the three main Hasidic dynasties in Poland aspired to a more worldly society, sending their children to secular Jewish academies, wearing stylish clothing and enjoying opera houses and foreign travel if they had the means. The young might be active in political circles and support their own Jewish candidates for elections.

The followers of the Rebbe of Belz, on the other hand, believed in the Rebbe's policy of loyalty to the Polish government, and immersion in Torah study rather than the pursuit of worldly affairs. The Rebbe shunned modern thought which departed from Torah teachings. It was rumored by the faithful that the Rebbe lived on air, eating but one spare meal a day, and meditating for days at a time. In those quiet moments, it was said in hushed tones, the Rebbe of Belz spoke directly with God!

When the Rebbe and his entourage traveled in the vicinity of Tomaszov, they would dine with Jona's family, and often spend the night. Feverish preparations took place when the Rebbe was due. Even though the Rebbe ate simply, Idele, the cook, screamed at the kosher butcher to bring her only the best cuts of meat. Her pots were bubbling at dawn and her ovens emitted the tantalizing aroma of baking bread. The children were fed in the kitchen in the evening and admonished to be quiet while the Rebbe was present.

Jona, like the rest of the household, was in awe of the Rebbe. He peeked into the dining room unobserved, marveling at the Rebbe's flowing white beard, and deep but soft voice. The Rebbe looked very old to Jona, as old as the God he imagined in Heaven.

The Belzer Rebbe consulted with Srulke on practical matters concerning his far-flung congregations. Hearing his needs, Srulke would write drafts for substantial sums to be placed at the Rebbe's disposal. Srulke also raised funds from other Hasidim for the Rebbe.

The Belzer Rebbe held court at Jona's house. Impoverished

Jews couldn't travel the forty-odd miles to the court at Belz. Hearing the Rebbe was in Tomaszov, they would wait patiently in line outside the house until Srulke waved them upstairs. Based on the many interpretations by former sages, the Rebbe would decide which ruling applied to the questions before him. These courts could go on for hours.

When the Rebbe heard that Jona had started heder, he called him forward for a blessing. Srulke smiled happily.

But by age four, while Jona could read the letters on the melamed's board, sitting for hours was still painful. When he ran outside after school he could see children tossing a ball back and forth or riding a high-wheel bike.

"Who are these children and why do they play all day when we can't? I want a bicycle, too!" he said, raising his face up to the teacher.

"Those are gentile children. You're a Jewish child. Be quiet and study your letters tonight," the teacher scolded.

Jews used the term "goyim" for those who were not Jewish. The Yiddish word's origin is Hebrew and means "nations" — those nations outside the Jewish nation. As such it has no other connotation. Its translation to English is "gentile."

Jona learned to read with some difficulty. But by the time he was seven, in a more advanced heder, he had not only mastered the Hebrew writing, but he could translate many of the words into Yiddish fairly well.

Yiddish, using Hebrew letters, was the language of the Jews of Poland and much of Europe and Russia. Those in small towns hardly knew the native language. They had Yiddish books, plays and newspapers. Hebrew was not spoken either. It was a holy tongue, reserved only for reading the Torah and other sacred books.

In 1917, when Jona was seven, major changes occurred in Europe. For many decades, parts of Poland had been divided among several European powers. But now, thanks to developments resulting from the Russian Revolution and the onset of

World War I, Polish patriots found an opportunity to reunite their country. However, other forces looked at Poland's open borders as an opportunity to gain control of undefended territory.

General Simon Petliura of the Ukraine, was a ruthless soldier. He mounted a drive to annex the bordering Lubelski region to the territory he controlled. To enrich his legions, he sent his ragtag soldiers into the countryside to raid Jewish neighborhoods, counting on the Poles to stand aside while Jews were attacked. And he was proven correct. Now, Tomaszov lay directly in his path.

In one fateful day, Jona's secluded world would change for him for all time.

Chapter 3

HOME INVASION

Little was said in the children's presence about the troubles, but seven-year old Jona had overheard some curious remarks.

One day his father muttered to Uncle Herz — "It's Chmielnicki all over again." The name meant nothing to him. Then Jona observed his mother and Bayla, the Jewish maid, cover their faces with their hands and rock back and forth while they spoke in hushed voices. He had heard the word "pogrom" uttered by the rabbi in the little synagogue where he prayed. Jona wondered what was going on.

"Who is Chmielnicki?" he asked his mother.

"He was a Cossack horseman who hated Jews and who came through Poland and killed thousands of us," she answered shortly.

"Is he coming again?" Jona wanted to know.

"No, my child," his mother said kindly. "That was many, many years ago — before our time."

"So what is a pogrom?" Jona persisted

"You shouldn't know from it, I pray," his mother whispered.

"It's when Poles who envy Jews start a riot, and turn against us. Go away now, Jona," she demanded.

The adults spoke only in small groups of what might happen now that General Simon Petliura was attacking villages bordering the Ukraine.

Srulke brought back the news from Lemberg. Petliura had rampaged through Jewish towns, flinging children into the road, trampling them beneath their horses' hooves.

Reports that entire families had been shot or stabbed had reached into every Jewish enclave. The Jews prayed their town would be spared. But nothing was done by the authorities to protect them. And the Jews, themselves, had no plan of action. Ultimately, Petliura was responsible for the deaths of 100,000 Jews, before he was murdered, reportedly by a Jew.

For centuries, all the ills of Poland had been blamed on the Jews. Because of their skill at commerce, they had been welcome in Poland before the 12th century when Polish princes invited them to settle in the vast Polish countryside. They would form a merchant class in a still medieval nation that consisted of only peasants and nobles. Casimir the Just believed Jews would bring trade to the country, and encourage investment. The experiment worked. In a mostly agricultural land, the Jewish merchants found customers for the wheat and grain abroad and increased the export of these products. Jews became innkeepers and small tradesmen. Those who learned to read and write in Polish were hired as collecting agents for the nobles who owned the land the peasants farmed.

Because Jews were dealers rather than farmers, and collectors of taxes and rents, the peasants believed all Jews were wealthy. "Rich as a Jew," became a common expression. That the agent or merchant was merely a conduit for the money he handled, was overlooked. The Polish peasants saw Jews as exploiters of their poverty.

In the churches, it was no better. Poles were taught each Sunday that the Jews had condemned their Lord Jesus to death and therefore represented evil. This strong indictment, that supposedly came from Above, was seen as a sanction to plague and slander Jews at every turn. So, not surprisingly, when Petliura's bands smashed Jewish stores and murdered Jews in their path, they found the peasants cheering them on.

Jona had been playing with his young cousin, Uncle Herz's four-year-old son, Little Jona who lived on the top floor. The two were racing around in the open space behind the warehouse, when Yachad called them to supper. The cook was setting out platters of fragrant beef stew and bowls of soup.

Rachel, the young woman who was teaching Jona's older sisters, Pesha and Esther at home, was invited to stay for dinner, and Uncle Herz and his family were dining with them also.

Srulke was telling the diners about a young Hasid he met on the train coming back from a buying trip in Lemberg, as Lvov was then known. They knew many of the same people in the various local towns, and now Srulke was sharing news about these friends.

Bowls of hot vegetable soup were set down before them by the cook, and the conversation tapered off.

As they sipped their soup, a band of Petliura's Cossacks cantered down the road outside of Tomaszov. The Polish peasants in the field hailed the mounted horsemen, their eyes glittering with pride. The leader pulled up his horse.

"We're here for one thing — Jew gold!" the horseman yelled. "Where is the house of your richest Jew?"

The peasants pointed to the road leading to the main street in town, and described the house of Srulke Lerman.

"Go get the bloodsuckers!" one peasant called out, grinning and laughing as the band galloped away.

With a wave of his hand, the leader, followed by his troop, took off on the road to Jona's house.

Minutes passed. Suddenly the Lermans heard the sound of hoofbeats pounding on the hard-packed earth outside their house. The clank of metal rattling at the store downstairs brought Srulke and Herz to their feet.

Srulke pulled off the napkin around his neck, a look of fear in his eyes. Boots were heard on the steps.

In a moment, the door to their apartment was pushed open. A dozen armed men, waving swords and rifles rushed into the room.

Jona's father and his uncle stood before the Cossacks.

"Hold on now!" Srulke said hoarsely, raising one hand.

In response, a hulking horseman struck at Srulke's head with his rifle. Another slashed the uncle's raised arm with a sword. Blood ran down Jona's father's face and flowed onto his beard. Jona's Uncle Herz fell to the floor, blood pooling around him.

"Jyid!" yelled a Cossack. "You disgusting parasites and money-grubbers — it's our turn now. Let's go — open up your sacks of blood money — or we'll tear you apart!"

"Sacks, I don't have sacks of money," cried Jona's father, holding a napkin to his bleeding head and attempting to move toward the door. "Please, don't hurt anyone. Let me go down to the store and get you what we have."

Followed by several Cossacks, his father descended the stairs. With their leader gone, the other armed men began to leer at the young Jewish servant in the household and the teacher, Rachel. The horsemen pushed the women into another room. Fierce shrieks came from behind the door. Jona could make out Bayla's voice, and Rachel's, too. There was the sound of deep grunts and then sobbing.

Jona held his ears and moaned in terror. The others began crying and screaming "Gevalt! — help! help!" Two gunmen lined them up against the wall, holding them back with rifles.

"Shut your Jyid mouths," they commanded. Jona locked eyes with a hairy strong man. Eyes of hatred glared back.

Then they turned to Jona's Aunt Feiga who was nursing her infant son. "Get in the other room," demanded a Cossack.

"Please," cried the aunt, holding firmly to her infant, "have mercy!"

The Cossack answered through clenched teeth — "Let go of

the child! Let go and come with me," he screamed. And placing his sword along Feiga's breast, he made as if to sever it from the baby's mouth.

Jona and the others watched in horror. Little Jona Feldzon saw it all, too. Covering his eyes, he ran through the open door to the balcony that overlooked the street and leaped out. The Cossack backed off as the women began shrieking.

Now, other Jews, who were fearfully peering from their windows and workrooms, saw the boy fall. Several men and women ran out to help the child and tried to carry him away, but Cossacks surrounded them with drawn swords and pointed rifles.

Then Jews ran into the street in droves and began screaming — "Gevalt! Gevalt!" Jews from several blocks away streamed from their shops and homes to see what calamity had befallen the town. The clamor of their terrified voices filled the air and echoed down the narrow lanes.

Meanwhile, in Jona's house, a new horror was unfolding.

A Cossack had spied the delicate gold earrings on Jona's sister's ears. Esther had received them for her recent twelfth birthday. The Cossack tried to take off the earrings, but his clumsy fingers couldn't find the way to unscrew the pin holding them. Raising his sword, he made a motion to slice off Esther's ear.

"Let me try!" screamed Jona's mother. Pushing herself between the horseman and her daughter, she unscrewed the pins.

But Jona Lerman had enough. He broke into a run, and galloping down the steps, fled through an open door to the street.

What did he think he was doing? He didn't know. He was only a little boy — but he felt he had to do something. He just couldn't watch and wait to be next.

Now he saw what seemed like hundreds of people, young, old, all in the road, yelling — "Gevalt! Gevalt!" "Help! Help!" Several kneeled on the ground. More raised their hands in the air. Jona kept running. Rifle bullets flew over his head but he didn't stop. He ran through the gentile neighborhood to the outskirts of the town, into the forest. He leaped to grab the limb of the largest tree, and climbed up into its higher branches. There he stayed all night, crouched into a ball to keep from the cold, hidden by the leaves.

Chapter 4

VOICES IN THE NIGHT

In the morning the sun was shining. Jona didn't know what to do. Should he try to go home? Was it safe? Was his family alive? Perhaps he was destined to die in that tree. Suddenly, from a way off, he heard his sister's voice. — "Jona, Jona — where are you?" Esther called.

When she came closer, Jona called back — "Here I am, Esther."

"Oh, thank God," Esther intoned.

Jona climbed down from the tree and let his sister hold his hand. It felt warm and comforting. Jona uttered no words; he was bewildered by what he had seen. They walked along in silence until they entered the doorway of their mother's store.

Then Jona learned that a rival army, under French General Haller, had run Petliura's band off into the forest and saved the town from further destruction. Srulke and his eldest son, Shlomo, and a helper, were trying to straighten out the store. Not content with taking a large sum of money, the Cossacks had tried to wreck everything in sight. Shelves were lying on the floor; containers were split open, their contents spewed on the ground. The countertop had a crack in its middle where it had been hacked at by a sword.

The men looked up from their brooms and nodded to Esther. His father shook his head as the pair went up the staircase to the living area.

Upstairs, Jona's uncle was lying bandaged from the blows he had received. His younger cousin, little Jona, lay helpless in his bed. He had broken his leg in the fall from the second floor window. A doctor had come to set his leg and had given him a medicine to help relieve the pain.

Jona's mother and his aunt were setting the main room back to some kind of order. But Jona saw that the handsome dining table had been broken in two; its splintered halves rested against a wall. The women hugged Jona, but they had no time for him, busy as they were with their two patients.

"Where is Pesha?" asked Jona. "And how are Rachel and Bayla?" From Pesha's room he heard crying.

"Go, go with Grandpa, Jona," his mother said. And his white-haired grandfather, Aaron Feldzon, came from the kitchen and took him to a table for some hot soup and bread.

"Zaida," Jona asked quietly, after he finished his meal, "why did they do this to us? When I was running — I saw an awful thing." Jona's brown eyes looked deep into the sunken eyes of his grandfather.

"Eat more, Jona," urged the old man, "don't bother about such things."

But Jona was not to be silenced. "It was Reb Leibish, Leibish," he whimpered. Leibish was one of the congregation's holiest members. He fasted Monday and Thursday and seemed to pray continually, only going to his home to sleep.

"Those soldiers made him dance with his pants down and they were relieving themselves on him! On Reb Leibish! Zaida. Why would they — " Jona began to sob.

"Enough, Jona! — these things happen."

"But why, Zaida! Why the Jews? When I ran through the gentiles' streets, they were sitting outside, drinking, eating, laughing. Only we, we were hurt. Why Zaida?"

"They were very bad people — those soldiers — to do that to Leibish. I didn't know....ach poor Leibush," Zaida said, shaking his head.

"But why us — why Reb Leibish?"

"It was God's will, Jona," his grandfather said firmly. "We mustn't question — but God will pay them back."

But Jona was a boy who did question — not always aloud. Sometimes just to himself. Why couldn't the Jews do anything to punish the Cossacks? How dare they enter his home and give orders! His father gave the orders — not these dirty men. And how powerful was his father, really, if he had to bow down to these robbers — and beg, beg them for mercy? And more basic, although the idea was just beginning to form — why should his people live in a place where they were treated like bugs to be smashed under-foot?

What if Haller's army hadn't come to chase away Petliura? Would all of them be dead?

Timidly, Jona approached his mother with some of these questions.

"Shah," she said. "You're too young to bother your mind with such matters. We must live our lives according to Torah — and God will watch over — you see how He sent us Haller's army. Meanwhile," his mother added, "we try to help each other. You know how at Purim we lay money on the table and the needy come by for their share. And my pushke — that's for the poor people in the Holy Land who deserve our help because they pray for us all. Go study, Jona, and don't ask so many questions." And she gently pushed him away. But that night, and every night, as Jona lay his head on his pillow in his dark room, he heard the screams of the women locked in with the Cossacks, and the cries of "Gevalt! Gevalt!" ringing in his ears. Whole streets of Jews were shouting for help, and no one to listen.

It didn't seem right or fair for people he knew to be treated like that. Finally, he put himself to sleep dreaming that one day he would find a way to put a stop to it.

Chapter 5

SCHOOLBOY

The community put a brave face on the Cossacks' raid, thanking God for its rescue by a rival force of horsemen. The Jews tried to forget their precarious position in a changing Poland.

Bayla returned to her duties in the Lerman household, pale and listless after spending a month away in another town with her married sister. Malka, the girls' tutor, did not return. Esther and Pesha wrote loving letters to her, but she remained in her own home, her mother said, often not leaving her room for days at a time.

That summer, as she had done before, Yachad arranged a wedding between an orphan girl and a penniless boy. The members of the shul contributed small sums toward household goods for the couple, and Yachad and Srulke put on a wedding feast that brought smiles to everyone's face. There was dancing among the black-robed men to the blasting of klezmer music. To Jona's wonder, the groom was hoisted up on a chair by the young men of the shul, and paraded around the room to clapping and song. The women danced, too, in their separate space. Jona, and the children, ran from one celebration to another. Each was equally fervent and joyful. Jona did not think it odd that only later that night would the newlyweds be permitted to be together in privacy for the first time.

The wedding served to renew community spirit and soothe wounded souls after the brutal raid by Petliura's band. At least, through their religious observances the Jews of Srulke's shul felt they had some control over their lives.

That fall, Jona began classes in the Polish public school. Now that Poland was reconstituted as a nation, the government ordered all children to attend and to speak and learn in Polish.

Jona knew a few words of Polish from the gentile woman who came to clean the house. He and the other Jewish children spoke Yiddish at home. Parents who were in business might know enough Polish to carry on trade with other Poles, but the language was rarely spoken among Jews when they were together. Now their children were faced with learning the language which employed a different alphabet.

When the teacher gave directions in Polish, the Jewish children were mystified at first. But they followed the others and tried to learn.

The gentile children made fun of the Jews, not only for their stumbling speech but because they had long sidelocks which they pushed behind their ears, and strings that hung down over their waists. The fringes were worn so "that you shall look upon them, and remember all the commandments of the Lord."

The Jewish children tried to hide their earlocks and fringes and to speak competent Polish, but the taunting didn't stop.

Pavel, a blond husky youth, kicked Jona on the playing field one afternoon and called him a "dirty bloodsucker." Jona felt his temper flare. He turned and punched the larger boy in the face. The two boys began to tangle. A teacher pulled them apart and sent them to their classroom to copy a long passage on proper student conduct.

Every time their gazes met, as they worked on their papers, the boys made angry faces at one another. At one point, Jona was ready to jump out of his seat. But Pavel began to pull down his eyelids with his pinkie fingers while stretching his mouth with his thumbs, then sticking out his tongue.

Pavel looked so crazy, Jona burst out laughing.

Then Pavel broke up, and the two boys were soon writhing from laughter. An angry teacher burst into the room, grabbed the boys' papers and told them curtly to go home.

But Jona saw an opportunity to question the Polish youth as they left the school.

"Why do you call us bloodsuckers?" Jona asked Pavel in a level voice.

"Because you Jyids make money from our hard work. You don't sweat. We do! We plow and seed, and thresh, and then your father takes our grain and gives us a few zloti. You Jyids never get your hands dirty. Look, I have hard hands," the boy said, thrusting his callused palms toward Jona. "Let me see your hands," he demanded.

Jona looked at his own white palms. Pavel touched the soft places under Jona fingers. Jona touched the hard yellow calluses on Pavel's palm.

"Still," Jona said weakly. "My father pays good money for your wood or grain. Sometimes he cannot sell it for as much as he thought. I know, because my mother yells at him — 'Srulke, you paid too much. We lost money.'"

"Yeah, but in the shops the Jyids overcharge for yarn and — and scissors my momma has got to have, and we have to buy from them — where else can we go?" Pavel countered.

Jona shook his head. "It's the same thing," he said. "My mother buys one fruit, but you want another and it lays in the shop and rots. She tries to guess right. To be fair. My parents are no bloodsuckers," Jona said, taking the path away from Pavel, disheartened and confused.

"Ah," he said to his friend, Jacob Lanel, the next day. "The Poles hate us — to them we can't do anything right. Why do we stay here?"

"Jona, people hate the Jews everywhere," his nine-year-old pal said philosophically. "And where else can we go? At least here we have each other."

His friend Jacob was very smart. His father was a melamed who taught his pupils in his home. Reb Lanel earned very little; the family lived in one room. The walls of Jacob's cottage were rough gray plaster. In Jona's house the walls were smooth and white-washed yearly. Jacob wore clothing handed down from his older brother that already seemed worn out.

Jona noticed these differences. He also observed wistfully that Jacob and his older brother could discuss questions they had with their father without being told to "hush."

The year he was ten, Jona was no longer the youngest in the

family. His baby brother Shmuel was born.

As Shmuel grew, Jona happily answered his questions. Sometimes these questions led him to the age old response — "That's the way it's always been." Now Jona wondered, does that mean it must always be this way?

Poland provided six years of schooling for their children at that time. At thirteen, school ended for most Poles. Gentile boys with good grades, whose families could afford it, might go on to the high school in Tomaszov. But for a Jewish boy, where almost everyone was devoted to Hasidic doctrine, the only further education was to study with the adult Torah scholars at the shul each day. These men read the commentaries on the Torah from early morning until the working men came in for evening prayers.

While they attended public school, Jona and Jacob, and his cousin Little Jona, spent their afternoons at the Talmud Torah where they learned to memorize the different points of view of rabbinical scholars through the ages.

Now Jona and Jacob were considered prepared enough to study with the holy men all day. Srulke contributed to the synagogue to enable his son to study with the elders. But what of Jacob? Would he be able to go with him? Jona was gratified to learn that as a melamed's son, Jacob was included in the study hall as long as he wished to take part. Jona admired Jacob and had fun with him. He felt he could tell Jacob anything.

Most of their age-mates however were sent off to learn a trade, working for room and board with a butcher, tailor or blacksmith. Some went to work as haulers or wagon drivers, some as mill-hands.

Jona began his study with the scholars, remaining after the morning minyon until the men came at dusk for evening prayers. Srulke always asked at the end of a day what tractate they read and how Jona had participated.

"I took part," Jona would say to reassure his father.

For a week the elders would read a section of the commentaries and ask the boys for a verbatim recital of the viewpoint of different rabbis as recorded in the Talmud. Their task was to memorize — never to question. Although there were many decisions that intrigued him, Jona waited until he had Jacob alone to try out his thinking.

"They'd look daggers at me, and tell my father," he told Jacob after giving him his theory about stealing, a discussion that they read that day. "I don't believe people that find a valuable in the street will proclaim it and seek the owner. A few, maybe, but not everyone obeys that law."

"Throw some chachka in front of the shul in the morning, and see if whoever picks it up searches about to find the owner," Jacob suggested devilishly.

"Yeah, yeah," laughed Jona. "I'll find something at home and we'll put all this theory to a test.'

"No you won't," said Jacob. "Causing another to sin, is also a sin."

"I know," Jona admitted. I'm all talk — no action," Jona shrugged.

The next day it was study as usual. Jona wouldn't dare voice his doubts in the study hall. Besides there were new pages to learn. There were books upon books. He would look at the stack high up on a shelf and lament what he had yet to go through.

Occasionally, there was a boy who gobbled up the opinions and quoted them without hesitation. Then the elders smiled. A true student had been found. The heritage would continue.

Srulke Lerman had long ago given up hope that his older son would become such a scholar.

"He has a good mind," Srulke would say, "but it's all for business."

Shlomo had left the local shul already, and had married a young woman from Bilgoray. He was now working with her family there. Srulke pinned his hopes on Jona.

But Jona would rather be outdoors — chopping wood — a job Jews of his community felt belonged only to gentiles, than sitting with his nose in a book. Though he was restless and resentful in those sessions, he later acknowledged that it was from those books that he developed a code of honor which he would carry with him always.

However, he was on a collision course with his father.

When the older men took a break to smoke, Jona and his fellow students would leap out of their seats and run outside to kick around a ball they had made out of rags and tape. On snowy days, the boys would squirrel themselves under the stairs and play cards.

Srulke Lerman learned that his son was the first to jump up, and the last to take his seat. The moment they returned home from prayers, he smacked Jona's face with the flat of his hand. Jona drew back, hurt and confused. He was studying every day. Wasn't that enough?

Srulke's disappointment must have been keen. Here he was, one of the few men in the community well able to support his son at the finest yeshiva in Poland when Jona was deemed ready and Jona was playing cards! He had to face the fact that his second son would not be a Torah scholar either.

Jona was relieved one Saturday morning, soon after his thirteenth birthday, when he was called up to read from the Torah.

His father celebrated by downing a shot glass of whiskey.

"Good," he said at last, "now your sins fall on your own head — not mine."

The men of the congregation shook Jona's hand. Now he was one of them. He had been reading Torah since childhood, so it was no special achievement to read to the congregation.

Jona was accepted that day as part of the team that was to redeem the world through prayer and good deeds. Jona felt he had put on a suit of itchy clothing. He wasn't sure he could comfortably fill the role assigned to him, especially when it came to ritual. He would try. At least his misdeeds and misgivings would no longer harm anyone but himself. The Hasidic community kept a tight rein on its young men. They were the most vulnerable to outside influences as they went about finding a place for themselves. The so called "enlightened society" was to be feared by the faithful.

Those young men who went to cities to find jobs were joining unions and various movements aimed at achieving Jewish rights in Polish society and better conditions for working people. There was talk of returning to Zion without waiting for the Messiah.

Even among the most pious there were signs of breaking away from traditions held dear. Shlomo came visiting from Bilgoray with his face clean-shaven. Srulke admonished him in front of the other men at evening prayers. Shlomo reddened. Later he spoke up to his father,

"I'm a married man, not a child. I must dress as I need to."

Srulke looked quizzically at his son. What was happening? Other fathers also complained about their children.

The elders shook their heads. How could they control these new stirrings? They thought they had found a way when Asher died. The burial in the bog would reestablish their authority. The pole covered with pitch would be a stark reminder for years to come. Instead, the pole had been buried with sacred rites.

What lay ahead for this community that wished so fervently to remain as it had been for generations?

Chapter 6

ONE TOO MANY

After Asher was buried for the second time, the faithful remained in their homes for the seven days of mourning as their rabbi decreed.

It was a hardship for most everyone. The shopkeepers passed milk and supplies to those feeding children and the ill, otherwise the community was like a ghost town. A traveling story-teller came to the shul mystified.

"What has happened here? A plague? Some calamity?" he asked.

"We are in mourning," said the caretaker. "Come back in a few weeks. Some one will want you by then."

The magid turned away. He knocked at the door of a friendly house where he had spent a few days only months before telling the family stories for a few zlotis and bed and board. He was given a brief meal and told about the storm.

"Burial for a pole. Yes," he mumbled to himself as he went on his way. Surely a new tale would be added to his offerings.

The Belzer Rebbe was told of the happenings in Tomaszov. He nodded knowingly and approved the rabbi's decision.

The faithful saved all year to visit Belz, to pray with the rabbi. When a visitor returned home, it was with pride that he might declare — "The Belzer Rebbe blessed the bread — and then passed a piece to me!" Until someone else came along with the same report, that worthy had a special status in the community.

It was just after the holiday of Succot that a new calamity befell the Hasidim. The Rebbe of Belz was gravely ill.

Jona came from his studies in the prayer house to find his father on the telephone, one of only a few in the Jewish section of Tomaszov.

Srulke was pleading with the person on the other end to arrange for a famous doctor, a professor of medicine in Lemberg, to come to Belz and save the Rebbe. He knew he was asking an extraordinary favor. Jona heard his father agree that, normally, one needed to wait several months just to see the professor. And then one went to him. He understood. But this was the Rebbe of Belz, Srulke said urgently.

Only a few days before, it had been Yom Kippur, the annual holy day when "who shall live and who shall die" during the coming year was sealed in a sacred book. Jona understood this precept literally, as he did all the Scriptures. Did this mean the Rebbe had not been entered in the Book of Life and would die? Jona was fearful.

Yet, here was his father trying to intervene.

Jona's father had good connections in Lemberg, and after hours on the phone, he was able to find someone who could persuade the doctor to go to Belz and see the Rebbe.

Jona was very proud of his father. When the doctor's diagnosis and remedies saved the patient, Srulke became a hero to the Jews of Tomaszov.

But Jona was confused, and he dared to question his father.

"If it is written on Rosh Hashanah, who shall live and who shall die, and sealed on Yom Kippur, Tata — if the Rebbe was to live — we could put him in the basement and he would recover. Why did we need the professor?"

His father's hand shot out, and he hit Jona in the face.

"Are you mocking me?" He spat. "That's one too many questions you ask. How dare you question God's will?" Then shaking his head and looking at Jona with his deep-set sad eyes, his father turned away.

Jona felt the blood rush to his face, but it wasn't his father's blow. It was from anger.

In the mind of such a religious man, it was not possible to doubt. It was obvious to Srulke that God meant for the Rebbe to live and with the doctor's help. But Jona wondered — if his father hadn't gotten the doctor — what then? And if man was able to alter his fate — why should he not do so whenever he could?

These questions tormented him, but to whom could he turn for answers? Then the day came that would change his life — and that of many other young people in Tomaszov.

Jona met Natan.

Chapter 7

THE MAN FROM WARSAW

During the year that he was fifteen, word was whispered among the boys in the study hall of the shul that a Zionist from Warsaw wanted to speak to them. A few boys had a vague idea of what a Zionist was. The others were intrigued by the notion that someone from Poland's major city had summoned them.

The meeting was secret. They must somehow get away to a clearing in the forest where the man would meet them that evening. Jona and Jacob and ten or twelve others turned up.

Natan, the man from Warsaw, was not so many years older than his audience. He was clean-shaven, well built and wore the sleeves of his work clothes rolled up like a laborer.

He spoke first of the centuries of persecution that Jews had suffered in European countries. He recalled present-day pogroms, restrictions and quotas on where Jews could live and what work they could do. The boys could relate to these stories.

Jews were loyal to the countries in which they lived, Natan pointed out, but even so, they were preyed upon by Russians and Poles. Thought of as a separate people, Jews had lost control of their destiny. Although they were a "nation," they had no country to call their own.

It's true that thousands had left Poland for America, he said, but there was discrimination there as well — a lynching, quotas and cross-burnings.

For decades, Jewish leaders had been working to create a homeland where Jews could live in peace; a place of their own to go to when they were not welcome elsewhere.

Jona's heart began beating faster. Where could this be? he wondered. He leaned forward to catch every word.

Jews had once ruled the lands around the Jordan River; the north kingdom they called Israel, the south Judea. Natan went on. That place was modern-day Palestine with its center in Jerusalem.

Jona's hopes plummeted. The Messiah had to come before Jews could return to the land of Israel — Eretz Yisroel — every Hasid knew that! What was this man saying?

Natan went on, unperturbed by the open-mouthed boys before him. Before the Great World War, he said, Turkey had ruled Palestine. Turkey discouraged Jews from settling there and those who did were not treated as equals. But Turkey had been on the losing side in the Great War, and now England was in control of Palestine.

Natan explained that the League of Nations had just approved a mandate for Britain to rule Palestine. This was great news because through the efforts of a Jew in England, Chaim Weizmann, a declaration had been signed by Lord Balfour, the British prime minister, that said: "His Majesty's Government view with favour the establishment in Palestine of a national home for the Jewish people, and will use their best endeavours to facilitate the achievement of this object..."   Natan read the words to them slowly.

" 'National home' means we can buy land in Palestine and have a hand in governing our own affairs. Even though we are a small minority among the Arabs, the mandate will protect us. It's a tremendous break-through!" Natan shouted, spreading wide his fingers.

"But the Messiah," one boy whispered. The others nodded. "When God says we are redeemed, He will build a paper bridge over the oceans so that Jews from all the world will come to Eretz Yisroel! The Messiah must lead us!" the youth recited with authority.

"I know. I know. But that's God's work. This is our work. Our Torah celebrates life," Natan declared. "The Jewish People must live! Establishing a homeland will do that. Once we worshiped in the Temple. When it was destroyed, we worshiped in a new way. Now we must do our work on earth in a newer way still. Remember when God told Abraham -'Get thee out!' — that would be God's message today.

"Our people should not be ground down as they are here. We respect the observant, pious Jews in Palestine. We don't expect them to pioneer the land. But a new breed is rising so that the Jewish people may be strong once again!"

Jona's thoughts whirled. Was this the answer he sought? A place where Jews could be safe, welcomed. His eyes glowed with excitement. He and Jacob clenched their fists and raised their arms to show Natan they were with him.

Young people were needed in Palestine to reclaim the desert-poor land they would purchase, Natan went on. Once again, the land could be rich in milk and honey if young strong people would come to Palestine to prepare the homeland.

"We who want to return to that ancient hill in Jerusalem, Mount Zion, where once David reigned, are called Zionists," Natan declared. "We need more people like you to become Zionists."

The boys listened wide-eyed to all Natan told them. Some had heard the term "Zionist" cursed in their households. "Socialists and free-thinkers," they had been called. But they listened on.

To prepare to be pioneers, boys, and girls too, should go hiking on days off; should exercise every day; and learn about farming. He invited the boys to ask their parents for permission to play soccer on the field near the high school twice a week after class. A man from a Zionist training school in Warsaw, run by the Halutz Hazair — the Young Pioneer movement — was coming to Tomaszov to start a sports club for young people.

Some of the boys shrugged their shoulders. Jewish boys did not do farm work. They studied and maybe later went into business. But they never worked the fields. That was for peasants.

But Jona was jubilant. Here was the kind of life he wished to live. No one to call him a parasite — he too would have calluses on his hands, earning his bread by the sweat of his brow. And as for the Jews to have a homeland, a place where they could live without fear, this was the only solution to raids and rules set up to be broken through bribes and deceptions.

His father's reaction to Jona's enthusiastic tale of the lecture, however, was an angry one.

"Don't you understand this man is speaking blasphemy," Srulke barked. "I'll sign no paper for a Zionist," he said bitterly. "When the Messiah comes, it'll be time enough for Jews to go to Palestine."

"But every year at Passover we say 'next year in Jerusalem,' " Jona said quietly. "Now we can make this a reality."

"Unacceptable," answered his father. "That hope is our wish for the Messianic Age, which we must earn, nothing more. Besides," said his father, "you don't know what you're talking about in Palestine. The so-called pioneers are starving there. Every year, some come home. They're sick and impoverished. Arabs kill the Jews there. The man didn't tell you that, did he? He's a trouble-maker, he should be drummed out of town."

There was no more to be said.

If his father would not talk further, Jona would seek out Natan. He found him at the house of the family tailor who was not a Hasid.

"Why won't my father answer my questions?" Jona asked plaintively. "Once when I wondered how he could save the Rebbe if who should live and who should die was already sealed on Yom Kippur—he hit me. Doesn't he ever question himself?"

"He doesn't believe in questions, so he doesn't know how to answer you," Natan said softly. "This mind-set was good for its time. Redemption by the Messiah gave people something to hope for. But now we have Zion, a land to hope for. It's hard to find people to rethink their beliefs, that's why Zionism is for you and your friends who are not afraid.

"I have a book for you," Natan said after a moment. "It'll answer most of your questions. But I wouldn't make a big display of it in your home. Keep it under wraps."

Jona stayed up nearly the entire night reading that book by

candle-light. The Yiddish volume described the origins of the many religions of the world and the different beliefs in God. He was amazed to discover that other peoples believed in many gods. Some even offered these gods human sacrifices, a practice condemned by the early Jews through their story of the Binding of Isaac in the Holy Scriptures. Several religions proclaimed life on Earth was merely preparation for life in the hereafter. Jona was too deeply involved in day-to-day tussles with life on Earth to contemplate the unknown.

He concluded that Judaism was a reasonable belief, putting responsibilities on people to care for the unfortunate during their lifetimes. He especially appreciated the fairness in several laws that specified one must pay his workmen in a timely fashion and feed his animals, before sitting down to his own meal. He discovered that many rules, although based on the Torah, were merely customs which differed among Jews in other parts of the world. Then he felt better. It was good to have a code of one's own, but it was also good to be free to learn about the world and discover answers for yourself. This he was ready to do.

Despite the objections of the religious leaders of Tomaszov, a Young Pioneer soccer club started, and Jona managed to get out on the field most days that a game was organized. When his side won a match—Jona felt a glow.

His dream was crystallizing. First, join the Zionist group in town; then the kibbutz in Warsaw; finally, some day, become a pioneer in Eretz Yisroel. At night, in his narrow bed, he imagined life on the training kibbutz in Warsaw. He kept his dream to himself.

Until he met Natan, Jona hadn't known what his life's work would be. He wasn't cut out to be a Torah scholar—that was certain. Business didn't draw him. But now he had a long-range goal.

Jona set himself a regimen of exercise to strengthen his muscles, and to extend his ability to run long distances. He took pleasure in observing the farmers on his father's farms, to see how they managed plows and threshing. Secretly, he came out to the farm nearest his home and with the foreman's cooperation, learned to keep his seat riding bareback on one of the foreman's horses. Soon, he was galloping between the fields, sidelocks flying, knees pressed firmly against the sides of the powerful gray horse. It was so exhilarating to be in rhythm with the powerful animal, and yet to be able to guide it where he wished. As he rode he imagined he was in Palestine, galloping through the fields of a kibbutz with other pioneers.

On one of his secret visits, he chose a different horse to ride. The gray mare bit him on the arm.

"Is she jealous?" he laughed with the farmer. He had to conceal his black-and-blues from his family. He better not go back, he thought guiltily, but the thrill of the ride proved too strong for him to stop.

There was no doubt that attitudes were changing in Tomaszov, even if this was not true in his own family. The sports club soccer team had challenged the local high school boys to a match—and had won. On the way home, a gang of ruffians beat up the boys on the Jewish team. The boys fought back, but came home bloody.

When they showed up for the next match, the gentile boys were surprised. Jews were usually pale and weak they thought, hardly athletes and fighters. They looked at Jewish athletes with new interest for the first time.

The parents could not help conceal their pride when their sons won a match. Some parents, seeing that there was little in the city to offer their children, sanctioned their going to one of the training kibbutzim in Warsaw. Several older boys were already scrounging around for the fare to be able to go to Palestine.

Jona began actively leading the younger boys and girls in projects to raise funds for the travelers. When Josel Krellenbaum, an impoverished young man from a nearby town decided to go to Palestine, he appealed for help to the Young Pioneers. Jona and his friend Jacob volunteered to have their group earn money for the man's journey.

With several other boys and girls they hauled fallen limbs out of the nearby forest. Without asking, Jona borrowed an axe and a saw from his father's warehouse. The job of wood-cutter was a non-Jewish trade. Jewish boys never held an axe in their hands.

For years, Jona had wanted to try wielding an axe. First he sawed the tree limbs into smaller pieces. Then he stood the logs on end and tried splitting the thick trunks in half. It wasn't so easy. Flying chips could put out an eye. An axe could sever a toe. He had to be very careful and take aim.

He loved the feel of the saw in his hand as it cut deeper into the wood. There was a rhythm to it that kept him working even when the sweat dripped from his brow.

"Let me try," begged Yitzhak Blank, a younger boy with a gleam in his eye. Yitzhak was the ping-pong champ of the club. He had a steady hand and keen eye, and fell to chopping the logs in two without much trouble. Then he instructed the others. Boys lined up for a turn. Several went back to the forest to drag in more limbs, so there would be enough sawing and chopping work to go around. The sense of doing something daring was part of the thrill.

Soon they had a good pile of logs to sell from house to house. When the various clubs in the towns pooled their funds, they found they had met the goal and Josel was on his way. To Jona, it seemed that accomplishment brought him nearer to the homeland he dreamed of and he was deeply satisfied.

He returned the implements to the warehouse, wondering how much his father knew.

One evening, after a lecture at the sports club gathering hall, Jona and Jacob were walking two members, Frieda and Deborah, to their homes.

Jona took Deborah to the door of her house, knowing that her father was despised in the town as a thief.

Srulke heard that Jona had been to the thief's home.

"How could you go there!" he exploded. "My son fraternizing with a thief! Don't you realize you jeopardize our good name by going to that man's house?" Srulke demanded.

"Deborah is a friend. It has nothing to do with her father," Jona answered angrily.

"I forbid you to have anything to do with that family."

Srulke commanded. Jona walked away.

Not only his father was angry, the religious leaders of the town were outraged. The young people were dancing—boys with girls—and this was absolutely not sanctioned by the pious. Not only that—they were talking about Zionism as if it were an acceptable idea.

Complaints were directed to Jona's father. He demanded that Jona halt his activities. Father and son were barely speaking.

Soon after, there was turmoil once more in the Jewish section of town. A gang of wild farmer boys assaulted the rabbi of the second shul in Tomaszov. They cut off his beard to humiliate him, and then strung him up from a tree by his legs. The rabbi dangled there, upside down, for hours until a passing wood-cutter found him.

The whole Jewish community groaned in anguish. Special prayers were said in the shul, and women brought food to his household and offered help to the family. But Jona saw that nothing was done to find and punish the boys.

"We stand like goats," Jona said that night at dinner. "We should find those scum and beat them bloody."

"Be silent, Jona," his father warned. "With your tongue, you'll get us another pogrom. We'll be the ones beaten."

Later that night, Jona appealed to his older brother who was visiting.

"Tata and I see things so differently. It'll never change. Shlomo, I'll go crazy here," he said. "I want to go to the kibbutz in Warsaw and someday to Palestine. That's where the Jewish future is. Please help me get to Warsaw."

At first Shlomo tried to calm Jona. He offered to speak to their father. But Jona shook his head and threatened to go to

Warsaw on foot, if Shlomo would not help.

Shlomo was alarmed. Jona was a stubborn fellow. This was no idle threat. But his younger brother knew little of the world and with his small stature, Jona would be no match for big brutish Poles he might meet along the way. After many hours of pleadings, Jona showed Shlomo his sack, packed and ready to go. Shlomo gave in. Before he left for his own home, he handed Jona the necessary money to take the train to Warsaw.

The next morning when Yachad came up from her store after the early rush, she asked for Jona. He hadn't been to morning prayers, a customer told her. Idele, the cook hadn't seen him when she gave little Shmuel breakfast and walked him to heder. Was he still sleeping?

Yachad went to Jona's room. The drawers of his cupboard were pulled out and empty. His boots and shoes were gone.

"Jona has run away," she said resignedly. "You can oppose a child just so long."

Then she wailed—"Where is Jona?"

Chapter 8

JONA ON HIS OWN

Jona knocked on the farmhouse door. He hoped the kibbutzniks would not turn him away because he was hungry and weary. A wagon driver he found in a market near the train station had dropped him off at suppertime.

Ragged youths often arrived without warning. This one was well-equipped.

"You are from Natan's group, eh," said the curly-haired blonde woman who opened the door. "I hear you are a good worker." She laughed in a kind of mocking way. "We shall see."

Jona nodded his head sheepishly. He was shown a bunk in a dormitory, introduced to three other youths lounging there and told to report for dinner at 17:00 hours.

In the morning, he rose before dawn. He joined another boy

who was wrapping the leather straps of his tefillin around his arm, and did the same. They stood in a far corner of the room, so as not to wake their bunkmates while they said the morning prayers together.

"The others?" Jona asked his companion.

"They sleep," the youth, Moishe, said. "These are not Hasidim or Orthodox kibbutzniks here. You'll see everything from these Jews," he smiled, folding away his phylacteries.

In kibbutzim like this one, young men and women were being groomed for the work ahead in Palestine. Zionists of every persuasion ran these training programs, from those with totally secular socialistic philosophies, to religiously inspired labor party members. The goal was to put enough youth into Palestine so that a safe haven for Jews would be assured in the future.

Most of the enlistees were impoverished young people, but there were also intellectuals with college training and idealists from well-to-do families. All were treated alike. Jona was expected to be as capable of work as anyone else.

The men and women were there for a two-year training period. Then they would be off to Eretz Yisroel to work in a colony in Palestine. The British required that Jewish settlers have a certificate from the kibbutz, so that when they came into the country they could maintain themselves.

Jona was exuberant about being able to do manual labor, and anxious to prove himself. The best workers were the ones that were praised. But after the day of shoveling fertilizer into bins, blisters rose on his palms. He tried to use different parts of his hands when holding the shovel.

He glared at the blisters in shame. He wrapped a torn towel around his hands and continued work. The blisters broke, leaving raw skin. He hated himself for weakness. Finally, his group leader saw his hands and sent him to the kitchen to peel vegetables with the kitchen crew. His blisters healed. Now his fingertips were sore.

One week he was assigned to work in the laundry. Never had

he thought of the work that was involved in daily chores. Always, they had been done for him by a servant or his mother.

At an evening meeting in the kibbutz, a lecturer described the put-upon Jewish mother.

"Not only does she get up at dawn to warm the house, make the cereal, dress the youngsters, but she often has to mind the store—her work is never done," the speaker pointed out. Jona thought nostalgically of his mother, who though she had help, was constantly busy and never complained.

"Jewish mothers coddle their sons," accused the speaker. "Even the poorest won't let her boys lift a finger—and when they marry—the wives continue this pattern. This is why our men are often afraid to try new ideas—they are too comfortable with the old. We must change that," declared the kibbutznik.

Pioneer men and women would be equals in the homeland. They would work side by side, helping each other, the speaker declared. The kibbutzniks nodded in agreement.

Jona had to laugh. He guessed he was one of the "spoiled" boys. He missed the delicious home-cooked meals that required time and care to prepare, roasted meats and chicken, tasty stews and flaky pastries. The kibbutz kitchen had no time for such frills. The food was boiled or smoked and it was the same, day after day.

Jona also had to wrestle with the reality that Jews could be passionate about their Jewishness while not the least bit observant. Several smoked pipes or cigarettes on the Sabbath, and others ate "traife," non-kosher food.

One summer evening, a group from the kibbutz walked to the local village. Several boys and girls ate pastries from a village stand, food that he was sure was not prepared according to kosher rules. But his bunkmate, Yossie, went even further, he ate pork, flesh from a pig. And he seemed to enjoy it.

Jona gagged watching Yossie nibble the chunk of meat. He looked at his bunkmate during the night to see if he still lived. But Yossie sprang from his cot in the morning, and when they went to breakfast together, Jona asked him—"How could you do it?"

"Look, kashruth is humane and all that. Not boiling a goat in its mother's milk is certainly fair. Keeping milk from meat, not eating pork is okay if you want to remain apart. But I don't want to be apart. When I get to Palestine, I want to eat with Arabs and Turks and fancy Englishmen. I want to do everything!" said Yossie. "Besides, millions of people eat pork. But you better make sure it's cooked good to destroy the bugs. After that, it's cheap and tasty."

"But aside from being our law, and the way Jews live, kashruth kept us healthy during the plagues for that very reason. We didn't eat food with bugs," Jona retorted, remembering a history lesson in Talmud Torah.

"Yes, but they killed us for that too. When we didn't get sick, they accused Jews of witchcraft," Yossie countered.

Jona was thoughtful. He also wanted to "mix in." Yossie's words about Palestine thrilled him. But a homeland for Jews would follow Jewish laws? Wouldn't it, he wondered?

Nevertheless, as he reflected on his experience with Yossie, he began to doubt that God was so closely involved with the affairs of man. Three years before, when the pole went into the bathhouse, he had believed it was the sign of God's wrath. Now he remembered the young men clutching each other in triumph when Asher, the non-believer, was reburied.

They had smashed the mikvah! Jona realized. And his father had helped save the Rebbe! God expected men to change what they could! Zionism was a legitimate dream, no matter what his father thought.

Jona was back on the shovel in a few weeks time and he was proud of the calluses deepening on his hands. They were now as tough as the hands of the farmer boys in his class at school in Tomaszov, and he had no doubt that he could stand up to any of them in a fight. Moreover, he was a producer, not a parasite!

However, when his mother sent him money to come home

for Passover, Jona was deeply grateful. He had been away from home for eight months. He missed his family. He was as anxious to earn his certificate as any of the young kibbutzniks, but a few weeks' leave couldn't hurt.

Leave was granted, and Jona made his way home in time for the holiday. "Weakness has its price," Jona was often to tell himself for many years to come.

"Enough with the kibbutz," his father said after the first seder was over. "Come home, work for me, learn something about the business. It's grown, I need my son."

His father's warmth toward him was new to Jona. He thought how nice it would be to share the Sabbath once more with his family. He persuaded himself that he could prepare for life in Eretz Yisroel in Tomaszov just as well as at the kibbutz. He would teach the skills he had learned in Warsaw to the younger boys and girls in the local Zionist youth group.

His dream was as strong as ever, but the closeness of family and the comforts of home won out.

In the next few years, that decision was to have many repercussions for the dreamer.

Chapter 9

THWARTED

"It happens every spring in Tomaszov," Jona was reminding the boys in his youth group one evening. "The city is a collecting center for the Polish army. So men from around this province report here for physical exams and induction."

He swallowed. He didn't feel as determined as he sounded. He was finally taking the step he believed Jews should take, but this was uncharted territory. Still, he pushed himself on.

"The night before they are sworn in," he smirked, "these men think they own the town. They drink, and yell, and stagger through the streets. Jews who pass their way are preyed upon.

Year after year, some innocent person who had to be out, has been beaten, robbed, his beard ripped out."

"Last year, I remember," interrupted eager Yitzhak Blank. "The rabbi of our other shul was visiting a sick person. He got caught—was dragged away by the drunks, hung upside-down over a well and dropped head first into the water. They pulled him out just in time. Then they plunged him down again!"

"I was at the kibbutz last year, but I heard about it," Jona said angrily. "They left the rabbi on the ground, gasping for air. But this year it will be different.

"These louts are leaving town the next day, and they think Jews will do nothing. We're too scared. And the police—they're always somewhere else." Jona went on. "This year we'll be ready for them. I need volunteers—you big guys."

"Next year," laughed Jona gently at several boys barely thirteen who volunteered. "When you've had your spurt. If we give these bullies a good beating, we'll send a message that in Tomaszov, at least, you'd better leave the Jews alone."

Jona and the bigger boys made their plans. Would they be pounded by the drunk men, and a boy seriously hurt? Jona knew he'd be responsible. The community, his father would never forgive him.

But that's what kept us down, Jona told himself. They had to try. Pincus, a wagon driver who was an uncle of one of the boys, evened the odds. He slipped each boy a set of brass knuckles the night before induction day,

The Jewish youths hung back in the alley near the taverns where the Polish men gathered. Jona felt the cold metal of the brass warming in his hand. As the noise got louder inside the tavern, the door swung open. Several men came out into the darkness, calling to each other—"Let's go get some Jyids!"

The boys shadowed them, hanging back when there was no place further to hide. Suddenly, they heard yelps and screams— "Help, stop you hoodlums!"

The boys charged. They flailed away at the drunks. The men

were stunned. In short order the boys had them laid out on the ground.

"This is what Yids can do, you lummoxes," Jona shouted.

Then the boys disappeared.

But Jona's voice had been heard and recognized.

His father was visited the next day by a town official. Srulke Lerman defended his son, claiming he was home. But Jona's scraped knuckles told a different story, and after the official left with a contribution to his favorite charity, Jona's father lit into him.

"Do you realize you jeopardize the whole town with your reckless behavior. We take a beating once a year—so what. We can stand it. We have other things to do besides fight," his father said harshly.

"But I can't stand it, Tata," Jona countered. "We Jews are brave Macabbees, not goats to be lead to the slaughter. If we let them, worse will happen. We have to show we want respect."

"God respects the Jews, that's enough. Further, it's our duty to follow the laws of the nation in which we live. I have not suffered here. Look at all we have. This should be enough for you, Jona Lerman."

"Not for me," Jona declared. "Not for me."

Jews in the homeland were not afraid to fight, Jona thought, and that's where I belong. There is nothing for me in Tomaszov.

Jona sought out the youth leader in town to ask for his help in traveling to a kibbutz in Palestine as soon as possible. He was not prepared for the answer.

It was now ten years since the Balfour Declaration had been proclaimed, and the leader explained that the Arabs in Palestine were alarmed at the number of young Jews coming to the land.

Kibbutz after kibbutz was sprouting up on land bought from Arab landowners, most of whom lived elsewhere. Land was cleared of stones, swamp waters were soaked up by planting thirsty eucalyptus trees, desert tracts were made fertile by digging irrigation ditches. Fields were planted in crops, leafy green vegetation covering the land as far as the eye could see. Orchards and vineyards appeared where all had been dust before.

The Arab leaders had long ago feared that the presence of strong young Jews would eat into their advantage as the majority population. Eventually, the Arabs warned, this growing number of Jews would lead them to push for a Jewish controlled state.

The Jewish Agency in Palestine, responsible for the Jewish community there, declared its aim was only to live in peace with its neighbors. If the land was reclaimed, they explained, there would be room enough for all who wanted to come. But the Arabs demanded that the British stop the immigration of Jews at once.

The pioneers had friends in Britain who pleaded for them, but restrictions were put in place to pacify the Arabs, and one of them was a trap for Jona.

It was the requirement that pioneers have their two year certificate from a kibbutz in their native land before being allowed to apply for immigration to Palestine. Jona had only eight months behind him, and he was now seventeen.

Jona was in a bind. He could not go back to the kibbutz near Warsaw for another year, because by that time, he'd be eighteen. Polish boys reaching eighteen were not permitted to leave Poland. They had to remain in the country to be ready for army service at twenty-one or sooner. His parents could be fined and punished if their son left Poland after he turned eighteen.

If Jona remained past that age, he'd have to wait until his army service was over to try again. That was years away!

Jona realized there was not enough time for him to qualify for Palestine through regular channels.

"There must be another way," he groaned.

"There is a group that goes illegal into Palestine," the leader said, "but they want thousands of dollars to take someone."

"Thousands—I can't get thousands," Jona protested, raising his hands in frustration.

"I know," said his friend. "It's really for older people who can earn it back because they have enough funds to start a business."

"Is there no other way?" Jona asked desperately. "If I could just get out of Poland before my birthday—then I could find my way to Palestine."

"The countries are not looking for Jews right now," his friend laughed bitterly. "There is one, however," he added. Then his friend told him about Uruguay, a country in South America that welcomed Jews.

"And from there I could go to Palestine?" Jona asked.

"Yes, eventually. There are people doing it from there."

"I would work and support myself 'til I could go," Jona declared.

"But I have to warn you, Jona," the older man said, "the reports from the kibbutzim are not stories of paradise. Some settlements are short of food. Arabs are sniping at them on the road. And in the cities, there's very little work to be had. It's a real struggle there, my friend. Think carefully."

"The more you tell me—the more I want to go," Jona said, grinning.

"Very well, my pioneer. I'll contact someone who will help you, but you must get your passport as soon as possible," the friend warned.

"I know, I know," Jona whispered. "In three months, I turn eighteen. There's no time to lose."

Chapter 10

THE OBSTACLE COURSE

Jona's papers were all in order. Just in time, too, because July 14th was only a few days away, his eighteenth birthday. His father was barely speaking to him and in fact had left for Lemberg, not even waiting to say goodbye.

In three days he would leave for Uruguay.

"You don't speak their language," Idele, his mother's cook said to Jona while he took some lunch in the kitchen.

"Don't worry, Idele, they speak Yiddish there just as we do," Jona reassured her.

"Who even knows where Uruguay is," Idele lamented.

"Please, Idele, it's hard enough," said his mother. "So young to go to a wild place, who knows what will befall."

"Don't keep on, Mamala," Jona said for the tenth time. "There are Jews in Uruguay. I'm not the first. I'll be helped till I get settled. They want Jews there," he taunted them.

"I'm going to get my things together," he said rising.

A few moments later there was an eruption of noise from Jona's back bedroom. Drawers could be heard banging, doors slamming. Then Jona appeared, red-faced.

"It can't find it," he declared. "My passport—where is it?"

"Where did you put it?" asked his frightened mother.

"It was in my top drawer, at the front! I saw it there yesterday!" Jona spat out. "It's not there."

"Maybe in your clothing," his mother said, clasping her hands. "I don't know where your papers are, Jona," she said firmly, getting up to help him look.

She bent under his bed, she ransacked the laundry basket.

"It's not in any of those places," Jona yelled. "I know where I put it. Someone took my passport!"

He bounded down the stairs to the store below where his sister and her husband were working.

"My passport is gone!" Jona said through his teeth to his sister, so as not to startle the customers. "Who did it? Who took it?" He looked accusingly at Pesha and her husband.

Pesha spread her hands helplessly. Hershel shrugged his shoulders. "Who would do such a thing?" he frowned.

"I saw it yesterday—so it's not Tata, he's in Lemberg. I'm sunk," Jona said, sitting down on a step grunting. "Whoever did this knew there was no time left for me to get another set of papers—this took three months already. I can't go to Uruguay. I'm done for."

Angry and sullen, believing his sisters or parents had thwarted him, Jona went silently about the house, cursing his luck.

In time, he reconciled to his disaster, as he called it. I can't let this destroy me, he finally told himself. My dream is postponed, but not forgotten. I'll get there yet.

Jona returned to the kibbutz outside of Warsaw.

At night, after work, he read the great novels by Dostoyevski, Tolstoy and Checkov that had been translated into Yiddish. He poured over Theodor Herzl's "The Jewish State," which was instrumental in persuading European Jewry that they must have a piece of land to call their own once again. He read of the down-trodden Jew in the shtetls of Russia and Poland in stories by I. L. Peretz and Sholom Aleichem.

He also took classes in Esperanto, an international language constructed by a Russian physician who believed that national and racial hatred would disappear if everyone could understand everyone else. During that time, he developed notions of social justice, and came to believe that a basic foundation of one's government should be to protect equally all of its peoples.

A year later he came home and worked in the store.

Then, shortly before his twenty-first birthday, Jona was called to serve in the Polish army.

Jews dreaded the day their sons had to leave for service. For religious Jews, it meant their sons would be forced to eat non-kosher food. Only the most stalwart could hold out with a diet based only on vegetables and bread.

But that was the least of it. Jewish youths had never handled guns. Even more fearsome was the likelihood that they would be beaten by fellow soldiers or officers, the very ones who tormented Jews in their towns.

To escape serving, some boys took the name of another family, one without sons. The army exempted an only son. Other parents sent their sons away, before their eighteenth birthday, knowing they might never see them again. The boys, helped by relatives in England, Canada or the United States, would join a steady stream of impoverished Polish Jews, hoping for a better life abroad.

Occasionally, a frantic father would cut off the first joint of a boy's finger, the trigger finger, rendering him unfit for service.

Nevertheless, Jewish boys did serve in the Polish military, a few professionals, like doctors or engineers even becoming officers.

Jona was prepared to serve. He was confident of his physical strength from years of training. Though he was only of medium height, he was muscular and strong. He felt certain he could stand up to Jew baiters and give blow for blow.

And almost from the first day, he had to.

Mordecai, a Jewish recruit from his town, shy and clumsy, was being pushed aside in the food line by the other soldiers. Finally his plate was filled, and he moved toward a seat at Jona's table. As he neared, a soldier deliberately stuck out his foot in Mordecai's path. Over went the tray, spilling gravy over the soldier.

"Damn you, Jew," the soldier called out, wiping his shirt sleeve while kicking the fallen Mordecai.

Jona was on the soldier in seconds. "Get your damn foot away," he yelled, grabbing the soldier by the collar. "You tripped him deliberately!"

The soldier drew himself out of his seat. Much taller than Jona, he menaced a fist at Jona's jaw, but Jona ducked and, hauling back, landed a punch to the man's stomach.

Moments later, a sergeant appeared. Jona was accused of landing the first blow and with two soldiers escorting him, was whisked away and slammed into a lock-up.

But he wasn't silent. Jona demanded to see the officer in charge. There was something in his manner that frightened the sergeant. Soon after, he was shown into the captain's office where he made his case.

He was reprimanded, and cautioned, but no further action was taken.

But Jona wasn't satisfied. The soldier who tripped Mordecai got away without a reprimand. Stubborn, and careless about his own safety, Jona planned to get even.

During the night, when the huge man was deeply asleep, Jona crept up on him. Little by little, as the man turned on his bed, Jona pulled away the sheet covering his mattress. When it was finally free, he rolled it in a ball and threw it out the window. It blew away on the dusty parade ground.

The next morning, the stunned soldier looked everywhere for his sheet, desperate to find it before inspection. Standing at attention at his bare cot, the embarrassed soldier was marked down for "destroying government property," and made to do latrine duty for the next month. The other soldiers hooted at him when they went to wash up and saw him mopping and scrubbing.

"Jona, you're crazy!" said Mordecai, when Jona confided in him. "You'll get yourself killed."

"I can't stand it when Poles think they can get away with anything with Jews. It kills me little by little," Jona retorted. "It may be crazy, but it's something I've got to do. Let him know what it feels like to be shamed."

Shortly before the training program ended, Jona and several other men were called out from their barracks and told to report to the captain.

What now? Jona wondered.

The officer stood before them, pistol at his side, reading from a clipboard to the thirty men at attention.

"Because you displayed outstanding marksmanship, and physical prowess during training, as well as leadership ability, you men have been chosen for further training by our great Polish Army," he said, looking at them sternly over his glasses. "You will report to the under-officers' training school tomorrow morning."

A sergeant distributed written orders to each of the men.

"I expect you to merit the confidence the Polish Army has placed in you," the captain warned. "Dismissed!"

The men turned sharply and left the building, orders in hand. They showed no emotion as they stood at attention, but once dismissed, they beat each other on the shoulders, grinning broadly.

Jona was one of only seven Jewish recruits selected for the school. He was extremely satisfied to have been chosen. It justified to him his years of preparation for pioneering, and gave him the sense that at least in the military, some went beyond the prejudices of their countrymen.

In the next year, Jona became a skilled unit leader. He discovered he could win cooperation from other men, Jews and non-Jews alike. His straight-forward manner, and his willingness to explain and instruct won him a measure of the respect he so craved.

As for his religious life, it was all but forgotten.

One day he learned that his brigade would be having maneuvers near Tomaszov. He wrote home, suggesting a meeting place.

His mother was waiting when he arrived. She greeted him warmly, scarcely noticing the corporal's stripes on his uniform, or admiring how smart he looked in his square soldier's cap. The military was of no interest to her. As long as her son was well, that was what counted.

Yachad had brought along a wonderful basket of treats. Sitting on a park bench, he picnicked greedily on a chicken leg and bits of sausage, the most delicious food he had had in months. His mother didn't embarrass her son by asking him if this was the first meat he had eaten since leaving home.

But Jona did have a question for her. She had promised to send him some money for the expenses he might have above his pittance of a salary, but he had never received it.

"Ah," she breathed sadly, "you haven't been praying either."

This was true. But could his mother have known? He didn't press her further. Later, back at camp, he went through his bag to find his prayer book. He opened the cover. A neat pile of zlotis lay inside.

Chapter 11

THE FLOUR MILL

Jona completed his military service in 1933. In Germany, there were ominous developments. Adolf Hitler had taken power, becoming Chancellor. Within two months, a concentration camp was established in Dachau for political prisoners and "undesireables."

Hitler eliminated all opposition parties and nullified basic German laws. As dictator, he proclaimed he would restore Germany to its past glory and his first steps would be to get rid of the Jews.

Polish Jews who had resided for years in Germany were arrested and driven across the border to Poland. Poland was refusing them entry. They languished in transit camps.

Polish Jews were groaning again.

The Nuremberg Laws, soon enacted in Germany, removed Jews from their jobs. Doctors and lawyers, even those who had fought for Germany in the Great War, were ousted from their posts. Citizenship was revoked; property confiscated. The National Socialist goverment—the Nazis—justified their actions by screaming that Jews were sub-human vermin who must be be forced out of Germany. Judenrein—Free of Jews—was the new slogan.

In 1934, Germany signed a non-aggression pact with Poland, quickly amended by Hitler who annexed the Polish city of Gdansk. Poland, wary, asked Britain and France to agree to come to her aid should she ever be attacked. They agreed. The pressure was off for the moment.

The disciples of the Rebbe of Belz knew that many Poles sympathized with the Nazi regime. Conditions were likely to get worse before they got better. But the idea of leaving their familiar surroundings was inconceivable. Where would they find work, a place to live? Besides, their Rebbe cautioned, in other countries the Torah was not respected. It would be hard to be a pious Jew. So they told themselves that tyrants come and go, and this Hitler would go too.

Only a handful of Tomaszov's Jews listened to warnings by relatives abroad that Hitler was a menace whose aggression would eventually engulf them. With their help, these few packed up and left.

As for Jona, he returned home, prepared to immigrate to Palestine as soon as he could make arrangements.

But his father surprised him with a gift—a flour mill in Lezainsk, a town about 45 miles from Tomaszov.

Jona was stunned. How could his father do this to him!

"It is so simple," his father said. "You'll make a good living, find a nice girl, marry, settle down already."

There was a girl, Zosia Adler from Tomaszov. While he was in the army, they wrote to each other regularly, and they saw each other when he was home on leave. Zosia knew of his desire to go to Palestine; it was her desire too. But lacking funds and training, she could not hope to do so for years. During ardent moments in each others arms, Jona spoke of sending for her as soon as he was settled.

His father's gift was a chance to marry Zosia, to earn enough so they could emigrate together. Jona had to face it. Marriage was the farthest thing from his mind. He wanted to go now, and make his way alone.

Jona wiped his brow. "You know I wish to go to Palestine, Tata," he said slowly. "Riches don't interest me. Nor does marriage at this time."

But his mother jumped in. "How can you not try it, at least, Jona. Why should you give up all this for what—a desert?"

"Some of my friends are there already," Jona said wearily.

"Those friends?" his father grunted. "They had nothing here.

But you, you've got everything."

To refuse outright, was more than Jona could bring himself to do.

"All right," Jona whispered hoarsely "I'll go to the mill for a trial period."

His older sister Esther's first husband, Shiye Fuchs, who had never been strong, had died a few years earlier. She had remarried Yoshe Steinberg, and he was in charge of the mill. It was his job to teach Jona, the new owner, the business.

Jona was fascinated by the machinery for grinding wheat into flour; for bagging it; hoisting it into the warehouse and carting the 100 pound bags into trucks.

He watched the men at the machines and asked to try his hand at working each one. The workmen laughed, and stepped aside for the boss. This kind of boss was new to them, one who wanted to work, not just walk around, hands behind his back, or timing their rate of production.

But Esther's husband, Yoshe, called Jona to his office.

"You're to be a manager, not a worker, Jona. Stay with me—go over bills, talk to buyers. Forget the machines."

"Yosse with all due respect, aren't you concerned about your future here? How long will this mill be ours if Hitler starts to march?" Jona said, speaking from his heart.

Yosse answered sincerely. "There are just six hundred thousand Jews in Germany. Here we have three million. No one can force himself on three million people! We've been loyal Poles. The government won't allow the outrages that are taking place in Germany. You've got a good business here, Jona, don't throw it away."

"It's not for me," said Jona sadly. He would have to disappoint his father again. His future was in Palestine, not in the flour mill.

Now his mother had one request. "Before you leave us, please Jona, go with me to see the Belzer Rebbe."

Jona would do this one last thing. So the two went off to

Belz. The Rebbe, Issachar Dov, had died in 1927. His son Aaron became the Rebbe of Belz. Not much older than Srulke, the Rebbe was a thin scholarly man. He adhered closely to his father's ideals, supporting the Polish government even while the world was turning to quicksand about him.

Yachad spoke clearly. Her beloved son wants to leave the fold for Palestine—not to pray there—but to be a worker in the desert. Could the great Rebbe appeal to her son as she had not been able to do?

The Rebbe looked closely at Jona.

First, he announced that Jona's earlocks were not long enough. That meant he was snipping them, rather than letting them grow to their full length, as one of the laws commanded. Then he repeated the argument Jona had heard so often. When the Jews of the earth are good enough to one another and fulfill the task of mending the entire world, the Messiah, himself, will come and lead the people back to Eretz Yisroel. To go there before that time, to try to reclaim Zion without the Messiah, was to deny the word of God. The Jews in Poland, by observing every letter of the Law, were trying to hasten that day of redemption. Jona should remain to help. "Remember," said the Rebbe, "our sages instructed— " 'do not separate yourself from the community.'"

It was hard for Jona to deny his own deeply reverent parents, but to reject the Rebbe's words made him feel as if he was stepping off solid ground onto a thundering train. But he was twenty three. The time had come to take a stand.

"Esteemed Rebbe," Jona said boldly, looking directly at the man before him. "I will grow my earlocks. But I must go to Palestine to build the land for the Jewish people. It is something I believe in that will help the Jews. Rebbe, when the Messiah comes to Eretz Yisroel—he will find me there."

His mother caught her breath. Her face was as pale as the face of the Rebbe. She backed out of his study, with her head down. "I'm ashamed," she said to Jona.

He had to accept the heartache of dismaying his parents.

There were more restrictions now that thousands of German Jews were trying to enter Palestine. While arrangements were being made by his contacts, Jona returned to the mill and tried to assist his brother-in-law.

But one night going home to his lodgings, he came upon a scene that enraged him

A policeman was bellowing at a Jew using the sidewalk. Jona knew the man, Isaac. He purchased flour from the mill and made the sweet rolls that Jona bought for his breakfast.

It had been a rainy spring in the mill town and the roads were muddy. Isaac was laboriously pulling his little wagon, laden with several sacks of flour, along the planks that formed the sidewalk.

"You have no permission to use the sidewalk, Jew!" the policeman yelled. Put the wagon in the road — do it now!"

Isaac looked up dazed. How was he to drag the over-laden wagon through the soft mud in the road? But before he could answer, the policemen flung him down, overturned his cart, and made as if he would bash Isaac with it.

Jona sprinted toward the unsuspecting policeman and throwing his body against him, shoved him into the mud, then furiously kicked at him.

Passers-by stopped to gawk. To hit a Polish policeman was a capital crime. Jona could be hung!

Now deep fear took hold of him. He ran from the scene, dodging around the blocks to the railway station. He was friendly with the Catholic station-master and he blurted out what he had done.

"Jona, you're in great danger," the station master said, horrified. "I must hide you in my home. Quick!"

Jona paced back and forth in a darkened room of the station-master's house until the man was off duty. Then they called Jona's father. Once again, Srulke Lerman came to his son's rescue.

The police chief was summoned; there were many witnesses to what Jona had done, he said. A large sum of money was put in the chief's hand. The witnesses would forget what they saw, he assured them.

The officer, too, was compensated. He now declared that he had slipped in the mud—and Jona was only trying to pull him out.

Jona was mortified that he had been responsible for bribing the officials—something he abhorred. But what other recourse did he have.

"Forget it!" said his father. "You curb your temper — everything will be all right." But Jona shook his head. It was time to separate.

Jona bade a long goodbye to Zosia. He would grab any job he could find in Warsaw, saving his money for transportation to Palestine.

The Hasids in the shul now referred to Jona Lerman as a "crazy fellow."

"To leave a business like that, a place as a prince in the community. He's not a man without a future. His father owns a thousand acres. Seven mills. The wholesale business. To throw all that away for who knows what dangers among free-thinkers, non-believers." There was only one explanation: "Jona Lerman was meshuggah." Thus went the talk.

No one could speak to Srulke about it. He had crossed off his son. But in the family, the youngest, Shmuel, marveled silently at his oldest brother's bravery. He viewed travel to the distant land of Palestine as one of danger and romance.

Shmuel, now thirteen, dreamed of going to the gynasium in Lemberg for further study. He wondered when he would find the courage to tell his father his plans.

Jona took the next train to Warsaw where he accepted the lowly job of dishwasher in a restaurant. He saved every cent, sleeping in a cheap rooming house, eating left-over restaurant food. His earnings would pay for his tickets to Palestine.

After months of plunging grimy dishes into scalding water and scrubbing them with strong powders, Jona's hands were bleached white. But he had the sum required. He contacted Betar, a group that was taking emigres to Palestine who did not have legal papers.

There were train and ship tickets to be paid for, food and lodging costs while they waited for the boat, money for false papers, money for bribes. He was $200 short of the amount Betar would need.

"Blast it," Jona spat in frustration. He would have to appeal to his older brother again.

He wrote Shlomo: "I'm not coming back. I want to go. Please send $200."

Shlomo came to Warsaw with Jona Feldzon. They had the money he requested.

"You're giving up your business interests here, you know," Shlomo cautioned.

"My business is what I can make of it in our own land," Jona smiled at the two men.

They knew not to argue with him. They could see his excitement about leaving. Little Jona embraced him.

"Good luck my Groisse Jona," he said hoarsely.

"Good luck, and great success!" Shlomo said brightly.

They parted. From his father, there had not been a word.

PART II

A SOLDIER FOR
THE LAND OF ISRAEL

Chapter 12

ON TO PALESTINE

*"The Lord said to Abram:
'Leave your country, your kinsmen, and your
Father's house, and go to a country that I will
show you...'" Genesis 12.2*

"Belzec! Belzec!" called the conductor. Jona's train was chugging into a familiar station. He peered through the window to see if his parents had come to meet the train in its brief stop in the town near their home.

His father had a flourmill there. There was a railroad siding that went directly to the mill. It wouldn't take too much time out of Srulke's busy day to wait for his son.

Jona jumped down to the platform as the train slowed.

Ah! There was his mother and sister Esther.

Esther smiled at him, and handed him a basket of food for his journey. His mother looked into his eyes.

"You're going, son?" she asked.

"Yes, after nine years of wanting this, I'm finally able to realize my dream. I wish you'd understand and wish me well," Jona said stiffly.

"I wish you well, my son. But understand? That I cannot do," his mother said plaintively.

He asked after each family member. His young brother, his sisters' little children. All was well, they told him.

The whistle was blowing. Esther leaned toward him and whispered, "Zosia sends her love." He squeezed her hand, and then ran for his train. He raised his hand as he swung aboard. And he was gone.

Jona was one of 130 illegal travelers who met at the collecting point. Betar, the movement that followed the precepts of Vladimir Jabotinsky, had arranged the transportation. Each emigre had a false visa for Palestine, good enough to let the holder of it pass the scrutiny of border guards of the nations on their path.

They got safely through to Constanta, the Romanian port on the Black Sea. There they filed into the steerage deck of a sturdy vessel that would cross the Aegean Sea into the Mediterranean.

Jona and the others heaved a sigh of relief as they boarded the ship. The discomforts of steerage class, its narrow quarters below deck, the sound of the gears grinding through the night, were nothing to these zealots.

Not all the travelers were devotes of Jabotinsky. He believed that Jews should be prepared to fight to regain the homeland that rightfully belonged to them. Jona hoped to achieve a homeland through peaceful means. They argued their different viewpoints, sitting in the crowded salon that served as their mess.

Before dawn, most of the men and women were top-side, exercising. The Betar members were trained in military discipline. They led the routine. Jona relished the fresh salt air blowing across his brow, and a chance to flex his muscles, creaky from sitting in the small quarters allotted to the steerage passengers.

As they neared their destination, Palestine's port of Haifa, they went over the several strategies they would use to enter the British Mandate.

The first plan was to have the group pose as students on a traveling holiday. Convincing the British customs officials depended on how thorough the agents were that day. The steerage passengers did not exactly look the part of tourists as they gathered their rumpled clothing from the bins. Several could not muster the tie and coat and gloves needed to look like gentlemen scholars. And those that could, wore seedy jackets, pulled into shape, and shirts somewhat frayed around the collars. They stood out from the crisply dressed men with starched shirts and bowler hats, and the ladies in light lace gowns and large straw hats.

As they docked, Jona stretched his neck to see over the throng on deck. There was the port of Haifa gleaming in the sun. At last, Eretz Yisroel. His heart beat rapidly, and he took a deep breath, trying to contain himself.

The well-dressed men and women debarked without problems, but when the pioneers' turn came, the officials took time examining the group's documents, then handed them back to the leader—"Admission denied," said the British inspector.

"We're tourists," called out a few men and women.

"You can't fool us," the inspector rejoined. "Settlers—every one."

Crestfallen, the group backed off.

Plan B was now in force. The group went on to Alexandria. Egyptian customs welcomed them. No problem there. The Egyptians needed their business and doubted that this band of Jews would try to stay beyond the allotted time.

Now, the group split up. Jona's section went on to Egypt's Port Said, boarding in a youth hostel. Jona saw his first palm tree, his first camel, his first fez. His eyes darted everywhere. He was bewildered and enchanted at the same time. He also observed the poverty. People living in the street, beggars missing limbs. He was anxious for his turn to come to move on.

In groups of four, the illegals were taken into the heart of Palestine. The first section was taken by small plane outside of Cairo to a landing in the fields of a kibbutz. The four pioneers would scramble away to be sheltered by the kibbutzniks.

Those in Port Said would enter Palestine by train. When Jona's turn came, his group of four bought tickets for Syria, north of Palestine. British Customs passed the four because their destination was beyond Palestine's borders. However, the route the train traveled went through Palestine. When the conductor called "Haifa. Haifa next stop!" the travelers stepped off amid a throng of other passengers, and walked quickly away.

Once past the station, the four, two women, two men, ran whooping into a park, hugging the trees and each other.

At last they were in Eretz Yisroel!

Jona looked at his watch.

The time was three-thirty in the afternoon of August 20, 1934. It was a date forever engraved on his mind.

It had been nine years since he first heard of the Zionist Movement from the lips of the man from Warsaw. It had been his dream ever since.

Jona looked around grinning. He set down his old army bag with his clothing, and stooped to pick up some earth.

He felt as if all the land he could see was his. The dusty streets would yield the clay to mold an enormous vessel that one day would be filled with milk and honey. He stared at the dry earth in his hand as if it were gold. This was the ancient land of his people, where Abraham, the patriarch walked, holy land where, at last, Jews could once again determine their future, and he could shape his own. Thankfully, no British patrols were nearby to see the hugging and tears of each of the newcomers. Suspicious police would demand to see their papers. And they had none. Arrest and deportation would have followed.

The comrades shook hands, and two went off to meet friends already there.

Tovah, one of the young women Jona had met on the trip from Poland, was to be picked up in Haifa by her cousin. She insisted that Jona come with her. From there they would go to the kibbutz that had agreed to welcome the newcomers.

Her cousin took them to his home down the coast in Tel Aviv. Jona spent a pleasant few days seeing the sights of the growing city. He sent a letter home, describing the large synagogue he had visited in the center of town, and giving his next address— a kibbutz in the Jezreel Valley.

At the kibbutz, Jona felt at home at once. Hands were clasped in friendship. At supper in the large airy dining hall, Jona and Tovah were introduced to the members to greetings of "Shalom!" Those kibbutzniks from Jona's province in Poland rose to embrace him and make a place for him at their table. Over platters of cucumbers, tomatoes, green onions, fish and fresh-baked bread they asked for news from home. They played Jewish geography,

"Do you know, by chance, the Teichers from Bilgoray?" one kibbutznik asked.

"What do mean 'do I know?'" Jona laughed. "My brother Shlomo is married to Mattel Teicher!" And so it went.

The newcomers were assigned beds in the men's or women's dormitories, and put to work at once. Agriculture is labor intensive, and with few mechanized tools, there was a great need for workers.

Kibbutzniks worked for free, getting room and board, and clothing from the storeroom. Everyone was equal and chores were distributed by the leader according to the needs of the day. One day Jona fed chickens; another time he packed cases of fruit; then he worked in the fields. If his work was good, and his philosophy blended with that of the kibbutz, in a few months he might be accepted as a member.

In the evening, Jona and a few other kibbutzniks, took formal language practice, learning the words and idioms of modern Hebrew.

While most came from Yiddish-speaking countries, the settlers spoke all the languages of the Diaspora—Polish, Russian, English, Swedish and Arabic—Jews from the Middle East also sought refuge in Palestine. What language did they all really have in common, except Hebrew? But those ancient written words were in need of up-dating by several millenia. There were many tongue-twisting sessions before Jona could feel comfortable with his basic Hebrew vocabulary.

The kibbutzniks also made time for singing, dancing and games. Most were young people, after all. They danced the hora around a blazing campfire, singing the tunes, arms around one another's shoulders, until the embers burned low. Jona glowed in the warmth of the camaraderie in that kibbutz.

There were philosophical discussions too. Some were devotees of an early form of the Mapam Party which believed all means of production should be owned by the community. Others argued for the more moderate Mapai, the party affiliated with Halutz Hazair that Jona belonged to in Warsaw. They wanted private as well as communal investment.

These different factions grew out of the Labor and Zionist movements in Europe and Russia. Each faction had helped the young pioneers reach Palestine, and they brought their philosophies with them.

Both groups were alarmed by the growth of the "Revisionists," led by Vladimir Jabotinsky, which seemed entirely too confrontational. Betar opposed a British plan to cede a large area on the west bank of the Jordan River to TransJordan. No Jew would be allowed to settle there, the very area where ancient Jewish settlements had been located. Many kibbutzniks sided with Jabotinsky on this.

But there was also the Jabotinsky notion that said Jews were wasting their time being farmers. They should live in cities and keep shops, as they had done in the countries from which they came. The ideals of the kibbutzniks were to reclaim the land with their own sweat and toil. That's what fueled their idealism.

Some kibbutzniks thought Jabotinsky scored points in calling for organized patrols to protect the settlements, citing massacres and shootings by lawless Arabs. On the other hand, they rejected the revisionist idea that they should occupy Palestine by force.

"That's crazy. We can't fight the whole world," one tall man with thick eye-glasses said. "We can live peacefully with the Arabs. They are our cousins, after all. Remember Abraham had two sons. Ishmael was cast out to the desert but God promised that from him would come a great nation."

"It's just a family feud, is that it?" a woman added sarcastically.

"Forget religion," groaned another. "This is now. We have to get up to milk the cows at dawn. Shut up, kibbutzniks, and go to bed!"

Jona laughed along with the rest, excited by the give and take, and amazed at the complexity of ideas in the Jewish settlement.

On Saturdays, the day of rest, most of the kibbutzniks had free time. Jona would hitch a ride to Haifa, where some Tomaszovniks were living. Josel Krellenbaum, the man his sports club had helped send to Palestine when they were boys, was in Haifa. He was already becoming active in civic affairs in the city.

Jona also returned to Tel Aviv to meet with a few people from Tomaszov who had come over earlier, and a distant cousin who lived there. They all compared experiences, the pros and cons of working in the city versus farming on the collectives.

Jona was intrigued by the stories of those who were working in Haifa or Tel Aviv. The challenges they faced excited his imagination, as the work on the kibbutz had not.

Perhaps it was because he was stimulated by the activity of the busy streets of the few cities he had seen—Warsaw, Haifa, Alexandria. Now, Tel Aviv was most appealing to him. He liked its location against the broad beaches of the Mediterranean Sea. He felt at home in the tree-lined streets with their stone buildings.

Not that Tel Aviv was beautiful. There were many shacks on the beachfront, and plaster houses crowded together on crooked paths. But it was a place he wanted to know better.

The city had been founded in 1909 by Jews who lived in the ancient Arab town of Jaffa. They wanted to create a green suburb on the outskirts of the dusty city. Growth was slow until 1921. Then the Arabs in that ancient town turned on the Jews living there, stabbing and shooting. Whole families were massacred in the rampage. The survivors fled north several miles to Tel Aviv. The city had grown ever since. By 1934, everywhere Jona looked, a new building was going up or a new store opening.

Jona was impressed by the idealism of the kibbutzniks. Everything they had was shared. If the kibbutz showed a profit at the end of the season of planting and harvesting, the surplus was plowed back into the kibbutz—to improve the children's cottages, to purchase new sewing machines, to buy special eyeglasses for a member whose sight was failing.

But now that he was on his own, Jona felt the thrill of being free to choose for himself for the first time in his life. He wanted to take the reins of his future in his hands alone, to see where he could go.

He would give up the safety of the kibbutz to try his luck in Tel Aviv. Wages were low, but there was work to be had in the expanding city. He wasn't sure where he would fit in best as yet. But he was drawn to the idea of helping to build a growing city for the future of Palestine.

Tovah was disappointed when Jona said he wanted to leave the kibbutz. He knew she was fond of him. But he was wary of any ties, and still thinking of Zosia. He would miss the camaraderie of the kibbutz, but he was ready to take his chances in Tel Aviv.

Chapter 13

TEL AVIV

Thousands of single young people were pouring into Palestine in 1934. A householder with a room to spare was eager to rent to a newcomer. Jona found a place in a small brick bungalow at the edge of the city, the home of a seamstress, her husband and son. Later he discovered it was around the corner from David Ben Gurion's modest stucco house. Beyond those streets was sand and scrub.

Ben Gurion was an important figure, even then. He was the head of the Mapai Party as well as the executive council of the Jewish Agency that administered the affairs of the yishuv, the

Jewish community, in Palestine.

Born in Poland in 1886, Ben Gurion had come to Palestine at age twenty, working behind a plow on a kibbutz. He studied law in Constantinople, and then returned to Palestine. On the eve of the Great War, the ruling Turks threw him out of the country. He spent the war years in the United States where he met his wife, Paula. His sojourn in the U.S. was to be of great value in the future for it was there he made friends among influential Zionists.

He returned to Palestine once the British took over the Mandate, and by 1934, he was recognized as one of the most dynamic leaders in the yishuv.

Ben Gurion, a stocky silent man, was to prove the genius of the yishuv. He could chop his way through the dense thicket of conflicting opinions surrounding every issue to find the most productive direction. His skill was in keeping dissenters within the fold. Ben Gurion went to and from his cottage, deep in thought, but always he returned the greetings of his neighbors with "Shalom, shalom."

Work was not easy to find in the city, with the influx of over 40,000 Jewish immigrants that year, but through a man he knew from Tomaszov, who was established in the construction trade, Jona was able to find work as a painter's helper.

He started by painting doors, ceilings, and masonry. He learned to apply plaster to the cinderblock houses. He also absorbed some of the techniques of construction from watching the other workers around building sites and asking his inevitable questions.

Each day he "commuted" to work on an old bicycle he had purchased from his employer. One evening, from his window, he saw David Ben Gurion's young son near his bike. The next morning he found he had a flat tire. He patched it and pumped it up, and thought no more about it. But a few days later, the same thing happened. Another bike owner also complained of mysterious flat tires.

Jona hesitated to bother the head of the yishuv with his suspicions, it was just a boyish prank, after all. But Jona had to get to work in the morning. So when he chanced to see Ben Gurion the following day, after repairing still another flat tire, he called to him, "Shalom, David, a moment—" and told him of his problem.

"You see him do it, you give him a good smack on his backside," Ben Gurion responded. The two laughed, but after that no more bicycle tires in the neighborhood were damaged.

Jona had arrived in August and celebrated the Jewish holy days at the kibbutz. But now it was March, 1935, Purim in Tel Aviv!

In Tomaszov, Jona had felt uncomfortable at Purim when women came to the door to receive the money his mother had laid out on the table. How could they belittle themselves like that, he had wondered then. But now he understood. If one had children, it was different and terrible to be without. Those women could not afford pride. He smiled, thinking of his mother, who never appeared when the women came in to pick up their packages, so they might have some measure of privacy.

He, on the other hand, could bear any hardship, he laughed to himself, as long as he was living his dream. A growing commotion in the street interrupted his thoughts. Music and laughter could be heard.

Jona looked out toward the main road, and saw crowds of people. Nearly everyone wore masks or some outrageous costume. Girls wearing their mother's slips as a long gown, strings of beads at the neck and golden paper crowns on their heads, paraded as the heroine Queen Esther. Children ran around dressed as clowns or bears, shaking tambourines. The revelry filled the main street and even the side streets of the town.

"Come on out, Jona," called his landlady through the door. He joined her family as they mingled with the crowds.

Booths lined the nearby streets where all kinds of delicacies were sold. Hamantaschen of every description were passed around by local women, who urged Jona to "try my 'taschen!" The three-cornered pastries, representing the hat of Hamen, the villain of Purim, were filled with poppy seeds, or prunes, or plums, and Jona pronounced every one "Delicious, Bubbela!"

The dancing and parading, eating and drinking went on throughout the night. The whirling circles opened to include Jona or anyone who approached. Arabs danced along with the Jews. Sabras—those Jews born in Palestine—often broke into an Arab circle and danced with them as brothers.

Jona's heart was full. This was the life he had longed for, young, vibrant people, able to show their love for their heritage in the main streets of town, with no one to make them afraid.

The feeling of being at one with every stranger, moved Jona to write home:

"Dear Family, you think you have a Garden of Eden there. But it is here!"

To add to his joy, his boyhood friend from Tomaszov, Jacob Lanel, arrived in Tel Aviv. Jona at once asked his landlady for a cot so his friend could stay with him while he got settled.

Tall and handsome with straight brown hair, Jacob was both serious and funny and a great addition to Jona's circle of friends. Jona was able to get him work at the same job site, but as soon as the job was completed, the men would be laid off.

Jacob had a letter from Frieda Stuhl, a girl from their sports club in Tomaszov, who wrote that there were opportunities in Haifa where she was working.

"She knows a couple who can rent me a room and let me use their backyard for a laundry," Jacob said.

"A laundry?" protested Jona. "You're too smart to do laundry, Jacob."

"It's okay, it's where I'm doing laundry that counts—Eretz Yisroel. Besides, we're falling all over one another in this closet of yours," Jacob said laughing. "And we'll get together often. This is a small country, really."

In a few days, Jacob was on his way to Haifa. With Jacob

gone, a few weeks later when Passover approached, Jona was thrown into a great yearning for home. There he was in the city with a hundred acquaintances but no family to speak of. His one cousin was off to a kibbutz for the holiday, leaving him the key to her apartment, which he had agreed to watch for her. But he had no invitation to a seder meal, and when his landlady said "Join us," he was too proud to let on that he was alone.

He returned early from work to his lonely room dejected.

Suddenly, he heard a commotion outside his door. Opening it, he saw Jacob and Frieda from Haifa standing there.

"We were homesick," They said together.

"Ah," said Jona, "so was I. I'm so glad you came."

Hugging and kissing they danced around each other in the small room, laughing at the joy of being together. Then, miracle of miracles, five more Tomaszovniks who had settled in Jerusalem, called to Jona from the street. Now eight people were hugging and kissing for all the world to see.

"We'll have a seder after all," said one of the women, clapping her hands. By pooling their meager funds, Jona was able to ride off on his bike to Jaffa where the markets were still open. He bought eggs and chicken, matzohs and wine and vodka.

Borrowing his cousin's kitchen, they made a seder meal. It wasn't ready until eleven o'clock that night. But no matter, while the cooking was done, they had prayed the service, and lustily sang the songs, well aware that they were in the land where the story of Passover had its triumphant ending. Songs poured out of every window on the block, and again there was dancing in the streets.

To this very day, those who have been blessed with a long life and many seders since say—"Wasn't that a wonderful seder we had in Tel Aviv?"

Chapter 14

TO BUILD A CITY

Biking to and from his job, through the crowded streets and alleys, was a thrill to Jona. He loved the cosmopolitan flavor of the budding city. Among the throngs in the roadways, Orthodox Jews wearing broad-brimmed black hats passed swarthy businessmen with turbans wound around their heads. Turks, sporting the fez, jostled Arabs wearing a kafiah, a rope across the forehead held in place a light cloth that covered the back of the head and neck. A good headdress, thought Jona, whose own neck was burning from the hot summer sun.

Who were all these people now living together? Moslem, Jew, Christian? Did they have any national identity? If someone suggested to Jona that he was a Palestinian—he wouldn't agree. "I'm a Jew in Eretz Yisroel," he'd say.

After all, the Jews were the only ones who ever had a unified nation of their own on this soil, calling it Judea in the south, and Israel (Yisroel) in the north. In ancient times they crowned kings—Saul, David, and Solomon on land that included both the east and west banks of the Jordan river.

Each of these kings, and others after them, had an army, a system of government, taxing authority, judges and officials. King David moved the capital of Judea from Hebron to Jerusalem as a more central location in the kingdom. His son, King Solomon, built the Great Temple in Jerusalem. The Kingdom of Israel was eventually established by the northern tribes with its own rulers and armies, and its capital at Samaria. But this kingdom lasted only two hundred years.

As for Judea, it retained its sovereignty until 586 B.C. Then the city of Jerusalem was captured, the Temple destroyed, and the Jews exiled. A second Temple was built after, and the Jews were invited to return. This Temple, too was destroyed by the Romans in 70 A.D.

The valuable location, on trade routes from Africa to Europe to Asia, was a tempting prize that became a battleground for invading armies. Assyrians, Greeks and Romans had a turn at occupying the land. In modern times, it was the Turks, now it was the British.

People from all corners of the earth converged on this parched and hilly stretch of land along the Mediterranean Sea. Its name was derived from the chunk of coastal land called Philistea, now known as Gaza. Palestine became the name of the region. Under the Mandate, the West Bank land was assigned to a country the League of Nations created, Trans-Jordan. The name means "across the river Jordan."

Jona shared these stories with a young Arab laborer on the job. They both acknowledged that Jews lived in the territory throughout these centuries, along with those who migrated north from Arabia.

"We come from Syria," Abdul offered, introducing the history of the parallel Arab experience. "My father farms up the coast, grows grapes and figs, and vegetables. We have been here for three generations. We still go back and forth to Syria. Two brothers live there now. If asked, I'd say I was Syrian."

Jona wondered if Abdul had national hopes for Palestine. He could see a time when the British would leave, and Arab and Jew could establish a country of their own on this soil. He realized there were Jews who wanted only a Jewish State—but he and others could conceive of a place open to all Jews who needed a home, but which would include Arab residents as citizens and equal partners in a nation.

The Arabs from all the nations surrounding Palestine seemed bonded by their common language, Arabic, and their devotion to the Moslem faith, although some were Christian. But in the 1930s only a few Arab intellectuals discussed the question of a Palestinian identity. Living as they did, having ties to Egypt, to Syria, or Sudan, the average occupant of Palestine seemed unconcerned about national status.

The argument—who was here first—seemed foolish to Jona.

It was clear the Jewish tribes created a nation first; it was also clear that Arab landholders felt Jews were poised to create another one. They were becoming violently hostile to Jewish immigration.

When the first Jewish settlers came on the land, the Arab farmers looked on with curiosity. It was the effendi, the landlords, who encouraged the Moslem religious leaders to whip up trouble between the settlers and the Arabs.

"You'll be displaced. Our sacred sites will be destroyed by these Jews," the Arabs were warned. Guns were passed out by the effendi to encourage attacks on the settlers.

At first, the pioneers hired guards, neither Jew nor Moslem, for protection. Still, the kibbutzniks were ambushed, stabbed or shot as they went about their property. The guards were found sleeping, or had run away.

Joseph Trumpeldor, a veteran from the Russian army who had come to Palestine with Zabotinsky, had a plan.

"We are a different breed," he declared for all to hear. "We will guard our own property. Watch out!"

"Strength and courage!" were Trumpeldor's watchwords. In each kibbutz he organized a defense team, and trained a corps that could be called upon for help when needed. That corp responded when the settlement at Tel Hai in the upper Galilee was under attack in 1920. Just 40 years old, Trumpeldor died defending the settlement.

Haj Amin al-Husseini had been appointed head Moslem jurist by the British in Jerusalem in 1921. This made him the leader of the Moslem community. The Mufti used his power to promote increasingly aggressive attacks on Jewish settlements.

In 1929, while Jona was still in his father's house, he learned that Jewish settlers in Hebron, who lived near the tomb of the Patriarchs, had been attacked by an Arab band. Sixty-seven Jews had been murdered, including young yeshiva students at their studies. The assault gained worldwide attention. Srulke had slapped down a paper with the report in front of Jona.

"This is where you want to go!" he said to his son.

Jona knew the Jews fled the town, only to return two years later to try to resume their lives. Again, they were attacked. This time, the British cleared the town of Jews, a place that had been their first capital and that they revered and had lived in from ancient times. Hebron is the scene of passionate Arab-Jewish conflict even today.

By the 1930s, the defense force enlisted most young men and women. It had to remain secret to escape British attention: no uniforms for the volunteers, no identifications, no ceremonies. The volunteers would only defend, never fire first. "Haganah" is the Hebrew word for defense.

Jona liked the Arabs he had met on the job. He would never pick a fight with an Arab no more than he had ever started a fight with Poles. However, he was dismayed to learn of wanton killings of Jews reported almost weekly.

Soon after arriving in Tel Aviv, Jona asked an acquaintance on the job how he could join the Haganah.

The man said simply, "After work, follow me."

Chapter 15

THE OUTPOST

Even though he had had military training in Poland, Jona needed the specialized training the Haganah provided. He had to learn the brutal art of hand-to-hand fighting, how to wield a knife to disable an attacker.

The men were ever mindful that if a Jew was caught with a gun, he could be deported, imprisoned or hung. Jona, who still had no legal papers permitting him to live in Palestine, was especially vulnerable.

Not that there were many real guns around. They shared rifles for practice, when there was ammunition. It was an occasion when a gun was smuggled in from outside Palestine. The men gathered round to see it tested. If it worked, there would be claims on who should carry it that day.

The volunteers were not paid. An apartment was provided for those who were relocated, and they were given a small allowance for food, but that was it. They supplied their own clothes, which got torn up on the rocks.

"We accept this," Jona explained to Yitzhak Blank, one of his favorites from the youth group in Tomaszov, who had just arrived. Four years younger than Jona, he had made it to Palestine legally and was now rooming in with Jona. Yitzhak volunteered at once to join the Haganah.

With other recruits, they had visited the Trumpeldor Memorial, and recited the phrase "Strength and Courage!" It was a slogan they would need in the future.

Tired from their final weekend of training, the two men slept the moment they hit their beds. Jona was up at dawn weaving around Yitzhak's arm, out-stretched in sleep. Four working men shared the one bathroom. He wanted to have his shower and shave out of the way before the others woke. Jona yawned and stretched in the hallway. Bright sun was coming through the blinds. How wonderful it was to be in the land of his dreams with his boyhood friend nearby! Building the city by day and helping the yishuv by night, was his ideal of a worthy life.

Yitzhak had folded his cot by the time Jona returned. The teapot was boiling on their one-burner hot plate, and Yitzhak was slicing an orange. Riding the one bike between them, Yitzhak clinging to the rack across the back fender, they would report to their construction site. All day they moved along the scaffold plastering the cinder blocks put in place earlier by the masons.

Now qualified by the Haganah, Jona and Yitzhak were on call at night and often during daylight hours.

When they came back from work, they would look for a note on the door:

"Meet at 2 a.m. same place," it might say. Grabbing a few

hours of sleep, Jona and Yitzhak would be off to the waiting truck at the assembly point.

In those years, the Haganah helped the settlers with a vital task. Although the Jews had paid for the desert land they hoped to reclaim, settlements were not always established because of British objections, lack of funds or manpower.

Turkish law, still recognized, held that land without a house with a roof on it could be used for grazing. The real danger however, was that these vacant tracts were also places where Arab snipers could hide, harassing travelers on nearby roads.

The Jewish response was to occupy the property, on a minimal scale, with a stockade and tower, and do so within 24 hours, before their activity could be detected,

Walls were assembled beforehand, numbered and trucked at night to the location. Guided by shielded flashlights, men and women worked in silence through the night, positioning the walls on the wooden frames, nailing in the sections at dawn. Double stockade fences were put in place, with a corridor of dirt between. The roof of the bunkhouse was hoisted up by sunrise. The land was occupied!

Armed with a rifle, Jona took turns standing guard, or labored with the building crew until relieved by a daytime volunteer. As soon as the tower was up, the Haganah could watch the countryside for a Bedouin attack. At nightfall, 24-hours after they had begun the project, the searchlight in the tower, powered by an electric generator, would be turned on. The land was theirs!

Haganah men would return at night to ride around the settlement on horseback. There was a possibility of attack when the Bedouin realized what had happened. They would need permission from the settlers to graze their cattle from now on. And they understood that in time, more settlers would arrive and planting and farming begun. They would lose that grazing ground forever. And the British could do nothing about it.

After one of these overnight construction projects, Jona would report to work at his day job, slugging black coffee to keep sleep from his eyes. Finally, when the work day ended, he would return to his room, exhausted but fulfilled.

As he closed his eyes, he'd see the picture that returned to him so often—hundreds of people in the street —shouting "Gevalt! Gevalt!" begging for help! Now he could calm the frightened seven-year-old boy still inside him. Today I did what I came here to do, help build a homeland for the Jewish people.

Chapter 16

THE GUN IN THE TOILET

There were settlements so dangerous that the regular British police refused to guard them. The British were forced to deputize Jewish men to patrol these areas. A force of five auxiliary police, known as gafirs, wearing tall brimless hats, were deputized to patrol settlements near Haifa where Jona was assigned by the Haganah.

The Haganah was always on the lookout for ways to arm their men. When one of the gafirs was off duty, he would loan a Haganah volunteer his gun and uniform so that the volunteer could safely continue patrolling. Of course, if the imposter's true identity was discovered, the penalty was severe, death by hanging. Yet, time and again, Jona donned the fez and took a turn on patrol.

His family had no inkling of his activities, but standing guard, Jona imagined the scorn his father would heap on him if he could see him, a man from an Hasidic home, with a fez and gun.

It wasn't just bravado, however, Jona knew the mere presence of these uniformed patrols was enough to keep Arab marauders at bay. At other times, Jona patrolled in ordinary clothes, ready to pull a pistol on anyone assaulting Jews.

On assignment on the Tel Aviv-Jaffa border later that year, Jona's group was not protected by uniforms. At the border they patrolled the marketplace with weapons hidden, hoping to disarm any attacker preying on merchants and shoppers.

One day, Jona was meeting with several Haganah men in a home owned by a widow and her elderly mother. The men were sitting around the kitchen table discussing tactics, when one of their group, who was on duty in the marketplace, burst in shouting in terror.

"There was shooting in the market. They saw me with the pistol! They're coming here! What can we do!"

"Give me the gun," Jona said instantly.

Jumping up, he ran to the toilet and tossed it in. Then without missing a step, he entered the old woman's room where she was lying in bed.

"Please, Momma, come with me one minute," he said. Lifting her gently, he half-carried the woman to the bathroom where he plunked her down on the toilet.

"Sh-h, Momma," he said. "Stay—it won't be long." He closed the door as two British policemen banging on the hall door entered the apartment, demanding their weapons.

Jona's friends looked up from the kitchen table were they had spread out playing cards.

"We have no guns here," they told the police. "Go look," they shrugged.

Pulling drawers out, raising mattresses, the two police looked everywhere but found nothing. Finally one opened the bathroom door. Seeing the old woman sitting there—he backed off. "Oh, pardon, Madam," he said, red-faced. The disgusted policemen soon left.

"Jona, you saved us," breathed the grateful volunteer. "Whew—that was a close one."

"How did you think of all that so fast?" another friend marveled.

"I truly don't know." Jona smiled weakly, shaking his head. "But let's help our real heroine back to bed."

The others jumped up to help the frail woman and to thank her.

Chapter 17

ON THE ROAD TO NETANYA

By 1936, the British were embroiled in Arab accusations of leniency to Jews. The Jewish community was ignoring immigration restrictions, smuggling in Jews fleeing from Germany, Austria, Poland and Czechoslovakia.

When the Ottoman Empire crumbled in defeat in World War I, the British saw their chance to realize a long-held aim—to have a position at the crossroads of three continents—Africa, Europe and Asia. That spot was Palestine in the Middle East. By controlling Palestine, they could better protect India, their colony on the Indian Ocean. The Suez Canal in Egypt joins the Mediterranean to the Red Sea, the gateway to the Indian Ocean. There was also a valuable pipe line through which oil was sent from Iraq to the port of Haifa. Guarding that stream of oil was vital to Britain.

Their humanitarian pledge, to look with favor on the creation of the National Home for displaced Jews, helped win the mandate from the League of Nations. But Britain's interest in Jewish welfare rapidly disappeared when it conflicted with Arab demands. Although the Palestine Arabs were a heavy majority, they had no national governing structure. They took directions from the kings and sheiks of the Arab oil-rich states in the Middle East. And those chieftains looked at the growing yishuv as a threat to their power.

It was true the yishuv was expanding. Jona was one of 42,000 immigrants who came from Europe in 1934. The year before, when Hitler became chancellor in Germany, 30,000 well-educated and well-financed Germans had entered. A whopping 61,000 arrived in 1935. By 1936 there were 400,000 Jews in the yishuv, still only one-third of the total population of Palestine.

Interestingly, Arabs from Syria, Egypt, and Trans-Jordan, hearing it was buzzing with activity, were entering Palestine in record numbers, too. The Arab majority was not losing much ground. However, their leaders were convinced that demands for a Jewish state were not far off. They based their hostile actions on that premise.

According to Golda Meir, writing in her 1975 book "My Life,"... "the guiding principle behind the attitude of the Arabs in 1936 and 1937, was what it has been ever since: Decisions are made not on the basis of what is good for them, but on the basis of what is bad for us."

The riots started when an Arab shot four Jews in a movie house. In the next months, eighty Jewish men and women died in the uprisings. A general strike was called in April of 1936. Arabs refused to go to work Jewish-run businesses, or to ship to market perishable vegetables and dairy products. The port of Jaffa was closed to Jews. In the countryside, Arabs set fire to orchards and warehouses where they had worked. They derailed trains, destroyed rail lines, and overturned buses.

The Jewish community had its hands full. Citrus was rotting on the ground. Needed foodstuffs from abroad could not be purchased. Metal pipes and building materials would not be delivered.

Finally, the yishuv built a make-shift dock at Sde Dov, a cove in the Mediterranean Sea at Tel Aviv. The wooden dock could receive small boats. At least some supplies could now be shipped in and out.

In an effort to protect the civilian population, Haganah volunteers were put on duty night and day. It was also critical to patrol the oil supply pipeline which ran from Iraq to Haifa, a tempting Arab target.

Jona was posted on the roads and at settlements, around the clock. It was unrealistic to expect full-time work during this period. Off-duty, Jona and his Haganah friends tramped from job site to job site looking for a day's work, in vain.

The Histadrut, the yishuv's labor federation, offered welfare payments to the jobless volunteers.

"I didn't come here to take handouts," Jona retorted to an interviewer at the job center. "Find me work so I may support myself." But the worker spread his hands in frustration. In addition to local turmoil, a depression in the whole Middle East was keenly felt in the yishuv.

The Histadrut did provide work two days a week, moving rocks out of a stretch of sand to form a roadbed. Three workers shared one six-day-a-week job. About two days was all a man could take tugging rocks in the broiling sun while swatting mosquitos and wrenching muscles.

Many a night, Jona and Yitzhak, and their penniless comrades, would concoct a soup out of left-over vegetables they found in the marketplace as the merchants were closing. Onions, cabbage, wilted greens, beans and berries, all would go into the pot.

"This is awful," Jona would say as he stuffed himself.

"Considering it cost pennies—it's delicious," mumbled a hungry Yitzhak between mouthfuls.

One day, when he was off duty, as Jona was returning to his room after a fruitless search for work, a woman called to him.

"Can you clean out my septic tank?" she asked.

"Oh, yes," Jona responded, although he hadn't the slightest idea of what was involved.

The woman showed him the cover over the below-ground tank, and gave him several pails and a shovel. When he filled all the pails with the sludge from the tank, Jona used her wheelbarrow to bring the pails to a dumping ground. He made trips back and forth all afternoon.

"Oya," Jona grunted, after removing the last bucket of smelly stuff, "and I complained to Jacob that he was taking in laundry."

When he finished the job, though, the woman gave him seven piasters, a princely sum with which he could feed his Haganah comrades and himself for several days.

He returned to his room, hurrying to shower and change so he could buy a hunk of real meat for the pot. He could just taste the rich stew he would make. He had pocketed the precious coins in his trousers. He reached into the pocket—not there. He searched his shirt, his bedding—not there.

"What did I do?" he groaned in frustration. He went through his room, the shower, the road he walked. The piasters were gone. After hours of that disgusting work, he had nothing to show for it.

When Jona did find work, he would buy groceries from Label, a man from Tomaszov who opened a store nearby.

The man would measure every item carefully, never giving a grain more than Jona had asked to purchase. Nor did he ever offer to extend credit for future payment when he saw Jona had only a small sum to spend.

But one day, he greeted Jona effusively.

"Jona," he beamed, "take anything you want. No need to pay me now."

Jona raised his eyebrows in surprise.

"What's going on with Label?" Jona asked Label's wife when the grocer was out of hearing.

"Well, to tell the truth," Label's wife said slowly, "your parents sent some money to put in your account so you'd have enough for food."

Jona reddened. He was mortified. His father was coming to his rescue again.

Jona demanded the money. It was a huge sum—more than he might earn in two years of work! Was he foolish? Should he starve when he might buy land for speculation as others were doing, or go into business with such a sum.

Yet he was furious. He had to make it on his own. Not only that, he wanted to prove that the yishuv was thriving in Palestine. The Jewish presence was growing, the difficulties would be overcome in time. He couldn't let on that things were terrible for the settlers.

His father obviously thought otherwise. There was only one way to end it. Jona went to the post office and made out a money order to the small synagogue where his father prayed. "Use this for Passover matzos for the poor," he wrote.

It never occurred to him that this gift from his father meant Srulke still cared about his son's welfare, despite the many ways Jona had disappointed him. Nor did he stop to think how his father would feel to have his offering returned.

The donation to the shul had its desired affect. Poor people were helped and it was said about Jona that he must have struck it rich in Palestine if he could donate that much money to charity.

But there was a further repercussion. In Tomaszov, Zosia, now turned twenty-one, was under great pressure from her family to marry. Her father argued, "If Jona Lerman has enough money to pay for matzoh for the whole of Tomaszov, why doesn't he send for you?"

As Jona sipped his penny soup, some weeks later, he read Zosia's tearful letter explaining that her family insisted she accept the proposal of a well-to-do Tomaszov man.

"I must listen to them," she wrote, "but for me, it is Tisha B'Av."

Tisha B'Av, the ninth day of the Hebrew month of Av, is a day that commemorates the two destructions of the Great Temple in Jerusalem.

Jona held Zosia's letter close to his heart, thinking of the girl he had cared for.

But he consoled himself for failing her. Theirs had been a romantic dream. The reality of Palestine was harder than he had imagined. Zosia would make a fine wife and mother and forget him in time.

A few days later, Jona got a full-time job working for a wholesale grocer. As he stacked shelves and counted cans, it wasn't lost on him that he was doing the work he might have done in Poland with far greater financial rewards.

One day, a shipment of canned goods came in with one case dented and spoiled. He pointed it out to the grocer.

"Call the supplier. Tell him ten cases were spoiled," he told Jona. "Dent some more cans. The insurance will pay."

Jona stared at the man for a moment. Then he took his jacket and turned to leave.

"Where are you going, Jona?" asked the astonished owner.

"I came here to build a country—not to be a thief," Jona replied shortly.

That night, it was back to penny soup once again. Jona walked around hungry. A dull pain settled in on the crown of his head by mid-afternoon. Bread and tea for breakfast could hardly fuel him until the long awaited supper, a meal that left him bloated but far from full. He tried to push away visions that flashed before him of his mother's dinner table, its brimming fruit bowl, the platters of stew and potatoes steeped in rich gravy, his heaping plate. Get rid of that picture, Jona, he'd tell himself angrily. You didn't expect a picnic when you came here. But fear gripped him at times. If he fell ill, would he have to appeal to his family? Prove his father right when he had challenged him with— "They're starving there!" Yet when a friend who was working offered him something to eat, Jona would answer. "I just ate, thanks."

"The only person to whom I wasn't ashamed to admit I was hungry was Frieda Stuhl," Jona later recalled.

Frieda had come from Tomaszov a year before Jona and worked as a waitress. She met Monyu Pe'er; they fell in love and married. Though struggling to make a living, too, they always managed to have a full pot on the stove. Once when Jona was low in spirits, starting at dawn he rode his bike the sixty-five miles to their home in a suburb of Haifa. Frieda and Monyu fed him, and after an overnight stay, his courage revived, he pedaled home.

The Pe'er's baby Uri was born in 1937. They had just joined the Kibbutz Tel Josef. But Uri came down with a lung disease He needed to be near the city for treatment. Back they went to Haifa with Uri. Monyu got work in a flour mill.

"Frieda never complains, even when things are hard," Jona reported to friends from Tomaszov. "And she always had strength for others."

During 1937, Jona's detachment was sent to patrol a stretch of road between Tel Mond and Kfar Saba. This coastal road was a vital link between settlements and market towns. Villagers in cars and trucks traveled it every day. Arabs preyed on the travelers. Stabbings and sniper attacks were common.

Arab zealots could silently creep up on an unsuspecting traveler who paused to rest, knife him in the quiet darkness, take his goods and money, and slide away in the rocky scrub.

Jona was now a group leader, operating with his team from an apartment rented for them by the Haganah. When on duty on the rocky bluffs along the road, they would camp out in a barn near an orange grove. The strip of road would be guarded night and day. Simply by making their presence known, they discouraged attacks.

Dressed as an Arab, perched on a donkey, Jona would peer undetected at Arab villages at dusk to detect any signs of an action in preparation. His men, hidden in the hills, awaited his report.

Night patrol had its own dangers. Jona posted one soldier on a high point to observe the vehicles coming and going. Three others waited in the orange grove or slept in the barn in case of trouble. None of his team had encountered trouble so far. He prayed their luck would hold each time he went out on patrol.

Several of Jona's detachment were barely out of their teens. Some were older men, taking time from work and their families.

Amos, a burly carpenter, father of three, insisted on night patrol. When the Haganah sent him up with supplies for the men, he would insist on standing watch, then returning to his settlement in his rattle-trap truck the next morning.

"I can't leave work in daytime, I must serve at night to do my part," he explained to Jona.

One dark night, Jona assigned Amos the eight p.m. to midnight shift so Amos could get some sleep before dawn.

"Good," said Amos, shouldering the unit's rifle as he moved away. "Don't anyone forget Saturday," he smiled. "My son's Bar Mitzvah—it'll be Open House. Come anytime."

The three others shook their heads. "We'll be there," they whispered as he crept away to man the forward position. Amos's low whistle would signal the approach of marauders.

Jona stretched out in the orange grove. The sweet small of orange blossoms perfumed the air. Stars, like a belt of small crystals, girded the hills. It was so peaceful. This land could be so gorgeous, he thought, if only we could have peace with our Arab neighbors.

Jona checked on Amos at ten, bringing him a peeled orange. He knew it was hard to stay awake, peering into the darkness for hours, especially for one who had worked hard all day. But Amos was alert, signaling, "Thanks. All quiet." Jona returned to the grove. At almost twelve, he woke the two relief men.

"It's been quiet. I'm going up now," he said.

Bent at the waist, and carrying a grenade for protection, he moved up to Amos, whistling low. No whistle answered him. Jona crept closer, feeling along the ground. Finally, he saw Amos's form. Where was the rifle? It should be at his side!

A flash of fear shook him. "Amos?" he whispered hoarsely. No answer. He crawled closer. He felt something wet and sticky on the ground. His heart plummeted. He touched Amos. The man did not move. Ambushed! The thought tensed his whole body.

Jona turned Amos over. Amos, who only wanted peace, was dead, his mutilated penis protruding from his mouth.

Jona wretched and cried as he made his way back to the grove. For the first time, his faith was shaken. How would the Jewish people ever create a homeland amid such savage violence? But if not here, where? he told himself dismally.

He was disgusted, sad and angry. Waves of remorse washed

over him.

Would his people ever be safe anywhere in this world? he groaned. Was his leadership at fault? Should he have stayed with Amos, who surely must have fallen asleep? Or sent a different man? He nearly cried as he approached his men. You're their leader, he admonished himself. Other units had suffered tragic losses, too, and stayed on task. Resolve took over. The land would become a sanctuary for his people one day—Amos's death would not be in vain.

"Strength and courage," he said to himself. "Strength and courage," he repeated to his men as they carried Amos's lifeless body back to the base. The men echoed the words of Josef Trumpeldor as they struggled down the rocks with their comrade.

The officers would send a bereavement counselor to Amos's widow and children, Jona was told. No, Jona could not be spared to attend the funeral. He and his unit must go back to their post, expecially since they had proved themselves vulnerable!

But from now on, two men would guard the forward position. They would find the extra manpower for every unit, somehow.

Chapter 18

TOMASZOV

While the world powers were watching the Nazi menace grow, thousands of men and women like Jona and his comrades were battling to keep some little ground safe for those who could make it out of the hell Europe was becoming.

During the next year, Jona served in the Haganah on the outskirts of various settlements bordering the coastal road north of Tel Aviv. It was a period of round-the-clock duty. Only a scant allowance was given to the volunteers for their maintenance. Many times, his band was out of food, and had to glean corn or squash from the fields. But no one complained. Their only wish was for more arms and ammunition. Sometimes, during a skirmish, they had to flee, for lack of bullets.

Between 1934 and 1939, ships purchased or hired by the Haganah agents abroad or by Betar, set out to bring fleeing Jews to Palestine's shores. Although most were intercepted by the British, their passengers interned or sent away, some few ships did make it through. The makeshift dock in a small cove along the Mediterranean Sea near Tel Aviv served to land illegals. Row boats from the blacked out mother ship offshore would reach the wooden dock hidden by trees. Whole families would scamper from the boats up the beach, into the waiting arms of kibbutniks, who would spirit them away to their safe havens.

Most were refugees from western Poland, Austria, Czechoslovakia or Germany, smuggled through adjoining countries by a secret pipeline manned by Haganah agents and the agents of Betar.

The escapees had fearful stories to tell. Polish Jews expelled from Germany were in refugee camps hoping for relief that didn't come. Jews were beaten in the streets; Rabbis made to scrub sidewalks with a toothbrush; Jewish stores were boycotted; Jews were arrested and sent to work camps.

Jona questioned those from Poland for news of Tomaszov, Lubelski. It was rumored that some Jews from there were heading east to towns over the Russian border where they felt safer.

Letters from his sisters throughout 1937 said that the family was well. Shmuel was studying at the gymnasium in Lemberg. The Lermans were carrying on their business as usual. They had heard that in the yishuv things were not well—riots—unemployment. Was Jona okay?

His family never told him that their father was ailing. Perhaps they didn't know. Srulke was not one to pamper himself. Perhaps Srulke was beginning to fear the perils to come. But he, like the other Hasidim, was trapped by the Rebbe's insistence that one must remain in the community; that the rest of the world was hostile to the Torah. The other reality was that these millions of Polish Jews had nowhere to go.

At a conference in 1938 at Evian, France, concerning what to do with Jews who were trying to leave Austria, Poland and Germany, it became clear that no nation would open its gates to these fleeing Jews. Understanding this, Hitler felt he had a free rein to implement his horrific "final solution." The Jews of Europe were poised for disaster.

Srulke listened to his Rebbe, perhaps with mounting foreboding. For in 1938, Srulke Lerman died of a stroke. He was 56 years old. He had amassed a fortune in holdings. He had sustained hundreds of families by employing their sons. He had given generously to his little shul and to the Rebbe of Belz. He hadn't produced a rabbi among his three boys. But his name was revered by all who knew him.

Jona never learned the full extent of his father's conflict until decades later. All he knew was contained in the cable he received from his elder brother, Shlomo, saying their father had died.

Ah-h, thought Jona, I can never hear his good wishes for me now. If he could see me, lying in dust among the rocks, a gun in my hand, how could he ever bless me.

Now came a dilemma for Jona.

Shlomo wrote that if he could come home, he would be able to claim his share of the proceeds of the sale of the many properties controlled by their father and of the flour mill which was still in his name.

Jona sighed. His only motivation for returning to Poland would be to see that his mother was safe, and bring over whomever might wish to come. With money from the flourmill, he might be able to swing their entry, as they would be investors in Palestine, something the British looked upon with favor.

But he was still an illegal person in British eyes. Did he dare risk revealing that he had no papers! Yet, the choice was between taking a chance on being able to return or doing nothing and always regretting it.

Weighing each word carefully, Jona drafted a letter to the British High Commissioner. He explained that he wished to go to Poland and that he would return with a considerable sum for investment in an industry that would employ the many newcomers in the country.

Not long after, an official letter, embossed with the Royal Crown arrived for him. He tore it open. The high commissioner responded that he was free to leave, but he would have to wait for his turn to come up in the quota before he could return.

"Ha!" Jona laughed bitterly. "That'll be the year 2000." His reaction was instantaneous. He could never abandon his beloved Eretz Yisroel for all the money in the world. He would not go back.

It was a decision he never regretted, and one that probably saved his life. For if he had re-entered Poland in 1938, he might never have left there alive.

Chapter 19

LOVE AND WAR

In June 1939, Frieda Stuhl Pe'er wrote her family that she was coming to visit them in Tomaszov. She and Monyu had saved enough money for her to make the trip with little Uri.

"I want my folks to see their grandson" she wrote Jona. "They have few pleasures in their lives. I'll see your family, too, Jona."

A letter followed that one.

"I'm not going. My father wrote—'Something smells fishy. Don't come!' I'm worried."

The Stuhls had reason for warning their daughter. In August 1939, Germany and the Soviet Union signed a non-aggression pact which meant the two nations would split Poland between them once again. Tomaszov, Lubelski fell in the German sphere. The prospects for the Jews of Lubelski were disastrous.

With the pact, Hitler had neutralized Russia, a potential enemy. He was now free to march farther into central Europe.

Poland erupted at this German blow to her sovereignty. She appealed to Britain and France. They had pledged to defend Poland if she were attacked and now they agreed to uphold their commitment. Hitler used this as an excuse to terminate his non-aggression agreement with Poland.

On September 1st, the Germans swept into what was left of Poland. Now Frieda Pe'er and all the Tomaszovkis understood her father's warning.

Britain and France declared war on Germany on September 3rd. That same day, the Germans bombed Tomaszov.

Only later would Jona learn that Yachad's home and warehouse were reduced to ruins. Shaken, but unhurt otherwise, she was able to move in with her younger daughter Pesha.

Tomaszov's Jews fled. Those who could, took refuge over the border in the Russian zone.

Yachad and Pesha and her family bunked in with friends in a town just over the line until they could make further plans. Shmuel lived in Lemberg in the Ukraine, now in the Russian zone. Shmuel took his mother to live with him. Pesha found a place to stay near Lemberg, now called Lvov by the Russians. Esther and her family fled to another province, Galicia.

In Tel Aviv, The Palestine Post was sold out as it came off the presses. The English-speaking readers devoured its pages. The Yiddish and Hebrew dailies were grabbed as they came to the vendors. People read aloud to each other, standing in the street.

The two democratic nations, France and Britain had finally understood that Hitler, step by step, was taking over Europe. He had occupied the Rhineland in 1936; he had annexed Austria in 1938; in March 1939, he had taken parts of Czechoslovakia and Lithuania. Now in September, he was bombing Poland.

Winston Churchill, who would soon lead England through the bitter war, later characterized his nation's lack of response in graphic terms.

"An appeaser is one who feeds a crocodile," he grunted, "hoping it will eat him last."

Poland, too, marshaled her army to fight Hitler's invading force. Ill-equipped for modern warfare, Poland put up its cavalry, men on horseback with pistols at their sides, against Hitler's armored tanks delivering rapid fire blasts from its guns. In the ensuing days, Polish solders were slaughtered, among them their Jewish comrades at arms. Poland was forced to surrender soon after.

By June 1940, France had fallen to the Nazi onslaught. Europe was in turmoil.

Great Britain was now at war all alone against the Nazis. The British had enough to contend with without worrying about competing populations in Palestine. She declared martial law in the Mandate. Under British military rule, both Arabs and Jews hesitated to engage in skirmishes.

But while this threat to the colonists diminished, Britain's harsh policy toward the desperate Jewish refugees, pleading for a safe haven, only became more oppressive. To appease the Arabs, the British, in 1939, issued a White Paper which not only restricted the Jews' ability to purchase land in Palestine, but placed a quota on immigration at 15,000 Jews for each of five years. This was a pitiful number, when thousands, indeed millions would seek refuge in the months ahead. The Jews in Germany and Eastern Europe were in mortal danger of annihilation—but their brethren in Palestine were shackled to quotas.

The Jewish leadership accused the British of reneging on their promise to use its best effort to establish a homeland for the Jews. Ben Gurion pleaded and politicked with diplomats; they were polite but nothing changed.

The militant Irgun leaders, inheritors of the Jabotinsky policy of armed opposition, ridiculed Ben Gurion in vicious language, declaring that reason would never secure a homeland for the Jews. Britain held the power—yet it was thwarting the yishuv at every turn.

The Irgun would unhesitatingly use sabotage to oust the British once they were certain Hitler was beaten. Meanwhile its members would continue to join with the Haganah to bring in survivors from Europe.

Although Jona was still on call to the Haganah, during this period when there was a lull in Arab attacks on civilians, he was able to find a plastering job and work for weeks at a time without interruption. At night, at last, he could afford a plate of solid food to nourish him for the next day's work.

As he dressed for work one morning, he took an old pair of washed trousers from the bottom of his drawer. Coins fell out of one of the cuffs. He found the piasters he had misplaced months before.

"Son of a gun," he laughed, looking at the money. "Now that I don't need you—here you are!"

After work, Jona treated two Arab men from his crew to hummus and felafel, mid-eastern specialties made of chick peas. They had pressed a pita filled with hummus on him one day when he was hungry, and he remembered that kindness. As he stood around the outdoor stand with them, the world seemed bright again.

Always, he returned to his room hoping for a letter from his family. When there was nothing, he returned to reality. His family was in a war zone.

A friend from Tomaszov stopped by one night.

"I had a letter from Lvov," he said. "My family fled there after the Germans bombed Tomaszov. Most of the town has gone to Russian-occupied Galicia or the Ukraine for safety. They were certain your family, Jona, was in the Russian zone, although they haven't seen them."

Shmuel was in Lemberg-Lvov. That was reassuring. He told himself that's where his mother and sisters were amd Shlomo was too. But that didn't put an end to his anxiety. If the Germans advanced into Russia, would the Communists protect the Jews?

After enjoying the comradeship of Yitzhak Blank for a year, Yitzhak had moved out. He had been appointed a gafir, an auxiliary policeman, by the British. He was assigned to a collective farm near Haifa. Jona hoped Yitzhak would find a post near Tel Aviv. But Yitzhak wrote that at the farm he had met a "terrific special girl," and was getting married.

Jona was joyful for Yitzhak. Yet, he felt a stab of jealousy. He had no one to confide in any more.

Jona thought a change would lift his spirits. He asked to rent a small house that he heard was available on the property of a distinguished intellectual leader in the yishuv.

The cottage would give him some room to breathe, and to put up anyone who wanted to stay. He had no idea that that person lived just across the yard.

The night Jona moved in, Shulamit, the owner's daughter, whom he had seen at group outings, knocked on his door.

"Welcome, welcome," she said smiling. "I brought you a cake to celebrate."

Jona was more than pleased. He warmed at the thought of having a friend close by. She made herself comfortable at his table, and Jona offered to prepare dinner for the two of them from the ample supply of food he had just stowed away.

In his compact kitchen, they fashioned a feast—grilled lamb, flavored rice, wine, dessert. As they laughed together and praised their own cooking, a spark was lit between them.

Shulamit was a university graduate who taught at the local high school. She teased Jona about his limited interest in Hebrew literature, and offered to read with him in the evenings. Those sessions of sharing soon turned into intense lovemaking.

Jona had had many girlfriends before, but none so giving and responsive as Shulamit.

He was in a whirl of emotions. Everything looked gorgeous to him, the vast sky slowly brightening at dawn, the sparkling turquoise sea, and even the flowering weeds in the yard between their two houses.

"Look, Shulamit," Jona would say as he glanced outside his window, "even the butterflies are in love."

And Shulamit, Shulamit was the most beautiful. Dark hair framed her face, dark eyes smiled at him, full lips caressed him, best of all, this wonderful, modern woman seemed to love him as well.

In the midst of mounting chaos, his world had never been better. At his various jobs in the building industry, he was gaining expertise while providing needed shelter. At the end of a hard day's labor, there was Shulamit waiting for him. After dinner, they might read or visit friends or join a discussion at her family's house across the yard.

Often, there were college professors and Hebrew scholars in attendance. The discussions went on till late evening. Jona was impressed. But although he knew the passages of bibical lore they were exploring, he was not really interested in taking part. There were so many important issues at stake at the time that he couldn't see spending energy on philosophical concerns. He was a practical man, not a theoretical one.

Shulamit's father noted their growing interest in one another. He complained to his daughter that Jona was not a religious person, and warned her he was not to be considered as a potential husband. Shulamit would laugh and say they were just good friends. To Jona, she whispered that she loved him and that he should not mind her father's misgivings.

One issue, Jona believed critical, was protecting the yishuv and helping to rescue refugees. At a time when Jews in Europe were in peril he had little patience for philosophy, he told her.

Walking on the beach one Saturday with Shulamit and a few friends, Shulamit suddenly called out—"Look—a boat!"

There, some distance out on the calm Mediterranean Sea, was a battered freighter filled to the railings with people. Some were clambering down a ladder to a small boat alongside the freighter. They could make out its name — *Farita.*

"Refugees!" the friends breathed in unison. Without a word,

they scampered into the surf. As the boat neared shore, they grabbed the gunnels and pulled it onto the sand.

Landing refugees in darkness, was one thing. But this was in broad daylight, in an unprotected place. The British patrol would be on to them in minutes.

"Change clothes! Quick!" the settlers commanded in Yiddish, as they ran with the immigrants toward the shelter of some trees. Taking off their shirts, shorts, skirts and blouses, they gave them to the refugees, donning their heavy European clothing instead.

"Not you, Jona!" cried Shulamit—"you're still illegal — we have papers if we're caught. In those clothes you'll be picked up. Please, Jona!"

Jona paid no attention to Shulamit. Dressed again in a heavy jacket and pants rolled up at the ankle, he led the way through the bushes and behind shacks along the beachfront.

As they mingled with the weekend throngs coming to the beach, they heard the whistles and gun shots of the British who had spotted the *Farita*. Moments later, the ragtag group was taking back alleys to safe houses nearby.

There had been 850 refugees on the *Farita*. Those that remained on the freighter were taken off by the British, and placed in detention camps. Their numbers were subtracted from the measly 15,000 immigrants allowed to enter Palestine that year.

The *Farita*, marooned on a sandbar, rusted there for years. Everytime Jona spied the black hulk, poking out of the sands, it warmed his heart. At least some of his brethren had found safety in the yishuv.

Chapter 20

ARMS FOR THE HAGANAH

The war effort intensified in Palestine. There was a tremendous demand for foodstuffs as nations of the British Commonwealth began sending regiments to the Middle East, gearing up for battle against the Germans and Italians in North Africa.

For a few months, Jona worked for an owner of orange groves supplying the British troops with fruit. He counted boxes and kept records of trucks coming and going.

Every day new battalions were pouring into Palestine from New Zealand and Australia. By 1940, the defeated Polish and Free French soldiers also were being shipped to the Middle East, determined to continue fighting the Germans and Italians who had joined the Germans and had officially declared war on Britain.

Remnants of defeated Polish troops had fled to Belgium, where they participated in the unsuccessful attempts to hold back the advancing German army. Along with British and Free French troops, they had been rescued by a massive civilian boatlift from Dunkirk in May of 1940, and had been ferried across the English Channel to England. The Russians took other Polish troops captive.

In June of 1941, Hitler, against the advice of his generals, invaded Russia, declaring he could defeat the Soviets in six weeks. This was devastating news for those from Tomaszov. Their relatives were trapped in a zone now occupied by the Germans!

The silence from their families in the Russian zone was a black hole of worry in their daily lives. They could only hope that the Soviets would soon have the Germans on the run.

Jacob Lanel's response to the heartbreaking news was to join the Jewish Brigade of the British Army. Finally, Palestine's Jews had won permission from the British to form their own unit and the Jewish Agency sent out a call for volunteers.

Ben Gurion's son, Amos, the boy who surely had spiked Jona's bicycle, had not waited. Against his father's wishes, he had joined the British Army at the start of the war.

But word had come back to Jona that the British were utilizing the Jewish Brigade in only menial work. Jona believed his place was in Palestine. Bitterly, he thought of dangers in the yishuv.

The year before, the kibbutz, in which Yitzhak lived with his young wife was attacked by the Arabs. Married only a few months, his wife hearing shots, and knowing that Yitzhak was on post, went out to look for him. She was shot dead on the spot by a sniper.

It was vital to continue to protect the yishuv, and to hold up his end of the chain that was bringing refugees to shore. And finally, Jona found even a more direct way to help the yishuv.

Once the Russians were allied with the British, they were persuaded to release those Polish troops they had captured. They were needed in North Africa as a fighting force.

The Desert Fox—Hitler's General Rommel, and his Afrika Corps would soon arrive on the scene, determined to win control of shipping by occupying the Suez Canal on the Red Sea as well as the coast of North Africa on the Mediterranean. Whoever controlled the seas would control supplies for the forces. The British would have to make a major effort to defeat the Germans in Africa if they were to win the war.

Jona, with his knowledge of Polish, was soon recruited by a contractor who was setting up camps for the Polish troops. Meanwhile, the officers and men were housed in tents.

One day, Jona, who was measuring a site near the commanding officer's tent, heard a strangely familiar voice.

He poked his head inside. There sat the major who had been his commanding officer when he had been in the Polish army! He greeted the officer by name.

"Who are you—you son-of-a-bitch?" barked the Polish major.

Jona identified himself as a former corporal of his regiment, and asked if he could be of service.

The major thought a moment. "Yes, there is something you could do. How can we get our damned laundry done here?"

"I think I could arrange that, Major," said Jona confidently. "Ask your men to put their things in marked sacks, and I'll be back with a truck."

As soon as his regular work day ended, Jona made arrangements with a laundry in Tel Aviv that was willing to wash and iron the clothes. He borrowed a truck and driver from a friend and came back to a huge pile of khaki sacks, bulging with laundry.

In addition to his other work, Jona and his friends made a respectable sum as a laundry contractor for the Poles during the next months.

"Nobody would believe this," he told Jacob Lanel who was on leave. "First, I'm doing laundry. Then, my customer is my Polish commanding officer. And where are we? A continent away."

"The world is upside-down," Jacob smiled.

"I don't mind making some money from these characters," Jona said.

Seeing the need, Jona extended his laundry service up the coast to Ashdod and Gedera where more troops were stationed. At the height of his laundry "empire," as he called it, Jona employed over seventy Arab men who washed and ironed uniforms for the officers each week. Jona learned some Arabic, and when his truck appeared in the dusty Arab towns with a week's supply of work for villagers, he was greeted with "Salam, Jona!" and applause.

However, the extra income from his laundry business was nothing compared to the munition gold mine he had discovered.

Polish officers were very concerned with their prestige. Jona realized that the British were lavishly supplying the Poles with rifles and grenades so they could continue training for combat. But to the officers' chagrin, they were not issued sidearms. These small pistols were a serious status symbol for the Polish officer. Without his pistol, he felt his uniform was incomplete. Jona understood this at once, and put his knowledge to use.

He knew the Haganah had a full storehouse of pistols, but

few rifles and grenades. His Haganah officers were ecstatic when he suggested a trade was possible.

"Run with it, Jona," they told him.

The Polish officers were delighted also. They fell over each other delivering munitions, grenades and rifles to a nearby kibbutz, picking up their cherished side-arms in exchange.

The armaments went to units on kibbutzim and in small villages that had been defenseless before. These locations were increasingly vulnerable to Arab terror as they absorbed illegal refugees smuggled in by the Haganah. Arms not needed were warehoused for conflicts that were certain to arise in the future.

Jona had by now become a knowledgeable operator. He knew sources, he knew how to avoid the British, he knew how to keep several balls in the air at once.

There were Jews among the Polish soldiers who were delighted to find themselves in Palestine.

"How do we get out of this army and into the Haganah?" they would ask. And the answer would come back—"See Jona Lerman." Nine out of ten men simply deserted, volunteering for the Haganah. Jona made the contact for many of them.

Menachem Begin, a member of Betar in his youth, was with the Polish army when it came to Palestine. He joined up with his Irgun comrades.

The Irgun, unlike a guerrilla offshoot led by Abraham Stern, cooperated with the British until the British started winning the war. Then the Irgun, too, made its goal one of ending the British mandate.

Jona would tangle with the Irgun in the future, but that was when he was married and one war was over with another about to begin.

Chapter 21

HANNAH

When Jona was not on assignment with the Haganah, he was rushing around building air-raid shelters in Tel Aviv. The Vichy French, who sided with the Axis powers, and the Italians were bombing the coastal regions of Palestine. Tel Aviv was one of the first cities hit.

Terrified residents begged anyone they could find in the building trades to construct a bomb shelter for them. Brick and timber basement rooms were being fortified all over town. Jona bought up surplus lumber and recycled used supplies to do the work. He had more orders than he could handle. He was working for himself, at last.

In a burst of optimism, he proposed to Shulamit. They had been deeply involved with one another for two years; it was time to be open about it.

Shulamit knew her father would be displeased, and she hesitated to tell him. Jona offered to speak to her father, man to man.

"Let's not wait any longer," he begged Shulamit. "Tell your father you've made up your mind to marry me, that's it. He'll come around."

Shulamit promised to break the news to her father but weeks went by and she couldn't find the courage.

"Let's just go off and get married," Jona whispered one evening in his little house. "I can't stand this indecision any longer. I love you. Why are we waiting?"

But Shulamit put him off yet again. Jona was heartbroken. Perhaps she was letting him down slowly. Or really didn't know what she wanted. She said she loved him—but what did that mean to her? Not what it meant to Jona, he finally realized.

He couldn't stand being close to Shulamit, without a resolution. "I'm moving out," Jona said one day, hoping she would relent.

"Oh," she said wistfully, not protesting.

Jona took his baggage and books and wounded feelings and moved into a sleeping porch in a bungalow in another neighborhood. A short time later, Shulamit married a high school bible instructor.

He was mystified. This man was so different from Jona. Pale, stooped, quiet, everything Jona was not. Swallowing his pride, he manfully greeted Shulmait and her husband when they met.

Sometime later, when the bombing began again, Jona offered to build an air-raid shelter for Shulamit's family. Although her father thought it was unnecessary, Jona and a friend dug out a bunker for them without charge. Not long after, the sirens sounded. Shulamit's house was one of those hit in the raid. Jona was relieved to learn the family had taken shelter in the bunker and had emerged unharmed.

Jona's worries about his family returned to him with renewed force with the bombings. He suspected the worst.

The war was raging on all fronts. British cities were being bombed nightly by German planes. Troops were fighting in the Sahara desert, and in Italy. Russia had joined the Allied Forces, but her armies were retreating before the German blitz. America had been sending planes and supplies to the desperate British, and when she was finally forced to declare war after Pearl Harbor, there seemed hope for a quick end. But four more years of bitter battle lay ahead.

Reports that concentration camps were really extermination camps were on the lips of every survivor who managed to make it to the shores of Palestine. Horrible medical experiments were being conducted in these Nazi death camps, they said. The able-bodied were starved and worked to death. Older people, and children were sent to gas chambers by the thousands. Ovens burned night and day, cremating the remains of the victims.

After the war, inquiries by historians revealed that hard information about these atrocities was known in Britain and even in America. This information had been repressed by officials in countries around the globe who just couldn't handle the complications to the war effort if it was felt that they were fighting a war to save Jews. They were fighting to save themselves, the Jews would just have to be patient until that job was done.

Reports of the extermination of thousands of individuals—no one could imagine it was millions—continued to be questioned. But newspapers and officials ignored the nightmarish stories. Meanwhile, whole townsful of Jews, in Belgium, Holland, Greece, Italy, Rumania, Hungary, Poland, every country in Europe under the Nazi boot, were systematically being marched to their deaths.

The last Jona had heard from his family was in 1939 when they wrote they might go to Lvov. More than a million Polish Jews had fled the German sector for Soviet territory. It was rumored that the Soviets had shipped the Jews to Siberia.

At night, thoughts of his family suffering in the barren wastes of frozen Siberia made Jona toss in misery on his narrow bed. Who knew how they were faring? How would his mother survive the cold? If only they had understood that Zionism meant to save them—how different it all might have been, he sighed.

One day in 1943, there was a creased, soiled letter in his mailbox. The stamps bore printing in the Cyrillic Russian alphabet. He tore it open! It was from his older brother, Shlomo.

Jona's heart pounded. Shlomo was alive!

His brother wrote that in 1939 the Communist Soviets had sized up the Lerman family with their leather luggage and sturdy clothing and declared them "untrustworthy, filthy Capitalists." They were shoved on a train bound for the northern reaches of barren Siberia.

In summer, they were eaten up by swarms of black flies. In the freezing endless winter, there was little to eat. Shlomo's son had tried to sell his coat for food on the streets of the Siberian town, and was arrested as a "speculator." Thrown into prison, he perished there. Mattel, Shlomo's wife, developed cancer. There were no hospitals or medicine. He and his three girls tried to keep her warm; there was nothing else they could do for her. She, too, suffered and died.

"Ay, Brother," Jona moaned. He remembered Shlomo's gifts to him so he could go to the land of his dreams. He pictured the lively, sweet Mattel. "If only you could have come with me, he mourned."

Shlomo's letter came from Samarkand, a city in Uzbekistan, then a part of the Soviet Union. He and his three daughters had been sent there some time ago. It was warmer and conditions were much better. But food was in short supply, even if work was plentiful. "At least, there is mail service of some kind," he wrote.

Shlomo did not know the whereabouts of their mother, nor sister Esther and younger brother, Shmuel. He had not heard from Jona Feldzon or sister Pesha, either, but believed they were still in Siberia.

Soon after, another letter with a U.S.S.R. stamp arrived. This one came from Pesha, who wrote from Buharah, in the same region.

"There are many poor Jews here," she reported, "and one continually searches for food." But she and her husband, Hershel, their two daughters and a son were managing. Their cousin Jona Feldzon and his wife Esther were in Bisk; she heard from them, she was happy to say. She also met Tomaszov neighbors, the Arbesfelds who survived Siberian winters. Everyone she saw she asked about their mother and sister. "No word as yet," she wrote.

Jona's brow knit in frustration. He pinned his hopes on his family being somewhere in Russian territory. The Soviets might imprison Jews, but they didn't murder them. He announced his news to his friends from Tomaszov. They too had recently received letters from Russia. It was clear to all of them that while surviving, their relatives, along with Russian citizens, were probably starving.

"We must have a relief committee," Jona ordered. "We have

addresses. Let's get food to them!" Frieda Pe'er in Haifa alerted Tomaszovniks in her region.

No matter how little they had themselves, packages with canned food, dried fruit, clothing, soap and cigarettes, which could be bartered, were shipped out by the yishuv to the Russian towns. Many a time, Jona went without a meal so he could send his packages on. It stung him that from his sister Esther or his mother, Yachad, there was no word.

By 1943, the Allied Forces in North Africa had beaten the Desert Fox. Captured German soldiers were herded to prison camps, some of them glad to fall into Allied hands. Hitler was finally on the run in Russia. The tide was turning.

The final phase of the war in Europe would come on June 6, 1944 — D-Day, when the Allied Forces under General Dwight D. Eisenhower of the United States Army, invaded the beaches of Normandy in France. The invasion propelled the allied armies to eventual victory on V-E Day on May 9, 1945.

As British and American soldiers liberated the death camps, the stories of atrocities proved frighteningly true. Piles of corpses were found in the camps. Half-dead men and women were helped to shelters and slowly fed gruel to revive them.

Robert Daniell, a British tank commander, and his crew smashed the gates of the Bergen-Belsen concentration camp in April. Anne Frank had succumbed to typhus in that camp just weeks before. Daniell told his story to newsmen after the war.

He was given two hours to check out the camp that day. He saw hundreds of naked or nearly naked skeletal people lying on straw. He heard shots and saw guards shooting the weakened prisoners who, not quite dead, were writhing in agony. He told an interviewer, "I was so disgusted, I shot the guards with the last four rounds I had."

When British forces entered three days later, ten thousand corpses lay on the ground, murdered by guards as the liberators approached. So starved and sick were the remaining 38,500 prisoners, that only a third of them survived.

It was estimated that one million Jewish children had been murdered outright under Hitler's orders. Five million Jewish adults had been worked to death or simply sent to gas chambers. Even when Hitler knew the war was lost, he raged that all Jews must die.

"The things I saw beggar description..." General Eisenhower said after an inspection of the camps. "The visual evidence and the verbal testimony of starvation, cruelty and bestiality were overpowering. I made the visit deliberately in order to be in position to give first hand evidence of the things if ever, into the future, there develops a tendency to charge these allegations merely to propaganda."

In the yishuv, there was little celebration at war's end. Instead, there was ceaseless mourning as the stories were published about atrocities beyond belief. Even the most hopeful, realized it was likely their loved ones were gone forever.

The bright spot, was the return of the Jewish Brigade to the soil of the Land of Israel. The young men and women, hardened by battle, were hailed as they came down the ramp of their troop ships, the gold Star of David emblazoned on their shoulders.

It was not until late in the war that these troops were sent by the Allies to fight on the Italian front. They fought Germans at Casino and slogging through a treacherous gully, routed them in the small hamlet of Cuffiano. A plaque in that town states that this hamlet was liberated on April 11, 1945 by "The Habrigade HaYehudit."

Nearly 30,000 men and women from Palestine saw active duty on several fronts as members of the Jewish Brigade. Jacob Lanel was one of them. Jacob, however, elected not to return home, but to stay in Europe.

A new battle was about to unfold—the battle to bring the tortured survivors into a hostile Palestine. Jacob would work with the underground railroad, moving survivors from the camps over the difficult route to safe ports. There, ships manned by the

Haganah, paid for by the yishuv and the grieving Jews of the Diaspora, could ferry them to Palestine.

Jona, and the others in the yishuv, would be waiting for them with open arms.

"Thank God there is a place for them to come to," was the sentiment of the yishuv. The victorious British would certainly relent now that the truth was known.

Jews in Palestine were prepared to welcome the old, the sick, the wounded in body and spirit. No matter the sacrifice, these remnants of once vital Jewish communities would find a loving welcome in their ancient homeland.

The leaders of the yishuv were confident that Jews the world over would help. There was new energy in the yishuv as they prepared for an influx of survivors. Jona's construction business had evolved into a supply service for builders. He became a source for sand and gravel, used in the making of cement. Contractors sought him out for supplies. His know-how in the construction field was paying off.

Jona felt somewhat lighthearted one day and purchased tickets to a concert for the following week for himself and his friend Paula. Since his disastrous affair with Shulamit he had had a number of women friends. Several wanted to talk of marriage, but Jona backed off.

A few days later, Paula explained she couldn't make the date, and suggested he take Hannah, a young woman she worked with.

The evening of the concert, Jona combed his thick unruly hair, put on a freshly laundered shirt open at the collar, and set out to call for Hannah Ulmer at her parents' home in a middle-class section of Tel Aviv.

A pretty teen-ager answered his ring.

"Are you Jona Lerman?" she asked, a big sheepish grin on her glowing face. Jona nodded.

"I'm Hannah, Paula's friend. I hope it's all right. We thought you wouldn't want to waste the ticket."

Jona laughed. This Hannah was quite young. But he adjusted.

How could he hurt her feelings.

"What do you mean?" he said, cheerily. "Of course it's all right. It's wonderful! Let's go."

During the concert, Jona sensed Hannah looking at him instead of at the musicians. She liked him, he thought. Suddenly, it was a nice feeling. He grinned at her in the semi-darkness and patted her hand. He found himself quietly pleased. Who was this petite teen-ager that she should affect him so?

"When will you come again, Jona?" Hannah asked boldly as they stood at her door.

"You want to see me?" Jona said laughing. "But you're just a child—and I'm an old man already."

"I like older men," Hannah laughed, ducking her head in embarrassment. "I'm 19. I'm not a child—and I know my own mind. I like you Jona..."

"Then I'll come," Jona said brightly, surprising himself.

That night, Jona lay on his bed, Hannah's fresh young face, crowned by a wealth of curly light brown hair, shone like a beacon before him.

This is crazy, he told himself, I'm looking for another heartache. What does this girl know of the world? How could she be a partner for a man who has yet to struggle in a hostile land, a man whose obligations to the Haganah may yet be tested again?

He questioned his feelings and hers because he did not know Hannah's story, nor her determination.

Chapter 22

A PERILOUS JOURNEY

Hannah Ulmer was named Anny when she was born in 1925 in Vienna, Austria. She and her girlhood friend Judith Weiner, would walk home from school together through the tree-lined streets of their city to the ornate apartment houses they lived in near the synagogue.

One day in l936, they had good news for their parents. The eleven-year-old schoolmates had been accepted at the gymnasium—the elite high school for talented students who would be prepared there for college.

Austria was a democracy then, and it wasn't of concern that the girls were Jews; Judith's father a rabbi, and Anny's father a struggling salesman. Judith and Anny were accepted on merit, and enjoyed studying with their classmates from different parts of the city.

But democracy was fragile in Austria, and that year the government was thrown out by an anti-Jewish religious party sympathetic to the demented Austrian corporal who had become chancellor of Germany three years before, Adolf Hitler.

Jews were full citizens in Austria, enjoying all rights. But they understood, with the coming of the new regime, conditions would change for them. The question was—how soon?

When Hitler annexed Austria in March of l938, German troops goose-stepped through Vienna's streets. The Jews watched with frightened faces, as the Austrians cheered and waved banners.

The handwriting was on the wall, both literally and figuratively. Anti-Jewish slogans were written on walls near the synagogue. Jews were kept waiting for service in stores where they had been welcomed before. As a precaution, Anny's father, Oscar, made sure that their passports were in order.

That September, Anny, Judith and the other Jewish students were told Jews could no longer study in the gymnasium. They were sent to a high school far from their homes, jammed together with other Jewish students in an outmoded building.

Jewish families were informed they had to double up with other Jews and could not occupy a whole apartment for themselves.

Oscar Ulmer appealed to his sister to take them in, but she had married a Catholic, and had converted. Her daughter was a member of Hitler Youth, she said, and would report the presence of Jews in their home to the police if they stayed with her.

Anny's frightened parents tried to arrange for her to go on a children's transport to Palestine, but preference was given to those who could contribute the full cost of the relocation, and they did not have the funds. Judith Weiner was accepted however, and the girls parted with tearful kisses.

In Germany, a frantic Polish boy, Herschel Grynspan, whose parents were deported, went to a German official to protest. Rebuffed by a low-level officer, he shot him. The Germans seized on this to punish all Jews, supposedly in honor of the German 17th century religious leader, Martin Luther.

On November 9th and 10th 1938, a pogrom was instigated by German and Austrian authorities which had no equal. Modeled on Martin Luther's directive when the Jews refused to convert to Luther's brand of Christianity, it was followed to the letter, and then some — burn all synagogues and holy books; destroy Jewish homes; confiscate Jewish property.

With venom, the Nazi SS troops, and others in plain clothes beat Jews in the street, murdered ninety others, smashed store windows, and trashed and burned synagogues in every German town. It is known as the "night of broken glass"—Kristallnacht—in German.

In Vienna, shop windows of Jewish stores were smashed with crowbars, Jews were assaulted, synagogues burned. Rabbi Weiner was dragged from his home, and with bayonets pointed at his head, made to desecrate the altar of his synagogue.

Then Oscar Ulmer was arrested—taken away to a work camp. Fearful of the future, Anny and her mother moved in with an aunt. Six weeks later, Oscar returned, having bribed an SS guard he knew to let him go home for the weekend.

"Genia, Anny," he said to his wife and daughter the moment he arrived, "collect some clothes, we leave Austria today."

With their passports in hand, they went by train to the border of Czechoslovakia. They could go no further because they had no visa for that country. A railroad clerk whispered to wait on a bench in the station for nightfall, and then speak to a guard. She rubbed her fingers together as a signal a bribe would be accepted. Later that night, the family was able to slip aboard a train to Brno, a city in the Czech republic.

Oscar had been born in Czechoslovakia and was fluent in Czech. His brother still lived in Brno. But when Oscar called, the brother suggested they meet on a park bench. He said he was in no position to shelter Oscar. A combination of personal problems, and his state of denial that the signs of impending tragedy were all about, prompted him to turn his brother aside.

Crestfallen, the Ulmers found a rooming house where they could stay, falsely promising the proprietor that their temporary permits were on the way.

Meanwhile, Oscar contacted a Jewish organization to arrange passage to Palestine. It would take time, he was told. Organizations were moving Jews from Central Europe as fast as they could find ships and captains willing to make the trip.

Anny and her mother remained closeted in the tiny room all day. Only her father went out since he could speak Czech. He brought back food and newspapers.

Ten days passed. Now the rooming house owner was threatening to toss them out because the promised papers had never arrived. If police checked and found illegals living in her house, she could lose her license or worse, she told them angrily. They would have to leave the next day if the visas weren't delivered.

In desperation, Oscar went to the police station, showing records that his father had fought in the Czech army in the Great War, and declaring his intention to leave the country momentarily. The policeman in charge, besieged by desperate Jews with various stories, shrugged his shoulders, stamped a few papers and the Ulmers could breath again.

Days later, Betar, the Zionist organization, sent word there was room for them on a transport. But it would be a long dangerous journey, and children were not wanted. The hysterical parents finally hit on a strategy. They simply said their fourteen-year-old daughter, was sixteen. The frantic Ulmers were accepted.

Finally, one step ahead of Hitler's invasion of Czechoslovakia, passage was arranged on the Greek vessel, *Aghios Nicolaos*.

They went by train to Bratislava and then by boat on the Danube to Romania where the rusty freighter was waiting. The passengers numbered 750 including twelve children. It would be a crowded, dirty three-week journey, but the pay-off, freedom in Palestine, kept their spirits up.

Among the passengers were many artists, dancers and musicians. They shared their talents on deck in nice weather. Anny was enchanted listening to violinists play classical themes, or lively music for a few dancers to whirl about. Artists amused people by drawing caricatures of their fellow passengers or arguing about trends in modern art.

As they neared Tel Aviv, the passengers held their breath. The ship approached the three mile limit, still in international waters. The vessel's lights were out. It was 4 a.m. as the captain crossed into Palestinian territory. The *Nicolaos* inched toward shore, engines on slow.

Suddenly the sound of gun-fire filled the still night air. Two passengers were hit. A British patrol boat loomed out of the darkness. *The Nicolaos* was ordered to halt!

Instead, the captain reversed engines and raced for the three mile limit.

"I'll not surrender my boat!" he declared. "I only agreed to bring you here—not to get shot at." The passengers screamed in protest. But it was no use.

The captain steered across the Mediterranean for a Greek island—Kaeous—just offshore of the city of Salonika. Once in port, the Greeks refused to allow the refugees to land, and the captain announced he would go no further. The passengers were marooned aboard the crowded vessel.

Day by day, conditions worsened. Water, sanitary supplies, and food were running out. And then the weather turned hot. When they left Vienna in February, the Ulmers took only winter clothing. Now it was May, the temperature soared to 90 degrees at mid-day and they were dripping in the heat. Genia cut up a pair of pajamas, to make shorts and a top for Anny.

The refugees stood on deck calling to the people on shore for water, food. When the Jewish community of Salonika heard about the plight of the refugees, they came to their rescue. Every day for three months, the Jews of Salonika sent supplies by boat to the island where the ship was berthed. Bread, water, vegetables, and medicines were brought aboard, offering some comfort for the refugees broiling in the sun, or sweltering below deck.

During that time, babies were born, people died. Dysentery struck most people, including Genia. And no matter how hard they tried to stay clean and air their bedclothes, most everyone was plagued by lice.

Anny had been a sheltered child before that trip, but no more. She saw couples making love, others retching from illness, and crying in despair. She helped portion out food, and bring it to those too sick to go on deck. Three months had passed. When would it end!

Finally, after repeated appeals to the Jewish Agency in Palestine, and British citizen Chaim Weizmann, a new ship came for them, towing behind it a smaller fishing vessel. It was July 4, 1939. The world was in turmoil as Hitler's march continued. The story of the marooned ship attracted little attention. The press was busy with stories about Hitler's aggressions. As for the caring 80,000 Greek Jews of Salonika, all but a handful perished in Nazi death camps.

In ten days, the passengers were once again in sight of Haifa. Now they were commanded to transfer to dories, which would draw up to the fishing boat that would take them into port.

The overloaded boat headed for shore, jammed with over 700 souls standing packed together. The British were horrified when they saw the tilting boat as it neared the harbor. The boat would surely sink if sent away, and the people drowned. Despite the repercussions they would hear from the Arabs and their own government, the British port officials allowed the refugees to land.

Genia was carried by stretcher to a hospital. Anny was lodged in a woman's barracks; her father was assigned nearby to a men's barracks. When they met at the back fence to talk, Anny declared she was ready to go on to Tel Aviv and find their relatives. Genia's brother lived there with his wife and two daughters.

Her father was detained further, but Anny was given a bus ticket to Tel Aviv. When she arrived in the city, it was Friday afternoon, the Sabbath was approaching and buses had stopped running. Anny wore her heavy winter coat over her pajama outfit, she still had lice in her hair, and couldn't speak Hebrew. What was she to do?

At the bus stop, she observed a kindly man speaking Yiddish to other travelers and pointing them in the different directions. She didn't know Yiddish, but she asked him for help in German. Fortunately, he understood. She showed him the address her father had written down. The stranger said he lived near her uncle, and agreed to walk her there. Leery of going off with a man she didn't know, Anny decided she just had to take her chances. But all was well, and after walking in the heat halfway across the city, she arrived at her uncle's door.

Her Aunt Haya by marriage who opened the door had never met Anny or her family. Now she was confronted by a sweating disheveled girl in a heavy winter coat. Keeping her distance, she listened to Anny's explanation, then hustled her inside.

Haya washed Anny's hair with kerosene to kill the lice then shampooed it thoroughly. While Anny bathed, Haya took some light clothing from her wardrobe for Anny to change into. When her uncle came home, he admired the pretty young lady who stood before him and embraced her warmly. He arranged to go to her parents as soon as the Shabbat ended.

Various organizations, some religion-based, others purely

educational, most supported by Jews in the Diaspora, arose to assist the yishuv in settling-in the youth who arrived on Palestine's shores, many of them without parents. They needed to learn skills, to become fluent in Hebrew, simply to be housed and fed.

Anny agreed to go to a boarding school for refugees in B'nai B'rak, sponsored by the Mizrachi organization, not far from where her parents would settle in Tel Aviv. Now, instead of being too young, Anny was too old for the school's two-year program, which ended when girls were sixteen. Already fifteen, this time, she made herself one year younger to gain admission. At once she assumed her Hebrew name—Hannah. But at home, she was still called Anny.

Anny - Hannah learned Hebrew easily. She continued her high school studies for two years and then transferred to a Youth Aliyah school and graduated from there at eighteen.

Meanwhile her father was employed by the British, and worked in Gaza, coming home to Tel Aviv on weekends. Anny rejoined her parents after graduation, and attended business college, becoming a bookkeeper. She went to work in a small office and made friends with the other office assistant employed there.

Soon Anny's parents began to look around for a man for her to marry. Her father knew a young bus driver who was saving to buy a share in the bus company. This was considered a promising way to make a living at that time.

But after one meeting—Anny—now Hannah wrinkled her nose and said "Forget it."

Anny dated another man and was equally disenchanted.

"He hardly knows Hebrew, and he's not trying to learn," was her comment this time.

Then, one day, her co-worker in the office asked her if she'd like to meet a really nice guy, a friend of hers who spoke excellent Hebrew and had tickets to hear a Yemenite singer at the auditorium.

Anny shrugged. "Why not, I've had no luck so far," she said. And so it was that petite Anny - Hannah Ulmer answered the door that early spring evening, and found square-jawed, sturdy Jona Lerman waiting on the other side.

Chapter 23

SURPRISING NEWS

For ten years, Jona's true and constant love had been the homeland, to help build it in the best way he knew how. Whatever it asked of him, he was ready to give.

Now he was nearly thirty-four years old. It was time he gave his own life some direction and set down roots. For that he needed a willing partner.

He didn't have much to offer a girl, to be realistic. He seemed unable to think in terms of earning money other than by his own hard labor. If he had enough to meet his simple needs, he was satisfied. Now he began wondering if he had been wrong not to think ahead.

Several men he knew had become rich by speculating in land. He found this a distasteful pursuit. The land was to be reclaimed and tilled, made habitable for families—not to be turned over and over to the highest bidder.

He had been approached by a merchant who sold fruit from Syria to the troops. For a sum, the fruit dealer would purchase more produce than was ordered. The Syrian fruit was a fraction of the price it could sell for in Tel Aviv.

Jona had been laughed at when he refused to invest before. The merchant said the plan was fool-proof and pointed to investors who had tripled their money overnight. Breaking his resolve not to speculate, he advanced the man a portion of his savings. Weeks went by without hearing further. Finally, Jona realized the contact man had disappeared, along with Jona's money.

"I learned my lesson," he was to say to future friends with enticing schemes. "I don't go against my principles."

So, after ten years of work, all he had to show Anny was a one-room sleeping porch with a tiny refrigerator in the corner and a hot-plate on top of it. He had no possessions. True, he had a small business that was growing. And he was putting any profits he made back into it so it would grow even faster. But if the Haganah called—his business was over. Just like that.

Still, after a few evenings spent in Anny's company, that shining face beckoned him through the night. It would be wonderful to see her every day, and to come back to her at night—to build a home with someone he loved. To have little ones.

Girlfriends he had no trouble finding. Now he yearned for someone to share all aspects of his life. Anny was so bright and quick, young though she was, he felt confident with her. He would go forward. And Anny, if she would have him, was the sweet but strong girl who had won his heart.

With wonder, he saw her devotion to him grow. He couldn't imagine why he merited such affection, but he responded, taking great pleasure in pleasing her.

One cool day in April, she had a strange request—to go swimming in the sea. No water was too cold for Jona so he agreed. The two sat together on the nearly deserted beach in their street clothes, a breeze whipping the sand in their faces.

"So, Anny, let's take a dip," Jona said grinning, wondering at her grit. He stood and stripped down to his bathing trunks.

"It's too cold," Anny laughed.

"So why then did you want to go swimming?"

Anny buried her face in the towel that covered her knees.

Jona could barely hear her.

"I wanted to see your legs," she said between giggles. "I could never marry a man with bow-legs."

"And do I pass inspection?" he asked, turning in the sand.

Anny assured that his legs exceeded her hopes both in their muscular shape and their straight lines.

"Any more tests for me to pass?"

"No, no more. I love you without reservation."

However, when it came to her parents it was a different story.

"A man is here ten years —and he doesn't even have a house," Anny's father cried. "What's wrong with him?"

"Nothing, nothing, nothing," Anny shot back. "He's a wonderful brilliant person. He's not motivated by money, that's all. He gave up riches to come here and to stay here. It's people like Jona who made it possible for us to be saved."

"It's hard to be married to a poor man," her mother cautioned. "I know."

"Yes, Momma," Anny said gently. "When it comes time to make money, my Jona will do that too."

They were to be married in June and Jona and Anny were preparing invitations.

Anny used her Hebrew name. She printed: "Hannah Ulmer, daughter of Oscar and Genia Ulmer of Tel Aviv, and Jona Lerman, son of Yachad Lerman, —"

"What city shall I put here for your mother, Jona?"

"Ach, I don't know," he said painfully. "She must be somewhere in Europe."

"So shall I say 'somewhere in Europe?'"

"Yes," answered Jona—"that's all I know and that's what it should say —'Yachad Lerman, Somewhere in Europe.'"

It was not lost on him that some people from Tomaszov were locating relatives. The Displaced Persons Camps were circulating lists of survivors looking for family members. Jona combed the lists for mention of members of his family, his heart beating wildly. No one he knew was on it. Disciples of the Rebbe were so vulnerable — how could they save themselves? He thought mournfully.

"It's too soon," he was told. "The lists are just coming through. Try again."

Then, a few weeks before the wedding, Jona had a visitor. A religious friend from Tomaszov called on him at his office. The man, Hesh, looked uncomfortable as he shook Jona's hand, shifting his feet, not wanting to sit down.

"You have news from Tomaszov," Jona asked, a lump in his throat.

"I do," Hesh announced. "The Rebbe wants to see you."

"The Rebbe is here, in Palestine!" Jona said astonished. Hesh nodded his head, taking a deep breath.

"He got out! He came here!" Jona's eyes were blazing.

"It's a terrible story," said his informant, putting his hand up to ask Jona to reserve judgment.

"He didn't want to leave—but his disciples knew that to stay was certain death. The Nazi butchers killed the rabbi first when they took over a town, and the Germans were in Tomaszov, as you know. The Resistance was determined to save him. They dressed the Rebbe in a Hungarian officer's uniforms—cut off his beard—of course. They were hiding him—when the SS entered the residence."

Jona held his head as the man went on.

"The Gabbai, his assistant at services, was standing at the door when they burst in—demanding the Rebbe. You remember the Gabbai—Yakov Shia—a big tall fellow.

"When the SS asked for the Rebbe, he said—'I'm the Rabbi!' The SS cut him down with their machine guns! Like that!

"A brave, good man, the Gabbai," said Hesh after a moment. "He saved the Rebbe. He gave the Resistance time to get away. They hid the Rebbe in Sokol. Twelve of his family were murdered there. Ach. Finally he could be brought here.

"Are you all right, Jona, you don't speak?" Hesh said.

At this Jona smashed his fist down on his desk in fury. Hesh stepped back, pale. Jona had no words. He paced his office, anxious only to get rid of Hesh and deal with his anger out of his sight.

"What shall I tell the Rebbe?" Hesh asked meekly.

"He's here—and my mother is 'somewhere'—who knows her fate! She might have come here to safety as he did were it not for her devotion to him!

"Tell the Rebbe whatever you wish!" retorted Jona. "I'll not come to him."

Jona was torn in two — his pure devoted family had been betrayed. How many others did this devotion to an ideal of other-worldly redemption, betray?

Jona sat in his chair his head bent, covering his face with his hands, not speaking until Hesh quietly left. It washed over him that his mother, brother and sister were gone forever. He hadn't wanted to face it before. Suddenly, he was certain.

It took days before Jona could come to terms with what he had learned. Anger filled him poisoning what should have been a happy time. Finally, helped by Anny's loving patience, his fury subsided. He came to understand that like the rest of European Jewry, the Rebbe was the victim, not the villain.

As he struggled to turn his thoughts to his coming marriage, he knew he'd never lose the rush of anger that raced through him when he thought of the twist of fate that brought the Rebbe to Palestine without the Messiah, and doomed his family.

Chapter 24

THE SLEEPING PORCH

Jona took heart from the excitement of his approaching wedding. He invited his Haganah regulars, friends from the kibbutz, from the journey to Palestine, old friends from Tomaszov, Jacob, Frieda and her husband, Yitzhak and his second wife. Abdul, a bachelor friend from Jaffa with whom he occasionally went surf fishing, accepted with enthusiasm. He issued invitations to nine other Arab men with whom he did business. They were delighted to attend. As is Arab custom their wives were left at home.

Anny's childhood friend from Vienna, Judith Weiner, would be there. Her father, Rabbi Weiner, had gathered together the remnants of his congregation and created a new congregation in Tel Aviv. He volunteered to perform the ceremony and lend his small synagogue's hall for the wedding party.

Jona didn't own a suit to wear to the wedding. Strict rationing was in effect in the yishuv so that scarce supplies could be fairly distributed. Only by showing proof of their coming marriage was Jona able to purchase a gray flannel suit on the "white" market, and Anny the material for a long white gown to be made to order for her. On the black market, these clothes would have cost four times as much. She also had curly hair straightened into silken strands, a style favored at that time.

Jona purchased wine, whiskey, and vodka; while women friends prepared meats and vegetables, platters of fruit and cake. After the wedding vows were exchanged, Jona broke the paper-wrapped glass placed under his foot, with a resounding crack. Cheers went up and with a burst of joy, Jona gripped Anny and lifted her aloft like a great prize.

Breaking a glass at a wedding is a Jewish custom all over the world. The glass is smashed to commemorate the destruction of the Great Temple in Jerusalem so many centuries ago, and to remind the celebrants that joy often comes on the sacrifices of others.

To break the glass in the land of his ancient fathers, was a moment of great pride for Jona. But as the crumbled glass reminds celebrants of the tragedies of the past, so was Jona's joy diminished. For he had heard nothing from Poland, and he had no idea if his mother and sister Esther and his younger brother were dead or alive.

The wedding party went on for hours, fueled by the singing and clapping that kept people dancing the hora until past their strength. They flopped joyously into each other's arms, toasting the couple, and singing lustily till nearly dawn.

Early in the morning, before they returned to their small room, and still in their wedding attire, Jona and Anny collected the empty bottles left behind at the hall. Jona would redeem them the next day—every penny counted. Then they walked the two miles to their sleeping porch.

Anny had resigned her bookkeeping job in a local firm to help Jona run his small office. Now Jona was free to solicit more business, and purchase supplies—sand and gravel—at advantageous prices. He worked hard, delivering materials to job sites, day or night, as supplies were called for by the builders. And progress was being made. In the six months after their wedding, he was able to put aside a sum of money toward the expense of moving to larger quarters.

As it was, in the small-enclosed porch in which Anny and Jona started out, they had to put a chair on the table in order to make room for the sofa bed to be pulled out each night.

Preparing a meal on a hot plate was a real challenge for an experienced cook. Anny was cooking her first meals.

Chicken was hard to come by, but Anny had gotten one-half of a pullet at the market, and Jona was looking forward to dinner. When she placed a pale, stringy portion on his plate, he balked.

"What did you do to it!" Jona cried. "It looks like rags."

"I boiled it in the pot with a carrot," Anny answered bewildered.

"Well, this is terrible. You ruined the only piece of chicken we've been able to get. Can't you cook, Anny?"

"I can't cook, Jona. I've never cooked before," Anny confessed, her mouth turning down and tears forming. One look at her and Jona knew he'd over-reached. He gathered her to him.

"It's okay, Annila," he said softly. "I'm sorry. Cheer up. I'll tell you a story about another cook."

Anny didn't mind what he was saying, as long as she was nestled in his arms.

"One night at the kibbutz, someone said he wished he could have a slice of his mother's cheese cake. A girl in the group offered to make one. There was plenty of cream on hand and she'd get the ingredients together.

"The next evening she presented the group with a nice looking cake, which we readily consumed. But that night there was a constant stream of people back and forth from the latrines. We asked her what she put into that cake," Jona said chuckling. "Everything sounded all right until she came to the oil. Where did she get the oil? She saw a can marked oil in the barn and used that. The men all groaned—'That was machine oil, you bird-brain!'someone yelled. It took us a week to get over that cake," Jona laughed. Anny smiled a crooked smile.

"Did you think I was as stupid as that?" she cried.

"Oh, no, no, no!" Jona crooned, kissing her tenderly. "I love you, I love you," he sang. "I'll show you what to do, next time," he began. "You put some oil in the pan, very hot, then you brown the chicken.... well...let's eat now, Anny, give me some horse-radish."

Anny began laughing at him, and shaking her head. Jona blushed. "I'm sorry, I'm sorry," he cried. "I'm eating, I'm eating."

"It is pretty terrible," she said. Then they began laughing and crying together.

Soon there was something else to laugh at, trying to fit on the sofa bed. Even extended, it was hardly big enough for the two of them because Anny was expecting a child. Jona parted with the equivalent of a thousand dollars for key money to rent a three-room apartment. For that, all he got was the key. The rent was due each month as well. But apartments were at a premium in the crowded city, and Jona had no choice but to pay up.

One evening, Jona returned to their new home shouting for the whole block to hear.

"My brother is alive! Shmuel lives! Anny, Anny," Jona called, racing up the stairs to their rooms, a sheaf of pages in his hand.

A letter from Shmuel Lerman in Lublin, Poland had finally found its way to Jona in Tel Aviv.

Overcome by emotion, Jona handed the papers to Anny to read. As she scanned the letter, the smile on her face faded, and she began to cry, to cry for his lost family and for Jona who would go from joy to profound grief in a few short minutes.

"What's the matter, Bubela?" Jona said, taking the pages from Anny's hand. He sat down to read.

"This is good, Anny, why did you frighten me?" Jona protested. "Shmuel is married to Krisha, a woman who survived Auschwitz..."

Here, Jona stopped in his reading, sighing heavily, he went on.

Shmuel wrote that he had dropped his studies a year after their father died and was working in Lvov, hoping his family would come to him. His mother moved into his small apartment. Pesha and her family were nearby. Suddenly, the Russians put all Poles in the city on trains for Siberia.

"When I came from work I learned our mother was on a transport," Shmuel wrote, "I ran to the station and pushed myself on the train, and found her. I pulled her off—explaining that I was a citizen of Lvov, and she should be allowed to remain with me. Permission was granted."

Esther, their sister, her husband and the boys, who were elsewhere in the Russian zone, were also able to remain.

"We managed for the next eighteen months. Then the Germans broke their pact with the Soviets. They invaded Russia. The Russians pulled back, abandoning Lvov to advancing German troops. Esther's area was also overrun."

The Nazis, under orders to massacre "Juden," sent younger men to labor camps. Shmuel was arrested by the Germans and sent to a labor prison. Old people and people with children, were trucked to the Polish town of Belzec, just three miles from Tomaszov. His mother and sister must have suffered the fate of the other Polish Jews in that action.

Shmuel had learned a huge hangar had been built, right opposite the site of one of the Lerman mills! Shmuel described the devastating details—a diesel engine pumped carbon dioxide into the hangar until all were dead. The bodies were then burned and the bones and ashes spread on a field in which seedlings were planted, as if to mock the biblical phrase, "from dust you come and to dust you return."

"My effort to save our mother from Siberia, turned into her death sentence," Shmuel wrote, his letters pale on the page.

Jona put his head against the wall, sighing. His good-hearted mother's face was so clear to him—placing scoops of raisins before him, hugging him when he came home from heder, blessing the candles on Shabbat, rejoicing at the many weddings she had arranged. What had she ever done to deserve such cruelty?

And Esther, the sister that had taken him from the tree in the forest where he hid after Petliura's raid, how old was she? Thirty-six? And her boys, Yitzhak and Herschel—fifteen and—and eleven.

"Eleven!" Jona called out. "What could an eleven-year old do to a German?"

Even when they knew they were losing the war, the Germans kept on with their genocidal madness in Poland and in France, Holland, Italy, Hungary, and Greece. How could people in those countries who were aware of what was happening—stand by? Jona's thoughts whirled.

He forced himself to read on. Shmuel and some other Jewish men were imprisoned in a work camp. Later, the younger, stronger ones were sent to work in a quarry, where it was plain that given only soup and a chunk of bread a day, they would be worked to death.

"When we were somewhat away from the others, two guys and myself, jumped the guard, and ran for the woods," Shmuel wrote. He formed a group of fighters from escapees, and survived as part of a Jewish Partisan band, wreaking havoc on German installations wherever and whenever they could.

Shmuel and Krisha were on the top of the list for emigration to the United States. Jewish organizations were helping the survivors find new homes. To return to Poland was unthinkable, Shmuel wrote. He had been back to Lvov and Tomaszov, and found that Jewish survivors were loathed.

"The Poles have occupied our homes and taken over our businesses, they don't want to see us again." Some returning Jews have been killed by the Poles, he was told.

"No, my wife and I are bound for America, and someday, when we're settled in, we'll meet again, dear Brother."

However, Shmuel wrote that their older brother, Shlomo, had gone to live in Germany where the government had pledged to help survivors. Pesha Glanzer, the surviving sister, was on the list to come to Palestine. And this news buoyed Jona's spirits somewhat. At least, she had been spared. Some day soon, he hoped to have some family near him.

Not long after they received the letter, Jona and Anny's baby daughter was born. They named her Yael for Yachad and rejoiced in their good fortune for she was a healthy beautiful baby.

It was 1946, Jona and Anny were happily at home in their new location on a pleasant street around the corner from British headquarters.

But their comfort did not last long.

The Arabs in Palestine were screaming. Survivors of the Holocaust in Europe were coming to Palestine in a never-ending stream. The British navy was stopping boats at sea, turning them back, shelling the vessels if they did not heed warnings. One overloaded ship was sunk without concern for the pitiful passengers aboard. The Jewish Agency under Ben Gurion could only protest and protest again. Negotiation and persuasion were tried, with little to show for it.

The militant Irgun declared the negotiations were foolish. The British wanted Jews to perish. It would now go all out, employing terrorist tactics around the clock, with one aim in mind—ending the British mandate.

The British, in their zeal to keep out the desperate survivors and appease the Arabs, had moved thousands of soldiers into Palestine and arrested members of the Irgun, locking them up in the prison at Latrun.

Despite this, the Irgun escalated its attacks. On July 22, 1946, their operatives blew up a wing of the King David Hotel in Jerusalem, selected because British officers were quartered there. Jewish civilians also worked in the wing. Although the Irgun had attempted to warn occupants to evacuate the hotel, the warning was ignored.

"We don't take orders from Jews," the officer in charge was reputed to have said when told by phone to evacuate. Over ninety British, Arabs and Jews were killed, and many were wounded.

In this action which garnered worldwide attention, sympathies were with the British.

England had stood alone fighting Hitler until the United States joined the battle. Her cities had been bombed, thousands of civilians and fighting men had died. Slaughtering British soldiers was a no-win proposition.

But the Irgun, led by Menachem Begin, was unrelenting. When Jewish terrorists were hung from a line of gallows, British soldiers were ambushed and killed by the Irgun in reprisal.

The British posted guards around their headquarters in Tel Aviv. Soldiers in full battle dress stopped residents and demanded to see their passes. Barbed wire surrounded the entire block. The Lermans' little haven became a fragile nest in a war zone.

One afternoon, from his office nearby, Jona heard firing that seemed to come from his own apartment house. Jona held his breath. What was this? The British must have gone crazy!

He sprinted toward his street. As he neared his apartment house he saw firing coming from behind it. The British were firing back at an Irgun attack.

Dodging bullets and flying debris to reach home, Jona flung open the door and called for his wife and baby. No answer. Where were they?

Glass shards from a broken window littered the floor in the room where Yael slept. "Anny!" he wailed.

"Here, Jona," came a tiny voice. Anny and the baby were hiding in the bathroom. She had barely closed the door when a blast from British headquarters shattered the glass.

With his heart pounding, Jona held Anny close to him. He cradled his little baby in his arms. He kissed Anny wildly. "I thought I lost you!" he murmured, as she hugged him back.

British officials appeared at Anny's door the next morning.

"We're taking this apartment. Everyone must evacuate this building at once!" an officer declared.

Anny went white. These were the same words the Austrian soldiers had used in Vienna when she and her parents were forced to leave. How ironic. And here she thought she was free!

The families were loaded onto trucks and deposited at an abandoned British army barracks. They had to leave most of their possessions behind. The precious key money would be a complete loss if the apartment house were demolished. It was cold and ugly in the barracks, but people tried to help each other and Jona organized a committee to report to the mayor of Tel Aviv as to their needs.

Then an event took place that finally turned the tide.

The *Exodus*, a ship purchased by the Haganah and filled to the railings with 4500 survivors of the death camps, including 300 orphaned children, was approaching the port of Haifa when it was fired upon by British officers! The ship was boarded and escorted into the harbor under guard. The passengers could see the green hills of Haifa before them and cried out with longing as British soldiers assaulted them with hoses and tear gas.

The British exploded underwater charges near the boat to keep refugees from jumping over and swimming to shore. After days of futile resistance, the passengers were forcibly taken off the damaged boat, with the promise that they would be sent to the island of Cyprus, a British possession not far from Palestine where Jews were being detained behind barbed wire. The baggage of the passengers was even relabeled "Cyprus."

But Great Britain's anti-Zionist Foreign Minister, Ernest Bevin, countermanded the order. It was to be an historic miscalculation.

Chapter 25

THE STATE IS BORN

It was a trick! The boats to which the Jews were transferred sailed back to the displaced persons camps in Germany.

Such unbelievable cruelty to people who had barely survived the worst mass ethnic slaughter in history was simply not acceptable to most people. Public opinion weighed in on the side of the Jews this time. Bitterness toward England came from every quarter, including their own citizens.

Britain caved in. They had had enough of this mandate which brought them failure after failure. Moreover, they were no longer concerned about protecting India. That nation had won its independence from Great Britain. They were more concerned about their relations with the Arab states in the Middle East. Under the sands of Egypt, Saudi Arabia, Iraq, were huge oil fields. In the work of rebuilding its cities and industries, oil was of prime importance to the countries of Europe. Only Russia, at that time had known supplies of oil. It was folly to antagonize these Arab states for a piece of near worthless land—Palestine. And the Arab states made clear that the idea of a Jewish state in there midst would be fought to the last man.

The British wanted out of this unsolvable conflict. They had problems of their own at home. The British declared their intention to give up their mandate.

Meanwhile, in the halls of the United Nations organization, established by the victorious Allies after the end of the war, diplomats and technicians were poring over maps of Palestine, trying to find a way to divide that sliver of land between the Jews and Palestinian Arabs.

Plan after plan was rejected by the Jews. An internationalized Jerusalem was an anathema to the militant Irgun leaders. Time and again they declared, Jerusalem must be in Jewish hands, not divided. The loss of the southern area, the Negev, was unacceptable to Ben Gurion. As yishuv leader and head of the Jewish Agency, he was poised to compromise—if only the borders of the state could be defensible and Jerusalem could become the capital of the new state.

As it evolved, the partition plan gave the Jewish State threads of land up and down the coast and a triangle to the south—the barren Negev. Crowding it on all sides, was Arab territory, including the West Bank of the Jordan River, reassigned to Palestine, along with the Gaza strip on the sea. The map looked like a rag that had been torn and tattered. And Jerusalem was not part of Jewish territory! The city would be under United Nations' control. While the Jewish State would be hard to defend, at Ashdod and Afula it was barely three miles wide, the Jews would at least have sovereignty. And that was paramount, if they were going to bring in survivors.

The Jews sent word they would accept the partition. Arab residents were assured they would be able to become citizens of the state with all democratic rights.

Despite efforts to mollify them, the Arabs leaders were boiling. They declared they would reject any plan of partition. They pointed out that it was Europeans who murdered European Jews, not the Arabs. The U.N. was trying to redress the Holocaust by taking land from Arabs who had nothing to do with it. Furthermore, the Arabs were allotted only 45 percent of the land, whereas their population was greater.

When the British left, the whole land of Palestine must come under Arab rule, they declared. There would be no compromise. They too had secret treaties in which they had been promised sovereignty over all of Palestine.

Nevertheless, world sentiment favored the Jews. As the horrors of the Holocaust, the Shoah, the annihilation were revealed, giving the Jews a homeland at last, where the remnants of a people could find some peace, seemed only fair.

It was pointed out by Jewish and Christian spokemen that most of the territory had been the Jews' only homeland for centuries. And while they lived in Palestine after the Romans destroyed Jerusalem in the year 140 A.D., as well as in many other countries, for nearly two millenia they had dreamed of returning to Eretz Yisroel.

Besides, the Arabs had many countries they could call their own. The Jews had only one. It was also remembered that the Grand Mufti Haj Amin el Husseini and Arab leaders had actively supported Hitler's armies.

In what might be considered a modern day miracle—the Soviet Union, which usually vetoed U.N. resolutions supported by the United States—this time agreed with the U.S. in pressing for partition. The Soviets, unlike other Europeans, had their own oil supply. Besides, they wanted to have a future say in the Middle East, the crossroads of the continents.

On November 29, 1947, the members of the General Assembly in its temporary quarters in Queens, New York, met to take the fateful vote on its resolution for partition. A two-thirds majority of the voting members was needed.

France, who had been wavering for and against, cast a vote in favor—and a cheer went up. The Philippines changed their vote to yes. Tiny Iceland, which identified with a besieged people, voted yes. Liberia voted for partition.

The final tally was 33 in favor, 13 against, 10 abstentions, including Britain, and one not voting. With only three votes to spare, the resolution was adopted!

In New York City, Jews rejoiced, joined by many Christians. In the displaced persons camps, Jews were jubilant. The Jews in Palestine breathed deeply.

Jona, his family and friends were emotional, "Finally, finally," they said raising glasses, but no one was complacent about the decision. They knew the Arabs would be on their necks the next day, fighting partition from house to house if necessary.

Within days, the British set a date for their departure from Palestine; it was to be May 14, 1948 — six short months away. In that time, the Arabs would throw all their efforts into crippling the Jews' ability to fight back. Almost immediately, small settlements in the Negev came under attack. South of Jerusalem, a bloc of settlements around Hebron was invaded. Arab bands rampaged in Jerusalem, looting and burning Jewish stores. Bus passengers bound for Kfar Etzion were ambushed and murdered. Thirty-five Haganah men were killed trying to defend the settlements.

The Haganah called upon every volunteer it could muster to protect the settlements once again. Jona's building supply business would have to wait. They would have to live on moneys owed them by builders, but after those bills were paid, their income would virtually stop. Anny would be left with only a trickle of funds to manage the house. Jona hated that prospect, but Anny did not complain. Along with other housewives and mothers, she would struggle and worry, but never complain. To everyone they knew, no sacrifice seemed too hard. Their mission was so stupendous, a Jewish homeland restored for all time, that no sacrifice could stop them.

"Go, Jona," Anny said when he was called.

The position of the new state-to-be hung by a thread. Seven Arab nations, representing 45 million people, would be arrayed against 650,000 Jews. Arabs were purchasing used arms from Germany and Italy, and the British gave them munitions outright. They even permitted boatloads of arms consigned to Arabs to land.

When it came to the Jews, the agreed-on rules were strictly enforced. The yishuv was not permitted to import arms of any kind, and every shipment was searched diligently.

In the months ahead, the Haganah and the Palmach, a force of younger men and women, would scramble to prepare itself for an onslaught. Ben Gurion sent missions abroad to raise funds, and relied on a few savvy Jews to purchase arms in several European capitals.

A cat-and-mouse game was carried on by the Haganah. It employed every ruse it could think of to bring in arms. American Jews shipped machinery parts for making bullets, labeled "farm equipment for the kibbutzim." A steamroller would be packed with guns, the front and rear rollers welded shut, so it would pass inspection. Parts of three small planes were smuggled in this way—reassembled in a kibbutz storeroom later.

Under cover of darkness, boats laden with arms made landings at the secret dock at Sde Dov.

Jona's assignment, one evening, was to take a team into a busy shopping area and create a diversion that would tie up British patrols while a delivery was in progress.

"It hurts to tell you this," he told his men, "but we're going to break the windows of the Heftzibah department store tonight, and get the Brits to run after us. We'll keep them pinned down with our craziness until the drop is carried out."

So the normally peaceful businessmen, husbands and fathers flung rocks through the show windows of a store owned by Jews. As the glass crashed and fell, evening shoppers ran screaming, drawing the British police to the scene.

Jona's men fanned out, running this way and that, disrupting sidewalk vendors, causing cars to careen out of control and tying up the police force.

"What are you doing? Crazies!" bellowed an outraged flower vendor whose cart had over-turned, his goods strewn in the roadway. Jona knew the vendor, buying flowers from him to bring to Anny for the Sabbath.

"Jona!" the man shouted angrily as Jona approached at a run.

"Arms drop," Jona breathed as he ran by.

"Oh-h," said the vendor. And as Jona and his team disappeared in a dark alley, the vendor, seeing police approach, pointed them in the wrong direction.

The supplies were delivered without interruption.

Jona could return home to sleep when he was off duty and this gave him a chance to help Anny. Food was in very short supply during this time of mobilization. People stood for hours for a chance to buy an egg or a quarter of a chicken. Jona often spent his off-duty hours waiting on line so he could bring Anny and Yael something for the pot.

One night, while waiting his turn, a woman approached him. She told Jona she was Malka, a sister of Idele, who had been a cook in his family's home in Tomaszov. Jona warmly embraced her and asked after Idele.

"She is still in Europe, but she wrote if I ever saw you, to give you a message," the woman said slowly.

"So, tell," Jona said laughing.

"She is the one who took your passport when you were eighteen. She thought she was doing the right thing. She didn't want you to lose your inheritance."

Jona lowered his brows. The picture of the dining room with his whole family around the table came back to him. He wanted to reach out to them.

The woman began to whimper. "I hope I haven't hurt you, Jona," she said.

"No, no, no," Jona mumbled, patting her arm. "It's so long ago... I just wish I could ask those I wrongly accused for forgiveness," he said slowly. To himself, he thought—where is my inheritance now, and where is my family? This concern with material goods, where does it all end? He made his way home, mourning his lost family all over again.

As so often happened, during this emotional time, one was rocketed from sadness to joy.

Anny had good news for him. The British had vacated their compound near their apartment on Derek Petah Tikva, and the residents could return to their homes. Just in time, too, because Jona had received word that his sister Pesha and her family were on the way and Jona and Anny had promised to take them in.

Jona spent his days with his Haganah team and it was almost impossible for him to conduct business. When builders needed supplies, he was simply not available most days to deliver them. After awhile, they found other suppliers. Jona accepted this. Now that there was a true homeland in sight, the culmination of his dream, and the dream of thousands of others who had struggled in the yishuv, no effort would be spared to make it a reality.

The Jewish Agency had no official army organization as yet. The various undergound forces realized they would have to co-ordinate their efforts if they were to be effective against a much larger enemy force. But each military group had its own officers, and strongholds.

The Palmach, a trained force of young men and women, some of whom had served in combat in World War II and had experience with modern weaponry, was the most promising group. Veterans, like Jona, made up the ranks of the seasoned Haganah regulars. They had little training in advanced weaponry. Then, there was the Irgun, with its different agenda, able to run a guerrilla operation, and finally its offshoot, the Stern Group, fierce fighters, who used terrorist tactics to compensate for their small numbers.

It would not be easy to meld this assemblage into an effective fighting team. But it had to be done and soon.

On May 14, the British withdrew at Haifa. In this vacuum, with no country having control over Palestine, Ben Gurion immediately called the People's Council of the Jewish Agency into session at the Tel Aviv Museum on Rothschild Boulevard.

By 4 p.m., just before the Sabbath would put a stop to all business activity, the proclamation was ready. It was read by David Ben Gurion:

"...we, the members of the National Council.... by
virtue of our natural and historic right and of the
resolutions of the General Assembly of the United
Nations, do hereby proclaim the establishment of a Jewish
State in the Land of Israel—the State of Israel."

May 14, 1948, the fifth of Iyyar on the Jewish calendar, became Israel Independence Day from that time forward.

Ben Gurion, as head of the Provisional government, extended the hand of peace to Arab nations of the Middle East and declared that Israel was prepared to seek the advancement of the entire region.

Declaring itself a state is but one step in becoming a nation. Step two would make it a reality, acceptance by other nations of the world. Would they respond?

By the dawn of May 15, the wonderful word was out—shouted from the rooftops—"The U.S. has recognized us!" That action by President Harry S Truman was viewed widely as the greatest psychological boost to the birth of the nation.

The Soviet Union recognized Israel on May 18, and moreover, did not embargo arms sent to defend the newborn state, as did the U.S.

"Ah-h," cried Jona lifting his glass in a toast with Anny and their friends, "at last I'm legal."

Soon after, the first immigrants were able to land on Israeli soil without fear of guns, or hostile patrols.

All the nights that Jona had woken from sleep, hearing the cries of his childhood—"Gevalt! Gevalt!"; all the years of nerve-racking night patrol in the desert and at the dock; Amos's horrible death while guarding the road; the deceptions and constant struggle, all were endured for a single privilege, finally won.

To all Jews, anywhere in the world who asked to enter their ancient land, the only confirmation they now needed was the piece of paper that said: "The right to settle in Israel is hereby given."

Chapter 26

LATRUN

On the 15th of May 1948, the Israelis' War of Independence began. Winning the right to land by international agreement is one thing. Holding it, is another. Five well-equipped Arab armies attacked on all fronts. The Arabs vowed to push Israelis into the sea in ten days time.

As the British left, they seemed to do everything they could to aid the Arabs.

Jona's unit had no time for celebration. Every opportunity to prepare for the onslaught would have to be seized. Now they took part in one of the strangest operations of the war, if one can call it that.

The British were evacuating an army camp stocked with munitions. Instead of leaving by the regular exit that opened into an Arab village, they were forming up to exit through the Jewish settlement in order to block Jews from entering. The Arabs, from the village of Beit Nabala, could then pile in the main gate, and take over the fort with its store of supplies.

Jona's commanders had a plan. They stationed a small force of men on a hill near the camp facing Beit Nabala.

"The idea," Jona told Anny later, "was to make the Arabs think we had hundreds of men. All night we dug a tunnel. At dawn, we began marching into the hidden tunnel and out again at the other end. All the while, half of us were carrying broomsticks. We didn't have enough rifles to go around.

"It sounds like kids playing soldier—but it worked! The Arab villagers watched us from their houses. They must have believed thousands of armed men were going to come down on them. They never came near the camp. Most of the population ran away. We waited. When the British cleared out, we rushed in. The supplies were ours!"

Jona was gloating, but Anny was just relieved to see him in one piece and learn there had been no shooting on this latest mission. The people at home never knew what was happening to their men and women on the front lines. There were no casualty reports until an entire engagement ended.

The strategy that involved Jona's Haganah unit at that time made it critical to take the towns around Lydda and Ramle. Lydda was needed by the Israelis because it was where the Lod landing field was located. The Jewish forces had only eight Piper Cub planes when the war began, but more were coming in, if promises were kept. In Arab hands, attacks would be launched on the Jewish towns from Lydda, not to mention Jerusalem, already threatened by Trans-Jordan's Arab Legion.

By securing the Arab village of Nabala and Beit Dagun, with the help of the Haganah regulars, the Israelis were now in position to take Lydda and Ramle.

The newly minted Israelis knew they couldn't win a serious prolonged battle the way they were organized. From 45,000 Haganah men and women, 30,000 were volunteer guards at their settlements, and couldn't be called upon to fight elsewhere, leaving their villages undefended. However, 3000 young, well-trained Palmach troops, and smaller units of the Irgun and Stern groups were better prepared and eager for the test.

The entire Israeli force had barely one rifle or machine gun for each active duty soldier. The 2-inch mortars had only enough ammunition for three days. The air force was the eight Piper Cubs; the navy, 300 sailors and their beat-up boats. Ammunition, tanks, and mortars were desperately needed.

The Arab armies that would oppose the Israeli were not much better coordinated but they were better armed. There were villagers who acted in defense of their areas, and two somewhat trained scout groups. But the Arab Legion, comprised of 10,000 British-trained Bedouin, was a professional fighting force. Added to that were more than 30,000 Arab troops from Trans-Jordan Lebanon, Syria, Egypt and Iraq, with artillery, armored vehicles and air support.

One of the Israelis' first priorities was to keep running the electric power stations in Israeli controlled areas.

Jona was now a group commander. His men were assigned to join the units protecting the vitally needed Rutenberg Electric Station which was not far from the dock at Sde Dov. Rutenberg supplied Tel Aviv and the surrounding area with power and it was an inviting target for Egyptian bombers.

Armed with only long-range rifles, one of Jona's men managed to hit an Egyptian plane as it was diving toward the station. Amid cheers, the men saw the plane spiraling down toward the water.

If they could knock down a plane with a rifle—they could do anything. But optimism could go just so far.

Then, Jona's unit was ordered to another operation—back up a Palmach battalion clearing Jaffa of Arab defenders. His men ran from building to building for cover as they worked their way forward behind the Palmach. If there was shooting from inside a structure, they returned fire. They entered each building rifles at the ready. Women and children found inside, were to be escorted to safe areas.

Hordes of Arab civilians were already streaming south from the town, but the attack caught many others by surprise.

Rifle in hand, Jona entered a deserted house, ready to fire. Inside he saw an Arab man, dressed in work clothes, sitting at a table, a burning cigarette between his fingers. Jona stared, then shouted, "Stand up!" The man didn't move. He had been shot dead moments before.

Jona's stomach churned, no less than it had for Amos.

"An innocent person caught in this crazy war," Jona whispered. Inside he raged. Why couldn't the Arabs accept the partition! Why must I leave little Yael, perhaps never to return!

What was he to do though, except go on.

Jona's assignment was shifted again. Now he was to command a unit guarding the power sub-station near his home. He and his men were able to keep the station up and running while he was in charge.

In Haifa, though, it was a different story. The main electrical plant took a direct hit on May 15th as the British withdrew. Jona's boyhood friend, Jacob Lanel, after serving in the Jewish Brigade in Europe and helping to bring Jews to safety after the war, had finally returned to Haifa. At once, he reported to his gunnery unit in the Haganah. At his post on that night, he was wounded in the leg. He was taken to the hospital, but without lights and power the medics couldn't operate on the wounded. By the time power was restored, Jacob's leg had become gangrenous. Jacob, who loved to hike in the hills, to climb Mount Carmel, lost his leg above the knee.

For Jona, there were more battles to come. On May 24th, Jona was reassigned again—this time to the area around the police station at Latrun.

The Haganah had captured the station, but abandoned it when the men were needed to reinforce an area under direct attack. It was a costly decision. The Arabs immediately seized the unprotected station. Latrun was a key position. To have taken the chance of leaving it unprotected proves how desperate the Jewish forces were for manpower.

The village of Latrun sat astride the only road from Tel Aviv to Jerusalem. The force that controlled the station, controlled the road. The force that controlled the road controlled water and food being transported to Jerusalem.

Jerusalem was already under siege by the crack troops of the Arab Legion. Supply trucks crawling through the Valley of Ayalon on the way to Jerusalem could now be blown apart as they neared the fortified Arab installation. And they were. By the dozens.

The Israelis were ordered by Ben Gurion to retake Latrun at all costs. The Seventh Brigade was one of the units given the task. No soldier looking up from the valley to the station, perched on the hillside, could be optimistic about the assignment. The muzzles of mortars were trained in all directions. The Jews had only a meager supply of weapons.

But the Haganah would send men to help, and a group of recruits was scheduled to join the operation. If determination counted, they would succeed.

The recruits were immigrants, fresh from the D.P. camps. Few of these men and boys had had military training. Yet, those who had barely escaped Europe's horror were willingly putting their lives on the line for a new state whose bounty they had yet to enjoy.

The plan was to assault the hill under cover of darkness. Through the element of surprise, they hoped to overcome what they lacked in experience and equipment. If they were lucky, the hill could be occupied by the recruits before the Arabs were alerted. Then the other units would pile in. Jona's men were stationed in the hills at Deir Ayub, bordering Arab-held territory around Latrun.

But luck was against them that night of May 24th. The recruits were spotted by an Arab officer roaming the hillside. In moments, guns were firing down at them. Three recruits were hit.

Units below began firing back at the guns. One or two were disabled, but many others kept up the barrage. The immigrants continued to struggle up the hill, as their numbers dwindled.

At last, their commander saw the task was impossible.

"Back, move back!" he shouted in Hebrew. A Sabra, born in Palestine, it was the only language he knew. The recruits seemed not to hear. He waved his arm and shouted again. The men looked around in confusion. Several more were felled.

In horror, the seasoned soldiers shouted commands in Yiddish.

"Get down!" "Crawl!" "Keep your bellies on the ground," they chorused hoarsely.

Jona could see the debacle from the hill where his unit lay, protecting the outer flank of the attack zone. He and the others groaned in anguish as they saw the boys mowed down, some from friendly fire from the guns trying to protect their retreat. Others were felled as they pulled wounded comrades after them.

It was a terrible loss for the just-born state. Men and boys they hoped to shelter became victims once again.

More than one hundred lives were lost. The hill remained in Arab hands.

Jona's unit camped in the hills for the next few nights, waiting for the call to re-engage. They holed up between the monastery on one side of the road, and the Arab town of Deir Ayub, on the other. The second assault took place five days later.

Mickey Marcus, an American volunteer, who had been a colonel in World War II, coordinated the attack with the Israeli commanders. The plan was to employ newly acquired half-tracks and armored vehicles to smash the doors in the wall leading to the police station. Once inside the compound, the troops approaching from behind the station would surround it, forcing a surrender. Jona's group would defend the hill from attack and come down to assist once the station was in Israeli hands.

The Israel Defense Force today is considered one of the best well-trained, well-equipped tactical force in the world. But in 1948, it was not prepared for the complexities of mounting such a battle. The barrage from the firing half-tracks set the wall of the station on fire. In the glare of this fire, the armored trucks were illuminated. The Arab artillery in the station had no trouble focusing their guns on the trucks, They were destroyed, their flaming hulks incinerating those trapped inside. Jona and his comrades kept firing toward the gun emplacements, but the barrage continued. The grizzled veteran next to him was hit. He rolled down the embankment, his blood dotting the ground as he fell. Jona shouted for the medics but kept his eyes forward and his gun firing.

The reinforcements on the way to the battle ran into an ambush and had to withdraw. The second attack failed. Latrun remained in Arab hands. Jerusalem was cut off.

Chapter 27

THE STONE PILLOW

Jona and his unit were not sent home after Latrun. There would be no soft pillows for their weary heads. They were ordered to Beit Jiz instead. The Arab town had fallen to the Haganah and from it the men of the Palmach and Haganah would try to save Jerusalem.

The Jewish Quarter in the Old City of Jerusalem had already been overrun by the Arab Legion. Looters were sacking homes, trashing synagogues. The rabbis had thrown themselves on the mercy of the Jordanians.

But a population of 90,000 Jews lived beyond the medieval wall surrounding the Old City. The Jews in the new sections of the City of Jerusalem, in Yemin Moshe and Mea Shearim, were being bombed and strafed. Injured and hungry, they were cut off from food, medicine, and ammunition.

If the city was not re-supplied in a matter of days, some Jews were willing to talk surrender.

But surrender was not an option to Ben Gurion and the Zionists who had fought so long and hard for this sliver of land. A way had to be found around the blockade!

At last, the Israeli scouts discovered a shepherds' path through dry gullies that wound around the Judean hills. If they could get through the rocks and boulders in their way, a road could be leveled to the secure portion leading to Jerusalem.

The men who were moved up to Beit Jiz, accepted the challenge. In ten days they would have to carve a road to Jerusalem. If ever Jona wanted to build the homeland with his own two hands, this was his chance.

Jona and the men of the Haganah and Palmach labored like Pharaoh's slaves in Egypt. No taskmaster, wielding his whip, was over them; their whip was the need to complete the job before June 11th. That was the deadline for a U.N truce to go into effect. All combatants would stand in place at that time.

The road building would have to cease.

Even more urgent was getting flour to the bakers in Jerusalem's Jewish neighborhoods. The ration was down to four slices of bread a day. There was no milk and little water. Children were starving. The bakers warned, "Only three days' supply of flour remains."

Day and night, the men struggled in the dust behind the bull-dozer. They lifted away boulders the road-building equipment had broken up, dragged away-uprooted trees, and shoveled dirt over holes in the path.

The torturous winding road gained only one foot forward for every three feet cleared. At that rate, they would never finish in time to save the people of Jerusalem.

There was one other solution, to hand carry the sacks of rice, of flour, of medicine on their backs over the uncleared portion of the hills.

They would do it!

Working under searchlights, supply trucks from warehouses in Hulda and Tel Aviv crawled up on the just leveled portion of the road. Jona and the men lined up, unloading the sacks onto their backs. Augmented by volunteers, who had come out from Tel Aviv, they stumbled three miles through the night to the secure road beyond.

The civilians, older men, staggered under the weight. They tripped and fell over the rocks. One man died of a heart attack. The younger men, most of whom had worked all day on the shovels, were bone weary and breathless. But they struggled on, fifty to eighty-pound sacks on their shoulders.

Three miles to go. Then they saw the jeeps and mules wait-ing on the other side to complete the journey. Back went the men for another trip.

Trucks unloaded, the volunteers were taken back to Tel Aviv. The road crews flung themselves down into caves on the hill-side until called to take their turn at the shovels the next morn-ing.

The road crews, and the troops guarding them, were on short rations. Water trucks were only for Jerusalem.

"We gathered water from streams in our helmets," Jona later told Anny. We strained it through our sweaty shirts to remove stones and sand. Who knew what we were drinking? But a thirsty man can't be choosy. The work had to go on."

At night in the caves, bats hung overhead and scorpions and snakes slithered past the exhausted men. Jona heard hissing near his head. Slowly, he moved away, shoving other half-awake men from his path.

For the first time in years, he asked God's help. What would happen to his wife and baby!

A soldier at the mouth of the cave suddenly turned. He sized up the situation. Tip-toeing over, he struck, smashing his heavy boot on the snake's body, then crushing its head with the butt of his rifle. Jona waved thanks, and went on sleeping.

The next day, struggling in the dust with his shovel, Jona found himself shivering in the hot sun though sweat poured from his brow. He asked the medics for medicine, drank it down, and went on with his work.

"For three weeks, I had a stone for a pillow," Jona told Anny. "Though, Anny, please understand, I was no different than the others. We all worked to our utmost. Not a man complained," he insisted, "If you couldn't take it, you weren't there. Those who were there were there to the finish—the completion of that road and the finish of the fight."

True, they worked like slaves, but unlike Pharaoh's slaves, these men were building a temple for the living, not the dead.

Slowly the "Burma Road" grew. Named after the lifeline road that was built during World War II, this lifeline to Jerusalem became a path to eventual victory.

And at last, by the first week of June, food and supplies, hauled by convoys of trucks from Tel Aviv, began to move straight on through to Jerusalem. The wounded could be treated, the children fed, the city defended.

Then the break came

On June 11th, the U.N. called the cease-fire. The Egyptians were only 25 miles from Tel Aviv. Jerusalem was still in danger. Israel desperately needed to re-group and plan new strategies. But why would the Arabs accept a cease-fire?

For one, Egypt's army had not expected a real fight, but the settlements were standing up to any assault the Egyptians could mount. Its army was not prepared to fight from settlement to settlement. The Syrians had withdrawn their forces, and the Iraqis were under-manned. The Arabs, too, needed to re-plan.

When the truce held, the commanders released the men.

"Go home, get cleaned up, get some rest. We'll call you soon enough," the men were told.

The next night Jona made it home and tapped on the door. Anny gasped with delight, and wanted to embrace him.

"Ay, Anny, I'm full of lice. Please bring me kerosene so I can wash them off."

Scrubbing himself out in the garden, he turned into a shiny blackened man. He threw his clothes in the trash heap and naked headed inside for thorough washing in a blessed shower. Kisses and conversation would have to wait till morning. Anny understood—just happy to have him home.

Jona fell on the first bed he had seen in weeks, and slept for twenty-four hours.

On June 20th, Jona was called up again.

This time for a heart-breaking mission—to fire on fellow Jews.

The decision to fire on the ship *Altalena* is still debated, and Jona recalls it as the most terrible moment of his life in the homeland.

A problem arose in the fledgling nation. While the truce was in place, the Irgun was bringing in arms, Sten guns, rifles, and ammunition, on the freighter *Altalena*.

Although Menachem Begin, head of the Irgun fighters, had pledged to join his forces to the regular army in formation, there was suspicion that he would do so only under his own terms—

and if this were not possible, might mount a coup in Tel Aviv and try to take over the stressed government of Ben Gurion.

The ideological differences—that still exist today—involved compromise versus rigidity.

Ben Gurion was for compromise, accepting the principle of a shared Jerusalem, for example, and then working toward a better solution.

Begin and his followers believed that because of their determination that Jerusalem and the whole of the ancient land of Israel should be in Jewish hands, they would eventually succeed in winning control of the city. And this was the time to take a stand.

Ben Gurion favored eventual discussion through a democratic process. For Begin, some items were beyond compromise. Jerusalem was one of them. Begin made no secret of his disagreements with the Prime Minister and his Mapai Party.

Now, with Ben Gurion's knowledge, a ship bearing arms and 500 trained reinforcements for the Irgun, was approaching Tel Aviv. Begin wanted a portion of the supplies for his own men defending Jerusalem. The remainder was to go to the other forces.

Ben Gurion distrusted the Irgun. He feared a coup and if not that, a division of loyalties at a time when unity was paramount. He ordered the Palmach to take command of the landing.

Jona and his Haganah unit were sent to the hill overlooking the small port. They were told to fire on the boats bringing the munitions to shore from the larger ship. Jona gritted his teeth. How could he do this? Jews firing on Jews? He set his sights on the keel of a small boat, make enough holes and the boat would founder, he told himself.

The Irgun fired back. The boats kept coming! A canon was wheeled into place on the hill, its muzzle trained on the Irgun.

Jona and several others began to cry with shame as the first ball was shoved into the canon. It exploded at the clutch of men on the dock. Ammunition and bodies flew into the air. Moments later, the Irgun commanders raised their hands in surrender.

"It was the worst thing I have ever done," Jona declares after many years of mulling over that night. "I feel it in my heart today—so terrible it was to fire on our own—yet I believe Ben Gurion was right, We needed to act with one voice."

Twelve men died that fateful day. Much needed munitions were exploded. The Palmach took over the ship and kept the supplies that remained. Begin agreed to subordinate his forces to that of the provisional government. Once the permanent government was established through the elective process, those with his ideals expressed their feelings through a consortium of parties in a democratic Israel.

Soon after the night of the *Altalena*, Jona went to the Israel Defense Force recruiting station and enlisted in the regular army. He had seen his comrades shot and maimed. He had endured strained muscles, fevers and sores, but otherwise was unharmed. His luck could hold out only so long.

The Haganah had no system for compensating the widows of men who died, but the army was being established on the principles of a regular force in an independent nation. His wife and daughter would be protected.

Jona was thirty-eight years old. He had fought long enough. He and other Israelis wanted desperately to get on with their lives, but they had to see the State firmly established first.

The army offered Jona a commission as a captain if he would enlist for two years. There was status in being an officer, better pay, contacts, and the thrill of being an insider. He could have had it.

Yitzhak Blank, whose first wife had died during an Arab attack on their kibbutz, accepted a commission. He commanded forces in the north of Israel, and eventually rose to the rank of colonel. But Jona hoped the armistice was only months away. He wanted to go home.

He didn't give a pin for status. His goal was service. Given the rank of sergeant major, he so impressed his commanding officer with his zeal, that Jona was sent to recruit men and women for the communications wing of the army. He also was placed in charge of Arab prisoners. To be a jail warden was not to his liking but he made it his business to see that their rights were respected. There was hatred expressed toward these Arab soldiers by Israelis in the camp. Jona was challenged when he insisted that they be given the proper food, and have a chance to pray. "They are dogs," he was told. "What are you worrying about them for?"

"I don't love them," Jona said. "But watch out! We'll have to live with them. Let's learn how."

Once he put his own life on the line for them.

The Stern Group was still functioning as an underground force. When Count Folke Bernadotte, the U.N. mediator in the peace talks, suggested that Israel relinquish the Negev, give back Lydda and Ramle to the Arabs, and allow the U.N. to control Jerusalem, he enraged the Israelis. But no one expected that he would be murdered. Yet tragically, in September, 1949, this is what happened

The international community was up in arms. The new state was mortified that this had happened. Known members of the Stern Gang were immediately arrested and imprisoned. They were sent to an army prison camp where Jona's Arab prisoners were at work cleaning old bricks to be reused in building a mess hall.

Somehow, the Jewish prisoners, brandishing guns, were able to escape. The Arab work battalion was in their path as they ran. The Arabs, seeing the armed men running toward them, cowered in terror.

Jona, who was armed, thought of attempting to block the escapees, using the Arabs as a barrier. But he would be shot, along with the Arabs. This escape was beyond his scope.

He flung open a warehouse door and shoved the Arabs inside, standing guard at the entrance until the escapees had passed.

"The Arab prisoners were my responsibility," he later told

his superior officers. "In that tense situation, anything could have happened. My first duty was to protect them."

The officers shrugged. Jona's strained allegiances were a preview of complex Arab-Israeli relationships that would face the new State.

Jona soon felt this on a personal level. In Jaffa on an errand one day, he dropped in at Abdul's house in what was now a nearly deserted Arab neighborhood. Abdul's mother greeted him warmly, but Abdul coming into the room pointedly looked up and down at Jona in his Israeli army uniform.

"Get out!" he shouted, eyes blazing. "You're not welcome here!"

Jona gaped at him. Abdul's mother admonished her son, but Abdul stood firm, pointing to the door. Jona felt as if he had been slammed in the face. He turned and left.

Not long after, he had to deal with the animosity of Jew versus Jew.

Once the camp mess hall was completed, he was instructed to hire religious men to supervise the kashering of food in the kitchens. These were ultra-Orthodox Jews who refused to serve in the army.

Jona and his driver were taking several soldiers and two of the religious men to the camp when he heard cursing and yelling in the back seats. The Israeli soldiers shouted, "These fanatics are praying that Israel lose the war!"

"Creating a state before the Messiah comes is a sin!" the ultra-Orthodox shouted back. Those were fighting words for soldiers who were daily putting their lives on the line. From then on, Jona kept the two groups apart.

What a place! Jona thought. Arab friends curse us, and now Jews do the same. These Ultras let us fight for them while they study and pray. They'll all come around eventually, he tried to assure himself.

While Jona was relegated to duties behind the lines, younger men were fighting the War of Independence on the northern and southern boundaries of their assigned territories. By January, they had penetrated to the tip of the Negev at what is now Eilat, and had the Egyptians trapped in Gaza. Egypt was begging other Arab states for reinforcements. Britain took steps to come to her aid. Then a cease-fire was proposed.

Ben Gurion, who had brooked no compromises throughout the war, was willing to agree to an armistice. The agreement was signed with Egypt on February 24, 1949. Israel would leave the Gaza strip in Egyptian hands, but her control of the Negev was assured. Israel withdrew from an area it had taken in Lebanon, and signed an agreement with that nation in March. Jordan followed in April, and Syria in July. The war was over.

Jona was released from the army. He had served nearly as long as he would have if he had accepted the commission. No matter. The job was done. He could go home to his wife and daughter.

Four thousand of his comrades-in-arms had died in the War of Independence. Two thousand civilians had been killed. Thousands of Arabs had needlessly lost their lives. But the nation was established, and the territory gained by Israel gave her more robust borders, and a larger corridor to Jerusalem, as well as much of the new city.

Satisfied that he had accomplished what he set out to do— help establish the Jewish homeland, Jona wished only to work and see Israel blossom as a free democratic nation. The only problem was, he had no business and no job, and Anny was pregnant again.

Chapter 28

CHICKEN FEED

If the one million Arabs in Palestine had accepted the U.N. Partition Plan, they would have enjoyed a solid territory in the north around Safed, a band of land touching Trans-Jordan and a chunk of the Negev at the Egyptian border, running north along the sea past Ashdod.

The armistice lines were far more restrictive. The whole of the barren Negev was in Israeli hands except for a strip along the sea, Egyptian Gaza. Israeli territory extended north to encompass the Arab towns of Afula and Nazareth, and while the coastal corridor was but ten miles wide at many points, it was wider than in the original plan. However, the bulge of land on the west bank of the Jordan River, including parts of ancient Samaria and Judea, was won back by Jordan.

The Arabs called for the elimination of the new state, and refused to sign peace treaties with the Israelis that had been agreed upon at the armistice. Israel would have to keep all its manpower on reserve. Each man was required to spend a month in the military each year, until the age of fifty-five.

One of the first actions taken by the Arab states was to exile Jews who lived in their countries. Thus was created a block of 800,000 refugees, most of whom immigrated to Israel over the next several years. Nearly as many Arabs fled the territories now occupied by Israel, to be housed for the next decades in U.N. camps in West Bank towns or in Jordan proper.

David Ben Gurion, the Prime Minister, welcomed the truce. Arabs came back over the border to return to their homes. Additional thousands, who had not fled, remained in Israel, becoming citizens.

The Israelis now would concentrate on their true mission of making welcome all Jews seeking a homeland.

Jona, as did thousands of other soldiers, turned to the Haganah for assistance. "We're not in the business of finding jobs," an official said.

Jona thought the leadership should be offering some assistance to their men and women who had given up their livelihoods and now were adrift, and he said so. But each volunteer was now on his own. Networking with one another, was the only recourse. The government later did provide benefits for veterans and their families, but by then Jona had made a connection.

An officer who had served with Jona, and who was impressed with his organizing skills, told him about the plight of the small farmers who were not attached to kibbutzim. He spoke of their need to have a better system for the distribution of feed for their chickens and animals.

To feed, house and clothe the refugees piling into the country from D.P. camps and from Yemen, Syria, Morocco and Algeria was an astounding task, and unique solutions were needed. To increase the supply of homegrown food, and give people an occupation, the government distributed chickens to those who were willing to try raising poultry. Householders were given eighteen chickens to start them off.

When a chicken farmer brought his eggs to the government warehouse, he received a ration coupon for a supply of feed for his flock. There were long lines to collect the sacks of feed, and the right supplies were not always ready.

Learning about this for the first time, Jona inquired if he could be a feed distributor. He felt certain he could organize a supply service if he could enlist the help of a friend who was an agronomist, Joel Sheftelowitz. A stout hearty man, Joel had studied crop production and field management in Germany before coming to Palestine. At present, he was the editor of a small magazine for farmers.

Jona knew nothing about mixing feed, but he knew that if a mistake was made, the flock could be lost. Jona made a beeline for Joel's editorial office in Tel Aviv.

"Jona," Joel said after hearing him out, "what a great opportunity! If we can get these people started on the right track, we'll boost our production of eggs and poultry. It would be a real service. I'll help you all I can."

Jona ran to the Haganah officials with his plan. "Just get me the permits so I can buy feed—and we'll go to work on a system for these farmers," he said.

With a respected agronomist like Joel Sheftelowitz involved, a Haganah official agreed to assist Jona to secure permits to operate a feed supply business.

When Jona was informed his permits were ready, he finally told the patient Anny what he had been up to.

"We're in the feed business!" he said triumphantly.

"Feed? Feed whom? A restaurant?" Anny asked puzzled.

"Yes, a restaurant—a restaurant for thousands of Israeli chickens!" Jona gushed.

Jona was given the address of a warehouse in Jaffa. Terrified Arabs had deserted the town during the war and their abandoned houses and shops were available.

Unlike some Jews who were grabbing Arab belongings left behind, Jona touched nothing. He put aside, in a large locked bin, everything he found in the space. He was prepared to vacate the warehouse should the owner return. The Arabs' plight reminded him of the Jews who had fled Poland to survive, only to be threatened by Poles who had taken over their stores and homes when they returned. He yelled this at the Jewish plunderers, but they ignored him.

In time, Arabs did return to Jaffa, although the owner of Jona's warehouse was not among them. Jona, meanwhile, hired a bookkeeper and a laborer, received his rations of feed, and he was in business!

In the coming months, Joel's advice was vital. Chickens need a balanced diet of proteins and minerals for eggs to develop and hatch. Manganese is essential, but an ounce too much of it—and the chicks could be poisoned.

Fishmeal is an important basic food for poultry, but often, it was not to be found. What to do? Joel would recommend a substitute that was available. He advised Jona to purchase dried fish, which was plentiful, and grind it into the mix. He set up charts for basic ingredients and their substitutes, so Jona and his worker could follow precise formulas.

Jona and Joel also visited poultry farmers to offer advice and encouragement. Grateful farmers, new at the work themselves, spread the word about Jona's feed service. Soon he was asked to also supply fodder for cattle.

News that the Arbesfeld's daughter Rivkah, a neighbor from Tomaszov, and her husband Moshe Goldstein, had arrived in Tel Aviv led Jona to suggest that they become chicken farmers. The Goldsteins, who met in a displaced persons camp, were only too glad to find work, leave the absorption center for new immigrants, and begin to establish themselves.

Jona's new business was grueling because there were so many small farmers to service, some needing only a few kilos of feed for a couple of dozen chickens or fodder for one lone cow. But gradually, the small farmers became reliable producers, bringing in more coupons for larger supplies of feed. Rivkah's chickens were producing so well that soon Moshe was able to look for work in construction while she tended the flock.

Meanwhile, this growing success meant that Jona's task was to keep his warehouse stocked. Truckmen brought supplies to the Jaffa warehouse at all hours of the day and night. If supplies arrived during the day, there were "tragers" available. These were teams of strong men whose job it was to unload the trucks. But often, Jona was called during the night. A ship with supplies he had ordered had just docked. Trucks would bring the feed to the warehouse by two in the morning. Could he accept the delivery then?

"Of course," Jona would say, wiping sleep from his eyes. He would call his helper and the two men would lift and stack heavy sacks throughout the night.

Often he would be wakened by a farmer whose cow was sick. Then Jona would rouse his faithful Joel for advice. The two friends would pile into Joel's ramshackle car, bumping along back roads, headlights on high, to drive to the ailing cow on a farm miles away.

Through this personal interest and the reliable service he offered, in two years' time, Jona had the largest feed supply business for the small farmer in the region. He also had an endless supply of eggs, brought to him by grateful farmers. In a time when meat was scarce, Anny became the Omelet Queen.

Food production in Israel was rising to meet the demands of an Israeli population that now included over a million Jews and thousands of Israeli Arabs. Visitors from all corners of the earth also came to see how the new state was faring in making the desert bloom. Israeli hotels were able to set an elaborate breakfast table laden with Israeli smoked fish, cheeses of all sorts, eggs and salad and fruit. Israeli exports of oranges, wines, dates and olives also helped bring cash into the struggling economy.

In his own little world, the population of the Lerman household was also expanding. Jona and Anny's daughter Yael was four years old when their son Israel was born. Named for Israel "Srulke" Lerman, he was a robust child, a smiling jolly baby. The three-room apartment was not enough space to contain him once he began walking.

One day, Anny's father announced that, as a government employee, he was eligible to buy a plot of land in a new suburb north of Tel Aviv. Jona volunteered to build a two-story house on the property, the ground floor for the parents and a second story for Jona and his growing family.

A solid stucco house soon rose out of the sand. Jona designed narrow windows to keep out blowing sand and the bright light of the sun. But he included deep porches on each floor to allow them to enjoy the outdoors in good weather

Topsoil was trucked in so a garden and fruit trees could be planted. Jona's new car would be parked in the garage at the head of the sandy driveway.

Anny clapped her hands that she would have a modern kitchen to work in.

"Now, I'll become a first-class cook, Jona," she smiled. "A baker, too."

"You're doing fine," he grinned, remembering their first spat over the chicken.

Jona had agreed to have furniture especially made for the apartment by a decorator and craftsman Anny's family knew. For its time, it would be a luxurious home.

Anny looked forward to sitting on the porch overlooking the ancient village of B'nai B'rak where she had spent her early years at school. The fruit trees, in time, would produce oranges and clementines for their breakfast.

Meanwhile, they were managing in their rented apartment. On Shabbat, family and friends would visit, or they might pick up Jacob Lanel for a ride into the forests where he had loved to hike. Jacob was in a nearby rehabilitation hospital learning to use an artificial leg.

David Ben Gurion had written Jacob a letter in May of 1949: "You gave to the war, not only your strength but a part of your body. The government feels obligated to prepare you to be able to continue working as well as before..."

Such concern buoyed Jacob's spirits as he struggled to make his thigh do the work of maneuvering his artificial knee, leg and ankle.

Unless peace was threatened, the Lermans were like any young family. Anny started a circle of young mothers who met to exchange ideas and enjoy watching their children play together. Yael attended kindergarten. Little Israel reminded Jona of himself as a child, always running about, and insisting "I do it myself!"

Jona was filled with pride in his family and his country. He invited Shlomo to visit from Munich. Jona wanted his brother to see that the $200 he had sent him to go to Palestine had been a good investment. Shlomo couldn't come then, but he sent his granddaughter for summer vacation.

Frieda Pe'er came to visit with her younger son Yonatan. Frieda was actively helping the refugees from North Africa coming into the country. Most were impoverished Jews with little education. Frieda helped find them places to live, jobs, and schooling for their many children. These Jews had different traditions from the European Jews. European Jews often looked down on them. But not Frieda.

"You have to prod them to take action. But they are learning," she said. "And we are learning from them. They are much closer to the middle-eastern way of thinking than we are. We need to understand this society too, so we can make this blend of Jews work."

Anny had to laugh because she had had her battles with the Moroccan vegetable man in their market.

"There's no such thing as a price. I don't know where the man gets the energy to bargain over each tomato."

The Lermans' spirits were high that summer. Who could imagine that in a day's time, they would be plunged into despair.

Little Israel had a bout of diarrhea early in the week. He was due to go for his two-year-old immunization shots. There was no polio vaccine at that time. These shots were for diseases that had already been conquered.

Anny queried the doctor about giving shots to Israel since he had not been his usual robust self. But the doctor said, "No problem."

That night, Anny heard Israel whimpering. She felt his head. It was hot. She tried to make him comfortable, wiping his forehead with cool washrags most of the night. Finally, he fell asleep. Just a reaction from the shots, Anny thought, and tumbled into bed.

In the morning, Anny went to Israel's crib. The child was still, and when she went to pick him up—his legs buckled under him. A wave of horror washed over her. She knew what the symptom meant. There had been an outbreak of polio that summer.

The pediatrician came quickly to Israel's bedside.

He turned to the white-faced parents,

"I'm sorry to say, it is polio."

The scourge that had hit the United States some years earlier arrived in Tel Aviv in the summer of 1952. Poliomyelitis—infantile paralysis — the dread disease usually struck young children, paralyzing their limbs and lungs.

The doctor gave orders to put hot compresses on the child and try to move him as little as possible.

For several days Anny and Jona, and Anny's parents, attended to the suffering child. There was no change so far.

"He's breathing so hard, Jona," Anny said, waking Jona one night.

He nearly burst out crying, looking at his little son, pulling his chest, and gasping for air.

"That's it!" Jona said. "We go to the hospital right now."

It was touch-and-go for a week. Children so small could not be placed in the only iron lung available. Made for adult patients, it would be too strong for their little lungs. Without a suitable machine, many children succumbed to the disease.

During that week, Anny and Jona met an army general and his wife whose child had to be placed in the lung in a last desperate effort to save the child. She died. They were devastated. The Lermans tried to comfort them, while watching and waiting for Israel to improve.

Israel managed to hold his own and was soon breathing normally. However, he had the most severe form of the disease, paralyzing his upper body and legs. Thankfully, his bodily functions were unimpaired.

Meanwhile, Anny's fearful parents took Yael to their apartment and watched her closely. The day before he took sick, Anny had seen Yael munching on an orange that Israel also had been eating. They were terrified she too could be stricken, but she continued healthy.

As soon as Israel's temperature subsided he was no longer contagious, so he was released from the hospital.

"When I picked him up to go home, it was like holding a little rag doll," Jona remembers. "Only his eyes blinked. The rest was still."

The Lermans were told that Israel's muscles would regain their strength in six to twelve weeks. Whatever muscles didn't come back by then, would be lost forever. To keep the muscles from atrophying, his limbs had to be moved for several hours a day.

Anny and Jona had to remain in their apartment in Tel Aviv. It was easier for the therapists to come there than to the new house some distance out of town. The therapists taught Anny what exercises to do. A large basin was filled with warm water from a hose attached to the kitchen sink. Israel was submerged in the water. It was very painful for him to have his muscles stretched, and when Anny took over, kneeling at his basin, it was wrenching for her to hear him cry and see his little face contorted in pain as she moved his legs and arms.

Jona drove from his feed warehouse in Jaffa to visit Yael each evening, and then came home to relieve Anny at the exercise routine. That year, the Israel Defense Forces excused him from serving his month in the reserve.

After a year of therapy, Israel could sit up with a supporting belt around his waist and shoulders. It was clear his leg muscles were useless.

"Will he ever walk again?" Anny whimpered in the night, against Jona's shoulder.

"Anny, what will be will be. We'll deal with it," Jona said sternly.

The Lermans moved into their portion of the new house. But all was ruined there for them. There were three steps leading to the walk to the new house. Then they had to climb up to the second floor. Once inside, there were more steps up to the bedrooms. Israel had to be carried up and down, endlessly.

The car was moved out of the garage so Israel and a few other disabled children could have therapy there together. Meanwhile, Israel had an operation to relieve muscle contractions in his thighs that were so painful.

The Lermans met with parents of other stricken children. Some youngsters recovered the use of all their limbs. Others were not so fortunate.

Jona talked to a man named Perlman at a clinic one day. The fathers compared notes. Perlman's son Yitzhak, like Israel, had not regained the use of his legs. The Perlmans were considering going to the United States for further treatment. Jona filed that information away.

At age three, Israel attended a nursery school for three hours a day. Jona carried him on his back through the sand. A sleep-in mother's helper was hired. The woman and Anny would carry Israel home from school each day. It was a life of drudgery and pain for each of them.

After a while, Israel was fitted with a brace that went across his back and closed with a latch. There was another brace for his legs that enclosed his hips. When it was locked, he could stand. With his little crutches, he was able to take a few steps.

At school, he begged to play in the sand with the other children. The teacher asked his parents what to do.

Anny and Jona chorused—"Let him."

They smiled, watching Israel sit in the sand and use his hands to fill a pail and then laboriously turn it over; it gave him so much pleasure. But Anny and Jona had to sit up at night, each wielding a toothbrush, cleaning the sand out of those latches on his braces so they would work the next day.

Anny and Jona were heartbroken. But they told each other—life had to go on.

"You can't cry in front of friends. You keep the sorrow to yourself. You must entertain your child and keep his spirits up. You must raise your daughter. You are fortunate that the grandparents are there to help," Anny would tell Jona, establishing a credo for them for the next years to come.

"We'll find a way to help our son," Jona said.

PART III

A NEW DIRECTION

Chapter 29

PIGEON

Between 1950 and 1952, two thousand children in Israel were struck down by polio. Eight hundred of those children died. The others recovered, though many, like Israel Lerman, were partially paralyzed.

Six-year-old Israeli, Yitzhak Perlman, lost the use of his legs, but his upper body strength enabled him to swing about on crutches. The world of music has been enriched by Perlman's wizardry on the violin. He is adored for his good humor and revered for his unfailing advocacy of access to public facilities for the disabled in Israel, the United States, and wherever he travels.

The State of Israel had many disabled, both young and old in the 1950s. Countries honor those who died fighting their battles, but often forget the wounded who endure lives of pain and frustration out of sight. But Prime Minister Ben Gurion did not forget.

In 1954 he brought a leading orthopedic surgeon from the United States to Israel to examine veterans and children who were disabled and to suggest therapy and treatment.

Some time earlier, a small group composed of parents of children with disabilities, had gathered in Anny and Jona's home to create an organization for their children. Their major goal was to establish a special school for the children. A group called Ilanshil came to their aid. It was composed of a journalist, a therapist, and Betty Dubiner, a philanthropist from Canada.

When Dr. Leo Mayer, the orthopedist, arrived in Israel, his visit was given wide publicity and Jona and hundreds of others asked to consult with the doctor.

Because Jona was president of a group affiliated with Ilanshil, he was given the courtesy of an appointment. Laden with X-ray pictures and files, Jona and Israel appeared for Israel's examination.

"I'd like to see your son in the United States," said the doctor, after studying the X-rays. "I think I can help him there."

Jona wanted to ask—will he walk again? But he simply said, "What can you do?"

"I have a plan for him—but it is a long-range plan. It will take time. You would have to be in the U.S.," the doctor answered.

"If it'll help my son, we'll go anywhere," Jona said.

Would Jona give up Israel, the land of his dreams? A place where he was a successful businessman, and had a standing in his community? A place where he had so many friends and loved ones? Could Jona do this?

Unthinkable before Israel became ill, now it was no contest for Jona. That same devotion he showered on his beloved land of Israel, he would transfer to his beloved son Israel.

"We must go to the U.S.," he told Anny when he returned that evening. Even after he explained that Dr. Mayer had a plan, she shook her head.

"How could we do that?" she cried. "We don't know the language. How will you earn a living? Where will we live? Jona, please, we've been uprooted before—it's so hard to make your way. How can you ask us to do that again?"

"I'm asking for our son—to give him a chance at a life," Jona said slowly.

"Who's to say their doctors are better than ours?" Anny argued.

"Listen, their president had polio. There was a great push in the U.S. to help such people. They have the wherewithal. We're just starting in some treatment areas. We have to give it a try," he insisted.

Anny was devastated. To leave her parents would be sad. Yael was so happy in school with many friends and activities. Anny had a comfortable home now in the wonderful new State of Israel. It was too much to ask.

"So, we'll learn English, starting right away," Jona said. "Like I learned Polish and Hebrew and Arabic. Yael already knows some words of English." Jona persisted.

At night he held Anny in his strong arms and soothed her. "You'll see. It'll be good, Annila," he whispered. Later, he lay awake wondering.

Jona took the necessary steps to begin the emigration process. He wrote to Shmuel, his youngest brother, who now went by the name of Miles and who had a successful farm in New Jersey. Miles immediately procured the proper papers for Jona to come to the U.S. He invited Jona to stay on his chicken farm in Vineland, New Jersey as long as he liked.

Jona Feldzon, Jona's younger cousin, now lived in Brooklyn, New York where he had a fabric business. He also promised to help in any way he could.

Jona took the final step—he sold his thriving feed supply company. From the sale, he had a substantial sum to start off with in the United States. Hopefully, in a year or two, or three, when treatment was completed, the Lermans could return to Israel. He wrote Miles that he was on his way. It was decided that Anny would remain in Israel with the children until Jona could get settled.

Now began perhaps the most daunting years of Jona's life. He would need all his skills of improvisation. Only his zeal to help his son, could keep him from utter despair

"When I got off the plane in New York, I could hardly be understood. I asked for directions, people laughed. It was very hard," Jona remembers.

Once Jona cleared Customs, there was Miles waiting for him. Jona had last seen Miles when his younger brother was a boy of fourteen. Now Miles was in his thirties, the father of two young children.

The brothers held each other for a long moment, and then stood back with eyes twinkling, looking each other over.

"You look like Momma," Jona laughed, delighted with his brother.

"Nah," Miles smiled. "But you look like Tata. A bit."

Off the brothers went to Miles' well-tended chicken farm in southern New Jersey. Krisha, Miles' wife, was a fine-looking attractive woman, very active in the community. She warmly welcomed Jona, and sympathized with Israel's need to regain as much muscle tone as possible. Her five-year old David, a year younger than Israel, rushed in and out again to play ball. She and Jona were silent a moment. Then he said, "A lovely boy."

"We're very lucky," answered Krisha. "We must help Izzy."

Jona was able to find an apartment nearby to receive Anny and the children. As soon as the paperwork was completed, she would be on her way.

But it was clear that to help Israel, they would have to live in New York City near the hospitals. Soon after Anny arrived, Jona went to the city to find an apartment and a means of making a living.

He would have settled for a job where he could learn English and get the feel of the city. Anny counseled him to find a business in which he could be his own boss.

"You're used to being on your own. You won't like it, Jona, listening to someone else. Besides, you have too much ability and experience to take a menial job. Find a business."

With money to invest, Jona looked for a situation where he could earn a salary as well as being an investor. Finally a business broker brought him a proposition. He could invest in a lease in an apartment house in Manhattan, and also work as the building's manager for a salary of $125 per week.

This sounded like a promising opportunity. The building, a multi-story structure on ll2th street in Manhattan seemed impressive. Jona agreed to invest half his capital with the company that had a long-term lease on the building.

By this time Anny had settled into the apartment he had rented in Manhattan.

Jona went off to work the first day with a springy step. His beloved partner, Anny, and his children were with him. He would come home to a family dinner. He had a business and a job.

Hey, this New York wasn't so bad after all.

But he returned that evening with a puzzled expression.

"It's a very nice building," he told Anny. "Marble floors, a fine lobby. But it's not apartments, people live in one room. The place is broken up. I sit behind a mesh screen in the lobby and listen to tenants' complaints all day.

"One woman came downstairs to tell me her toilet was stopped up. I had to lock my cage and go upstairs to her one room. I never saw anything like it before. People were lounging in the halls drinking, sleeping. Her room was a mess—clothes all over. Food strewn about. Her toilet was full of glass. It looked like a liquor bottle was broken in there."

He spared Anny the revelation that most of the people were desperate cases—put in the building by the city's social services agency because they had no place else to go.

The next day, the monthly rent was due. Residents stopped by all day to put their rent money in the opening of the cage. Jona thanked them, issued receipts and kept the records. Accompanied by a policeman, he went to the bank at the end of each day. When the next week came, though, he saw that some tenants still had not paid. He decided to call on one woman he had seen come into the building a few minutes earlier.

Jona knocked on her door. A woman's voice barked, "Who is it?"

Jona answered firmly—"Mr. Lerman reminding you about the rent—it was due last week."

The door was flung open and an angry disheveled woman stood before him holding a knife at his face.

Jona recoiled.

"You see this knife!" the woman yelled. "My husband just took someone's eye out with it. And I'll take out yours if you bother me again!"

Jona backed off. He went downstairs locked his cage left the building and paid a visit to the lawyer who had made the deal for him. It took some time, pressure and threats for Jona to get back his investment—but finally he did. Jona means "pigeon" in Hebrew and he felt like the pigeons he saw scratching the ground for food on the dirty streets of the city of New York.

At home, it was not much better. Anny complained that no one talked to her. People looked at Israel, sitting in his wheelchair, and turned away. There were no curb cuts then in the sidewalks, and it was a struggle letting his chair down at each crossing when she went shopping or to a park. The supermarket door was hard to open. She had to wedge her shoulder inside while she maneuvered Israel's chair. The clerks, many of whom had come recently from Puerto Rico and were learning English themselves, couldn't make out Anny's halting efforts.

"Where is borscht?" she asked a stock clerk.

"Brushes? Aisle 5."

She saw she was in cleaning supplies. How many times a day could she do this?

She was bewildered by the choices on the shelves, not knowing one brand from another. Once she found cans of tuna fish, but pictures of cats were on each of them. Until it snowed, and the sidewalks became slippery, she couldn't understand why the markets sold huge bags of salt. Jona heard a drumbeat of complaints from Anny most nights.

Yael was picking up English at school but she moped around at home.

"It's easier to leave a person than to leave your country," she said to Jona one day.

How the girl resented being torn from her roots!

Now he threw up his hands.

"You and your mother can go back if you like! I'm staying here with Israel until we go as far as we can with his treatment!"

The other two realized that is why they were in America. They kept their complaints to themselves, thereafter.

Jona lay awake at night wondering what would happen to them. Israel was about to go to the Hospital for Joint Diseases to be operated on by Dr. Mayer and his team. Suppose it didn't help and more operations were needed. His store of funds was being eaten up by the expenses, and he had no prospects for work or business. How could he take care of his wife and children, pay rent, buy food and clothes. He was a "greener"—an immigrant who was looked upon as a joke.

Would all his efforts to be a self-reliant, independent person, come to nothing?

Chapter 30

THE FACTORY

Jona investigated his next business offer very carefully. He found an ad in the Yiddish language newspaper, Forward, that sounded promising. An owner, who was getting too old to be active, was looking for someone to take over his embroidery business. The deal required a sixteen thousand-dollar investment plus the owner's full time attention.

Max, the retiring owner, took Jona to see his factory in an old building in the Bronx, another borough of the city. There women worked at sewing machines filling in patterns of flowers with shiny thread. First, workers pinned the patterns on the cloth and after the designs were filled in, other workers trimmed the material. The embroidered patch was later sewn on women's blouses or lingerie by the manufacturer.

The twenty factory workers spoke Italian or Spanish or a little English. "It'll be a tower of Babel," Jona thought, "with me and my broken English."

Jona demanded to meet the customers, manufacturers of women's clothing. Max took him to Madison Avenue in Manhattan where the women's clothing and lingerie industry was centered.

Almost every customer Jona met was a "landsman," a person from Poland who came to the U.S. as a child, or one whose parents did. Some greeted him in fluent Yiddish.

"I'm George Garfied, production manager," said one man, extending his hand.

Such a fancy name, Jona thought to himself, but I recognize the accent.

"You've spent time in Eretz Yisroel?" Jona asked.

"And in the Haganah," George added.

Jona embraced the man, grinning. They compared notes further. Garfield had been a driver for Ben Gurion. He also transported high explosives at night to sites where needed, headlights off to avoid detection.

And how had he come to Palestine? On the same freighter, the *Aghios Nicolaus*, as had Anny. George even remembered Anny's father and mother — and the "little girl with them."

"That little girl is my wife, Anny," Jona spurted with emotion. The whole factory stopped to gaze at the two men, suddenly laughing and kissing and speaking Hebrew. George arranged a time for him and his wife Susi to meet with the Lermans.

Finally, a friend in New York, Jona thought with pleasure.

Max's other customers were also encouraging to Jona.

"Listen," one business owner said, "it's a good deal for you. Max has a nice business, he could do more, but he's not strong any longer. With you, an energetic fellow, you'll do well, and we need your product."

Jona still hesitated. He was draining his money supply for household expenses and doctors' fees. He was fearful of committing too large a part of his funds to one proposition. Then he had an idea.

Max had a son he was very proud of. The man was an English teacher, but anxious to make more money, he had entered the sweater business. Now however, the business was bankrupt and Jack, the son, was out of work.

"Why not come into the business with me?" Jona suggested to Jack. "You speak excellent English and can deal with customers. I will run the factory."

Jack and his father liked the idea. This involvement of the

son meant that Jona would only own half of the business, but also would only have to contribute half of the sale price—eight thousand dollars, a sum he could more easily handle.

So the deal was made. Jona got along well with the employees. They saw that he was interested in their welfare, and so they responded by helping him learn the details of their work. Soon the factory floor was humming with busy hands at every station. Customers were treated to prompt deliveries of first quality supplies.

Sometimes, Jona noticed, Jack had to be prodded to check on a customer whose order was completed. Jona was anxious to keep the flow of work coming. On occasion, he'd call up a customer himself, and get an order. "Just send Jack in," the customer would say, "and we'll write it up." Jona would wonder why Jack had not made the call himself.

Nevertheless, in a year and a half, the work force had expanded to forty-eight people and to thirty-six sewing machines. Jona worked long hours, but he felt he was making progress.

Anny was grateful too that they had been able to move to a three-bedroom middle-income housing project in upper Manhattan. The first apartment they had rented was above a commercial garage. All night the metal garage door clanked open and shut as cars entered the building. Each clank jolted Anny awake. She couldn't wait to move.

The architect of the new building invited Anny to his office to understand Israel's special needs. Then he made adjustments to the floor plan so that Israel's wheelchair could go from room to room.

Israel was attending a special public school in midtown Manhattan for youngsters with disabilities. He was also the Poster Boy for the New York Philanthropic League. He posed, leaning on his crutches, with the then mayor of the city, Robert F. Wagner, Jr. The picture was all over town. His classmates were proud of him.

Anny and Israel rose before dawn to have time to put on his

braces before the school bus came at seven. Walking was difficult for Israel. Anny sighed as she locked the heavy metal supports in place. The pressure he needed to hold the braces firmly to his legs was painful, but it was the only way he could stand and maneuver.

Once a week, Anny boarded the bus with him. The Board of Education of the city required parents to help out in the classroom because these children needed so much assistance.

Izzy, as all the kids called him, made fine academic progress. He was popular among his classmates for his unfailing good humor. That summer, he enrolled in a sleepaway camp for children with polio.

Jona and Anny were exhausted. Yael, now a teenager, was out of school for the summer. Anny had an idea.

"A vacation would be good for us," she suggested one July morning. "Israel is happy at camp and in good hands, and Jona, you haven't had a break for months. How about it?"

Jona liked to please Yael and Anny. He had a competent forelady who could see to it that all the outstanding orders for the fall were completed, while Jack would secure more orders for the winter season. Jona would return refreshed and ready for the August rush on the new orders.

Miles had given Jona an old but serviceable car. The Lermans headed north to Canada. On the way back, Jona called the forelady for a report.

"Oh, all the orders were delivered," she said bruskly.

"And the new orders?" Jona asked anxiously.

"Well," said the woman, "there are no new orders. I sent the people home—there was no work, you see."

"Where was Jack?" Jona asked.

"He was here," the woman reported. "He didn't go downtown to customers. He was talking on the phone to his lodge friends about lodge business. What was I to do?"

"Call Jack," Jona said, "and tell him to be in the factory first thing Monday morning."

With Jack in tow, Jona visited all his manufacturers. They explained that none of the patterns had been cut, because they had placed no orders. Now their cutters were too busy to bother. Jona's factory would have to cut the patterns out themselves, if they wanted the business.

Jona saw no other way but to go out and buy a cutting machine. He couldn't let his business fall apart. There were too many people depending on him.

A cutter in a manufacturer's plant took his lunch hour to show Jona how to pile the cloth in stacks, and carefully guide the machine over the stenciled lines. After work, the two of them practiced together.

A cutter has to follow the pattern perfectly, otherwise the top cloth, and all the pieces underneath would be ruined. A slip of the blade could also sever the operator's finger or a hand. The job of cutter was the most skilled job in the industry.

"Only a crazy Israeli would try this. Suddenly I'm a cutter," Jona says remembering.

After a few practice trials, he began slowly cutting the material. Working till all hours, Jona cut into the stacks of cloth.

Two days later he told Jack, "Call up the pinners. There's enough work for them. This is Wednesday, on Friday, take the car and bring the sewers in to work."

In eight days, Jona had the factory up and running again at full speed. Then, privately, he spoke to Jack.

"I can't work with you any more, Jack," he said. "If I can't go away for ten days and trust you, we can't work together. You get out from here, or take the factory and give me my money back."

The father protested. "You're taking bread from my son's mouth."

"No," said Jona, "it's a healthy business. I'm giving it to him, just return my investment."

"You buy us out," the father countered. "Buy Jack's half."

This Jona was delighted to do. A system of notes was arranged for the payment of ten thousand dollars in one year's time, and once again, Jona was on his own and on his way!

Chapter 31

WORKSHOP

Jona subscribed to Israel's daily morning paper. It came a week late, but the news reaching him in New York was a drumbeat of attacks and counter attacks across Israel's borders.

How different life was for Americans, he thought. American borders were secure. People went to bed at night free from air-raid sirens. Workers left for jobs in the morning without fear of bombs exploding on their buses. Families vacationed in the countryside unafraid of ambushes and sniper fire.

In 1955, 260 Israelis had been killed. Squads of fedayeen, trained by Egypt, had been raiding settlements in the north and south of Israel. Gamal Abdel Nasser, Egypt's ruler, and the Arab world's most powerful leader, built air bases in the Sinai desert, his planes poised to attack Israel. Then in 1956, Nasser nationalized the Suez Canal! Now Egypt would control access to the vital waterway. France was furious and supported Israel's drive to secure her borders and access to the Canal.

After constant provocation on the Sinai border, the Israeli army penetrated the Egyptian desert in October 1956, controlling all roads to the canal. In seven days, they had captured the Sinai and Gaza.

This was a far different army than Jona had known. It had planes and paratroopers, armored vehicles, and a strong chain of command. Yet, Ben Gurion agreed to withdraw from the Sinai and Gaza, if a multi-national police force would patrol the terrain. They did so, on the promise that the Canal and the Straits of Tiran would remain open to shipping.

The Sinai Campaign led to an important development in world

affairs. The U.N. created an emergency force to keep the peace, a job it is attempting to do around the globe today.

Finally, there was a time of relative calm in Israel.

The energy that Israelis had spent on protection and resistance was now transferred to business, the family and acclimating the many newcomers to their new surroundings. For Anny and Jona, it was a welcome relief to know their friends and family in Israel were relatively safe, as they tried to make a life in America.

Jona made progress in his business, receiving orders in a timely fashion, and producing the goods he promised.

Early in 1960, Jona's accountant surprised him.

"You've made too much money. Your taxes will take most of it," the accountant warned.

"Too much money. Too many taxes. That's all right with me," Jona blurted, clearly pleased.

"You could put the excess back in the business, instead of paying the tax. The government encourages that."

"That sounds sensible. I've wanted to move downtown. Now I will."

Jona took a loft in a building in the Madison Avenue women's wear district. He bought forty high-speed sewing machines, modernized his office, and expanded his work force again.

George Garfield was pleased.

"Now we can have lunch together, Jona," he said.

"Who has time for lunch?" Jona shrugged.

"Well then, join B'nai B'rith, I'll get to see you there," George suggested.

B'nai B'rith, the oldest Jewish men's organization, was founded in 1843. It fought discrimination and was involved in fundraising for Israel. Jona signed on. He and George often were called upon to explain the latest difficulty facing their former homeland. Jona felt he was making a contribution in that setting. He even suggested a way of boosting attendance at meetings. While there were hundreds of members on the rolls, he saw that only a handful came to the meetings.

"Why not invite our wives? Make it a social night out." Jona suggested to George, who was lodge president at that time.

"We'll try it!" George said, enthusiastically. The next meeting advertised—"Wives Welcome, Refreshments Served." The meeting was a success and from then on wives were welcome.

One day a customer of Jona's appealed to him to join a men's club that raised funds for a hospital. Jona hesitated.

"It is only once a month. You'll meet people from the trade," the manufacturer insisted. Jona, always wishing to help in a good cause, agreed to join.

A few months later there was a drive on to recruit new members to the club. It was also Brotherhood Month. Special speakers were invited and the members pledged to do everything they could to further integration.

Jona proposed a person for membership who would answer both needs.

"In what way both needs?" the wary president asked.

"He's a professor at City College, a fine fellow, plays a good game of chess, my neighbor in the apartment house. He'll make a good member. As a black man, he could help integrate our club and we would learn a lot from him."

The members moved in their seats.

"We'll take it under advisement," the president said after a pause, smiling.

"What advisement?" Jona shot back. "Do I invite him or not?"

"Please, Jona. We'll discuss it in committee. Wait to hear from us."

Jona raised his eyebrows. Later, the chairman of the membership committee took him aside.

"Don't pursue this, Jona. He won't get in. It's an embarrassment. Drop it."

"You talk brotherhood yet you tell me 'he won't get in'. I'm not interested in talk when there's a chance for this group to make a difference. How can you be like that?" Jona said disgust showing on his face.

"You have to be realistic. Even if we all agree, someone will blackball - er - vote him down. It only takes one."

"Because you won't take a stand," accused Jona, "I resign from this club," he said.

"Come on, Jona, you're unreasonable," said the member. "These things take time. Besides, you just paid a hefty initiation fee!"

Jona looked at the man. "I have no patience for this kind of an organization. I have better things to do with my time."

And Jona resigned, despite pleas from the customer who had invited him. "Everyone likes you, Jona. Give it some time. Try again next year," the man said.

"No, my mind's made up," is all Jona would say.

"Jona's a man of principle," the customer would maintain. "A man ahead of his time. We just couldn't measure up to his standards."

Anny and Jona joined a synagogue in Washington Heights where they lived. They had not belonged to a synagogue in Israel. They felt little need to join. All the holidays were observed as part of the way of life of the country and the children studied the Scriptures in school as their own history.

In America, it was different. There was no national recognition of Jewish holidays nor were there religious teachings in the public schools. At the synagogue, Yael and Izzy would be with other young people from the temple's religious school for holiday celebrations, as well as learn about the Torah and Jewish history.

Moreover, in America, there were several different branches of Judaism to choose from. The one the Lermans selected encouraged questions about confusing Bible stories and held discussions about ideals and goals.

In Israel, the only officially recognized branch is Orthodox—ranging from the traditional Jews who are willing to serve in the military and mingle with the general population, to the "Black Hats," ultra-Orthodox extremists. Thousands of ultra-Orthodox Yeshiva students, with few exceptions, refuse to serve in the army and they actively confront Jews who do not follow their interpretations to the letter. They believe they are the guardians of "pure" Judaism.

Anny's father wrote her that the bus company in Tel Aviv was under siege by the ultra-Orthodox, the haredim.

"They demonstrated at the central bus station because buses began running before the end of the Sabbath. They also are carrying on in Jerusalem where buses were taking people to the beach on Shabbat."

"One thing about this country," remarked Jona, "everybody does his own thing, and there are no government officials representing religion. Ben Gurion never should have let the religious factions have representation in the Knesset. The State and Religion should be separate, as it is here."

"But, Jona," Anny countered, "if Israel is a Jewish state, how can it not observe the Sabbath?"

"That's a matter for a person to decide. Not for the government to say, 'do this; do that', Jona replied. "Meanwhile, your father writes these things and I feel good that there are no worse troubles there."

But Anny still thought about the little disabled children they left behind in Tel Aviv.

"That terrible truck you had to ride in," she reminded Izzy. "It had those hard benches, and the kids with braces were jostled all the way to the school in Jaffa."

Ilanshul had started the school, and Izzy was enrolled there until they left for America.

"It was an hour-and-a-half bumpy ride each way," Izzy remembered.

"We're going to get those children a proper bus," Anny vowed. "Everyone wants a television set. We'll have a raffle. That will be the prize. And we'll use the profits for the bus!"

No one was happier than Anny, when she had a project.

A 19–inch black-and-white television set was purchased—a big deal in those days. Raffle tickets were printed.

Anny was tireless. She approached women in the laundry room, at the supermarkets, on the park bench.

"Oh, Mrs. Greene, you sold the whole book of raffles! That's wonderful. Here, take another book. Yes. And here, give one to your sister. Thank you, thank you." That was Anny, day after day. Thousands of tickets were sold for that one TV.

In Brooklyn, the survivors of Tomaszov had formed a society, and they pledged to sell tickets too. In the end, a ambulance was purchased, outfitted with seats with cushions and springs, and a portable ramp for the wheelchairs and shipped to Tel Aviv. The Tomaszovniks put the name of their town on the vehicle.

"What did I care who got the credit!" Anny says. "The kids got their bus. That was the important thing."

Meanwhile, Yael was once again an enthusiastic person. She had displayed artistic talent as early as nursery school, and after primary school, she was admitted to the prestigious High School of Music and Art, now known as the LaGuardia High School of the Arts.

Izzy worked on school projects when he returned home in the afternoon, and began study for his Bar Mitzvah.

Anny now spent the days she was not at his school in her B'nai B'rith Women's group raising funds for a residential program in Israel which cared for children with severe emotional problems. What with wars, dislocations, missing parents, and cultural differences, many children were confused and angry. The special school, staffed by psychiatric professionals would go a long way to helping these youngsters.

Jona worked long hours at his embroidery factory. He was often there before the first employee clocked in, and was usually the one to turn off the lights at night.

Not only did he want to make the business successful in order to take care of his own family, he felt he had a responsibility to the families of his workers. Some nights, he lay awake worrying about payrolls, and cash flow, and changes in styles that might cut into demand for his goods.

Nevertheless, when a social worker from the city's department of labor came to ask him to include a training shop in his factory for workers with disabilities, Jona, thinking of Izzy's predicament, said yes.

A mentally challenged young woman was referred for a job. Jona and his forelady spoke with her for some minutes and decided to try to train her as a pinner. She was teamed up with a motherly Latino woman, who patiently instructed her. Eventually, the young woman did competent work at her own pace. Jona then took on several other people with disabilities

Six workers were eventually in the special program, They received "sheltered" wages, less than the other workers earned because of their need to work at their own comfort level.

The labor department was thrilled with Jona's special workshop. But the union to which his workers belonged had other ideas. They demanded that Jona, as their employer, pay their union dues and contribute the employer's portion of dues as well.

Jona argued that these workers had a special status under labor department standards for sheltered workers and should not be considered to have the same obligations as union members. But the union organizers said—"Rules are rules. Everyone must join and must pay dues."

At the same time, two groups of women in his shop got into a fight. Jona believed it was racially motivated. He tried to mollify the women, but they shouted at him—"Just butt out!"

That night, Jona took stock. His children's future education was provided for. He and Anny had enough savings to carry them for several years if they lived simply. Why should he put up with the responsibilities of his complicated business? Work, he could always find, but now he wanted peace as well.

Jona had always been sensitive to the charge of exploiter.

The mocking words of his childhood schoolmate—"bloodsucker, parasite,"—still haunted him.

He really would be happier earning what he could from his own sweat and toil, and not depend on the labor of others. He explained this to Anny. She was surprised. But she shook her head.

"Jona, you made this business what it is. If you want to give it up, it's your right. A living you'll always make."

Jona kissed Anny for understanding. His heart warmed, recalling how he had trust that the young girl he was marrying twenty years ago was steady and strong and loving. His belief in her was confirmed, over and over.

Once more, he appealed to the union representative to forego the rules for his sheltered workers.

"Impossible," said the union representative.

The official didn't count on Jona's stubborn streak when he thought he was being taken advantage of.

"Well, then, I'll close up," Jona said casually.

"Ha, ha, ha!" laughed the official. "And give up a business like this."

But the next day, Jona began selling his machines. The bookkeeper was instructed to total up everyone's pay, including vacation time owed, add in severance pay, and as soon as checks were cut, begin to send the workers home.

The union officials came screaming. But Jona's mind was made up. He closed his doors.

As he handed the keys to the empty loft back to the landlord, he squared his shoulders and left the building. Walking down Madison Avenue, Jona felt as though heavy chains had just been lifted from his shoulders. He sauntered down the street, a free man.

Chapter 32

NEW BATTLES

Jona, with the privilege of making his own priorities for the first time in years, now threw himself into work for his two Israels.

Izzy was having a hard time. The first operation had not been able to give him much added mobility. Now, at fourteen, he was experiencing the natural spurt of teen-age growth, but the arrangement of muscles and tendons did not allow sufficiently for his added height. His back was curving over.

Another hospital would operate to release these muscles and fuse Izzy's spine so he could sit and stand erect. It would be a complicated process, and the worst of it was that Izzy would be in a cast for two years!

"No, Abba," Israel said, using the Hebrew word for father, "no more operations. I'd rather die."

Jona's heart sank. "It will be hard, Israel, no question. But you must do it. We'll be there with you. You have a future, if it is done. Please, son—let us save you."

So finally, the boy agreed.

Jona and Anny were anguished for Izzy. He would suffer such pain, and for what? Just to hold his own. They felt so powerless. All they could do was live one day at a time.

Izzy was put in a "turtle cast" after the operation. It encased his whole back. He would have to lie on his stomach for twenty-six months! How could he be expected to submit to this torture? Anny would stay awake nights crying for her son.

She knew she couldn't properly care for him at home. Moreover, there was no local long-term care facility for youngsters at that time. He would have to go to a hospital across the Hudson River that handled adult patients.

It was hard to see him in that place with older, severly disabled men, some of whom cursed and cried out in their sleep, who had lost hope. Izzy, at fifteen and sixteen, saw more tragedy and misery in that hospital than a person sees in a lifetime. Anny and Jona were in torment every time they left him after a visit.

A bright spot for Izzy were the days a high school tutor came to the hospital. An up-beat young woman, she went over the textbooks for his courses with him, and gave him assignments. How much homework he did between sessions was open to question.

Jona and Anny drove the forty miles to be with Izzy twice during the week and over the weekend. They helped make his mealtimes more pleasant, to play board games with him, to wheel his bed to an outdoor patio in good weather.

Finally, the day came when the doctors said, "He's healed. We can take off the cast."

Everyone on the ward celebrated Izzy's first meal sitting up. Yael was home from college and so happy to see her brother smiling. But the boy still had a long way to go. Next stop was the Rusk Institute for physical therapy, so he could exercise his muscles and practice skills for daily living once again.

While Izzy was at Rusk, Anny and Jona accepted Miles' long-standing invitation to visit his home in Vineland, New Jersey.

It was a lovely ride across the state on a clear spring day. They passed newly tilled fields of the farming country. Already, pale green shoots of planted corn and vegetables were peeping through the dark earth.

The ride, alone, lifted their spirits. Perhaps Izzy could make a life for himself now that his back would be straight and his muscles working again.

"He'll finish high school and go to college," Jona declared as he drove.

"And then?" Anny asked.

"Don't worry, Anny. There are plenty of jobs a person in a wheelchair can do. And Izzy is spunky, like you. He'll be all right."

"I hope he can find a girl," whispered Anny.

"He will do that too. He's a handsome guy and he can father children. There will be a girl for him," Jona asserted, shaking his head as he turned the car into the long driveway leading to Miles and Krisha's house. They kissed as they climbed the front steps, as if to seal everything Jona had said.

Krisha ushered them into the large living room where they saw there were other guests already gathered. Miles was speaking to the philanthropists and businessmen there about the importance of purchasing Israel Bonds.

The State of Israel was gearing up for another conflict. Egypt's Nasser vowed to "erase our shame," referring to his defeat in the Sinai Campaign of 1956. With the help of the Soviets, he had built up a new arsenal of weapons and had won support from the other Arab nations "to drive Israel into the sea."

Miles' guests that Sunday listened closely. Before the discussion ended, the heads of foundations and charitable institutions had committed to major investments in Israel Bonds. The bonds would give the state some funding for its infrastructure and social needs while Israel prepared to re-arm.

Jona sensed the other men and women regarded his younger brother with esteem. Miles was surrounded by people Jona had only read about. Yet, he was looked up to by these powerful philanthropists as their equal.

Jona understood that Miles was an astute businessman who had gone into ventures that made him a great deal of money, but now Miles was reaching even beyond that. He was devoting himself to making the movers and shakers of society see the strategic importance of Israel to the United States as the only democratic nation in the Middle East. And his presentation was effective.

Miles was active in more than one arena. Jona knew he was bringing refugees from countries under the Soviet thumb to the Vineland area. He set them up as chicken farmers, but he expected them to work as hard as he had when he began, and not look for handouts.

Jona laughed with pride at his brother.

"Miles is clearly outstanding," he told Anny on the way home. "I am very impressed with him. He speaks so fine, hardly an accent. He's so knowledgeable. He's left me far behind."

"Jona, you had different challenges and different goals. Those you have met in outstanding ways, too."

"Ah, Anny," he said, "my devoted one, but there's a difference here. I am one of many thousands like me. Miles is another story. You shall see. He'll go further still."

Both brothers would have many opportunities to be of help to the Jewish homeland in the months ahead.

In 1967, it was clear that an attack on Israel was imminent. The Soviets had supplied the Egyptians with arms and aircraft. Syrian, Iraqi and Jordanian armies began massing on Israel's borders, their rallying cry, "Wipe out our shame!"

The U.N. had stationed peacekeeping forces on the southern-most tip of Egypt's Sinai desert, and on the Gaza strip. Egypt demanded that the peacekeeping force withdraw. At the very time when they were most needed, the U.N.'s secretary general, U Thant complied without hesitation. Israel went into all out preparations for an invasion.

Both of Frieda Pe'er's boys were in the service. Yitzhak Blank was on active duty. Jona felt he should do his part, too. He had a twinge of conscience about leaving Izzy in Anny's care alone, but despite this, he contacted the Israeli embassy offering to volunteer to serve once more in the Israel Defense Forces. He held both Israel and American citizenship. But he was now fifty-seven.

"We have younger men and women to fight," he was assured. "Raise funds, sell Israel Bonds instead."

Jona got the message. He went all out. As president of the B'nai B'rith lodge, he asked to address meetings of other lodges, of clubs and synagogue groups. Anny came along when he spoke. Sometimes she had to supply a word for him. His English was fluent but occasionally he got a question from a member of the audience who used a term he had not come across before.

Sometimes, he was challenged: "If you loved Israel so much, how come you're here?"

Jona hated that question because he didn't want sympathy or apologies. He would answer simply, "We came here to get treatment for an illness," and leave it at that.

Other objections came from a few Jews who felt they had given once, and that was enough.

"I'm an American—I give here," he was told.

"Listen," Jona would answer, "I love this country. It is a great land. But remember, the German Jews loved Germany and the Polish Jews were devoted to Poland, and look what happened. Now we have a homeland, if we lose it, where will the Russian Jews go if they are ever freed, and the Algerian Jews, and the Ethiopians? Think man. Stretch your giving budget this year. It's important for Jews and America. Besides, the bonds pay interest and they've never defaulted. It's an investment you can be proud of."

Mostly though, Jona was listened to with respect. World War II veterans themselves, his listeners could relate to a Haganah veteran who spoke from the heart.

Jona recruited other speakers to address different groups. Miles agreed to come to a B'nai B'rith rally on behalf of Israel Bonds. Jona had flyers made up and stuffed them in car windows to assure a good turnout from the neighborhood. It was a memorable night. People opened their checkbooks, and bought bonds on the spot.

When it was obvious that other nations were turning a deaf ear to Israel's plea for support, American Jews responded generously. The reality of the Jewish State had changed their lives. No longer were they "wandering Jews" without a home to call their own. Since 1948, Jews, regardless of where they lived, realized they had a place to go if ever they needed one. Nineteen years later, they were not going to let anything happen to that hard won privilege.

Not only did they buy bonds, 2500 American young people volunteered to go to Israel to do whatever was needed.

On the morning of June 5, 1967, the Israel air force struck. In its surprise attack, Israeli planes were able to destroy 309 out of 340 Egyptian combat aircraft on the ground, including 135 Russian-made MIGS. In an assault on the Mitla Pass near Suez, an entire Egyptian tank battlion was demolished.

Confused by the presence of a United States' intelligence ship off the Sinai coast, the Israelis bombed that vessel too, thinking it Egyptian. American Jews were mortified. Israel paid damages and apologized. War breeds tragic consequences, especially for the innocent.

It was the battles on the Jordanian front that were watched with bated breath by those who consider Jerusalem a most sacred city for three major faiths, Judaism, Christianity and Islam.

The Jordanians controlled the Old City with its churches of the many branches of the Christian faith, including the Stations of the Cross where Jesus was believed to have walked to his crucifixion. The only above ground remnant of the original Israelites' Second Temple was the portion of the wall that surrounds the Temple Mount. It had been desecrated by the Turks and Jordanians, who threw refuse over it. Jews could not even approach that wall once Jordan took over in 1948. However, the Israelis controlled the new sections of Jerusalem to the west. There 100,000 persons, most of them Jewish, resided.

On June 5, Jordanian troops began bombing across the armistice line into Israel. A fierce two-day battle ensued, in which Arab Legion troops fought bravely. But the Israeli air force was able to knock out so many Arab gunnery installations, that the IDF could clear each section of the Old City. Finally, after nearly 2000 years, the Western Wall was in Israel's hands once again.

Within six days, Israel was in control of the Sinai desert, the Golan Heights where bullets had rained on the settlements below, and the West Bank territory on the Jordan River.

But the Kotel, the Western Wall, had emotional appeal beyond the mere conquering of land. Jews wept when they could touch that wall of stones once more. Soldiers, who had been wounded in the Six-Day War, came to the site in their bandages to see the place that is a symbolic center of Jewish identity.

Standing before it, tucking little folded messages between its stones, both secular and religious Jews can feel the pull of centuries of Jewish history. The wall makes real their connection to their forefathers.

Perhaps land won by Israel in the Six-Day War would be more significant for future diplomacy, but access to that ancient site is an emotional high for Jews the world over.

With Israel victorious on all fronts, the cabinet of the Parliament is on record as having voted to give back the Sinai and other areas if the Arabs would come to the peace table. But it was not to be. The Soviets offered to re-arm the Arab states, and they refused to talk peace.

Chapter 33

WEDDINGS

Jona found a new business. A woman who imported gold chains was looking for a partner

"What do you know about the jewelry business?" George Garfield quizzed him.

"Nothing," grinned Jona. "To tell the truth, I don't know gold from silver. I never paid attention. Now, I'll pay, and learn."

"You'll pay and pay," George warned, looking worried. "There are sharpies out there."

But gold chains were the rage in New York then. The importers couldn't get enough of them to meet the demand. Jona went to Italy with his new partner where he met the jewelry suppliers and learned how to judge fine work and weigh gold. He picked up a little Italian to show the artisans that he was trying to learn.

Best of all, the new business gave him freedom to plan his time.

That summer, the Lermans went to Israel. Izzy was strong again. True, he used a wheelchair. Walking was just too great a strain. But he maneuvered his chair with agility.

"Israel is a lovely human being—that's what counts," Jona would say. "If only he didn't have pain..." Jona and Anny would sigh to each other.

In Tel Aviv, the Lermans visited friends and family. They still owned the villa with Anny's parents. The children and their grandparents rejoiced to be together.

They spent time with Jacob Lanel who had married and worked as a bookkeeper for a company that manufactured cooking oils. He was anxious to show the Lermans the forests that had grown up since their earlier visit. Izzy was thrilled with the excursions to crystal waterfalls, and to caverns in the countryside.

Jona and Anny met with their friends from Ilanshil, now simply called Ilan. One of them enlisted Jona's help with a difficult problem.

The Sephardic Jews from Algeria and Morocco who had disabled children resisted the help of social workers who wanted the youngsters to attend a special school.

"Jona, visit this man for us," the friend asked. "If you can get through to him, his countrymen might see the light."

Confident that he could win the man over, Jona approached the home of a poor Algerian refugee who had come to Israel several years before. There in the small darkened living-dining room, he saw a little boy, bent with palsy, strapped to a chair.

The father sat smoking his pipe.

Jona explained that there was a school nearby that would care for the child, where he would receive therapy and be with other children.

"Someone will pick him up and bring him back to you each

evening," he assured the father.

"You are kind," replied the man. "But we don't need it. My wife is here to take care of the boy."

"But he's alone here all day," Jona said patiently. "Your wife is busy. He would profit from being with other children, to have exercise, to learn."

"God will take care," the man said passively.

These were fighting words for Jona.

"It's better he sits there in a wet diaper!" Jona railed at the man.

"Yes, yes," repeated the father. "God's will."

Jona was exasperated. He left, and called his friend Frieda in Haifa. Frieda had been working with the Shephardi Jews since the first group arrived in 1950.

"Jona, they have such a different mind-set," she said calmly. "They are like their Arab countrymen. You have to bargain with them. Go back to the man. Offer him something to let his son go each day. Let me know what happens."

"You mean money, Frieda? We should pay him to let us take care of his child?"

"Yes, Jona, my dear," Frieda said patiently. "And not a few coins. Try the equivalent of five dollars."

Jona was baffled. Yet, he had an assignment. He did not like to fail. Back he went.

"The government has authorized me to pay you five dollars each day for allowing your son to attend our school," he said, sounding official.

The father took his pipe from his mouth, considered the offer for a moment.

"Six will be acceptable," he said finally.

Jona took the sum in Israeli lira from his own pocket.

"Tomorrow, the bus driver will come. He'll pick up your son, and in the afternoon, give you the money for the next day. Tomorrow!" he repeated, smiling at the youngster. The little boy in the chair smiled back.

Jona shook his head. He would report to the school what he had done. A fund would have to be set up to pay these parents until they saw the benefits for themselves.

A few days later, Jona was off on another mission, this one at the opposite end of the spectrum.

A friend of Miles', a leading philantropist, was in Israel to meet with Foreign Minister Golda Meir. He would like Jona to accompany him.

Jona demurred. "Golda speaks perfect English," he said. "What help can I be?"

"I'd feel comfortable with you there. We'll be talking about social programs. Later you could reflect with me and what we spoke about."

Jona was pleased to go along with the businessman. They met in Golda's kitchen.

"She was a plain-spoken woman, anyone could talk to her. Just a regular person," Jona often would say about that meeting.

After exchanging greetings in Hebrew with her, Jona sat to the side. Golda and the businessman discussed funds at his disposal for use in Israel for absorption programs. He had American dollars from contributors behind him, and some ideas for their use. The two worked together in harmony to craft a plan for the funds.

Jona felt a glow after being in the presence of this woman who had been a pioneer years before he arrived and had endured the harsh conditions of the early kibbutzniks. It was so typically Israeli for her to discuss millions of dollars in her kitchen, no fuss, no wood-paneled office at the top floor of a skyscraper. Just real people putting their heads together for the benefit of others.

Golda came from Poland as a little girl. Her family settled in Milwaukee. Fervent Zionists, she and her husband had immigrated to an impoverished Palestine in the 1920s. Golda had been Labor Minister and now Foreign Minister and desperately wanted to retire. Instead in March 1969, she was called upon to be Prime Minister.

Back home in the States, there were new challenges awaiting Jona. He found that his own partner was ready to retire.

"No problem," he told her. "I'm able to take over. Anny can help me in the office."

In the back of his mind was a proposal for Anny. The children were quite grown now. Perhaps they should consider returning to Israel to live. He could conduct business just as well from there, returning to the States as needed.

At the moment, though, it was premature to speak to Anny. Yael had news for them. She and Robert Morris were engaged!

Yael met fellow student, Robert Morris, in college. On school breaks, he was a frequent visitor in the Lerman home. Everyone liked Robbie, as he was called, and the Lermans were thrilled that Yael was so happy. Soon after their graduation, Yael and Robbie planned to be married.

Robbie's family offered their large synagogue in Great Neck for the wedding. The handsome sanctuary was decked out with trees and flowers. White gloved waiters stood ready in the banquet hall. Anny and Jona were a bit tense in the lavish formal surroundings.

But not so their daughter. Even her veil could not hide Yael's glowing face as she came down the aisle between both her parents. Her slim figure was sheathed in a satin wedding gown. The solemn groom in black tux, stood at the wedding canopy.

Her parents kissed Yael, then Jona took her hand and placed it in Robbie's. Robbie grinned.

Jona was smiling, too, but the lump in his throat felt as big as an apple.

The glass was broken and the couple embraced to claps and a few whistles. The guests filed out to a reception and an elegant dinner, the orchestra blared out show tunes, contemporary music, and later a spirited "Hava Nagila" to which young and old danced the hora, pounding their feet on the floor as they circled the bride and groom. Izzy sat smiling on the sidelines, happy for his sister.

Grandparents Genia and Oscar Ulmer from Israel were joined by relatives in the States. They shook their heads in wonder.

Miles was there with his wife Krisha, and their children, Jeanette and David. And so was Jona Feldzon and his family.

Was it possible that the two Jonas, who had fled in terror from Petliura's pogrom when they were small children, had survived hunger and war and dislocation to come together once again to enjoy this moment! Yes, it was amazing, they agreed, and due in large part to the bounty of America.

After the guests had departed, Jona and Anny took a floral bouquet from their table to bring home.

"But we do not have to collect empty bottles this time," Jona said jokingly, remembering their clean-up after their own wedding.

"No, my Jona," said Anny, tears in her eyes. "I said you could do anything you wanted, remember, and I was right."

"Yes, you were, little Anny," chimed in her father, embracing Jona.

"When we were fleeing for our lives from Vienna thirty years ago, I never imagined I would live to see such fine grandchildren and a celebration as splendid as this. I realize how fortunate we are," he said solemnly.

Two years later, Izzy brought home a pretty girl he had met in college. The two had left school to go into a candle-making business together. Now they wanted to marry. Although Rose was of a different faith, Anny and Jona gave them their blessing, and arranged their wedding.

Often, one of the satisfying pleasures of family gatherings is that close relatives, who hardly can make time to visit each other, have a chance to meet and catch up on each other's lives. At the weddings, Miles and Jona traded stories of their present interests.

Miles confided to Jona that he still anguished remembering the fate of their mother and Esther and her children. In his mind's eye, he could see his mother, walking arm-and-arm with him in Lemberg. With her determination and resourcefulness, perhaps she would have survived deportation to Russia. His dragging her from that train had sealed her doom,

The tragedy was never far from his thoughts. He was also troubled by another strand. Some historians had claimed that the Jews went to their deaths without attempting to resist. Yet, he knew thousands of stories of resistance.

Now he wished to translate this burden of memory into something lasting that would teach and explain to future generations how, growing from one restrictive rule to another, one lie to another, such a tragedy came to be. Future generations then would not let tyranny take over their humanity as it had so many Germans, Poles and Austrians.

He also was passionate about the need to demonstrate how Jews resisted their oppressors with arms, when possible, with sabotage when not, and to honor non-Jews who helped them.

Miles had been back to Poland, to Tomaszov. There he saw that the gravestones from the once cared-for cemetery had been ripped up to pave the road so Nazi trucks could travel. Miles could still make out the Hebrew inscriptions of people his family had known.

He visited the place in Belzec where half-a-million Jews had been cremated in the brief time that that killing field had been in existence. The bones of his mother, his sister, and of the Jews of Tomaszov and other towns and cities lay in that field. Poland, which once had hundreds of vibrant Jewish communities, had them no longer.

There had to be some memorial to those millions of all faiths who had perished under the boot of the Nazi terror.

Jona could not bring himself to return to Poland. For him, the hatred he had experienced as a young boy was still as fresh in his mind as if it happened only days ago. But Miles was determined to enable Poles, and all those who had permitted this genocidal persecution to take place, to acknowledge the consequences of standing idly by.

"How will you do this, Miles?" Jona asked thoughtfully.

Miles shared some of his recent activities with Jona.

From his base in New Jersey, Jona's younger brother had business contacts with influential leaders of industry. Miles had begun talking to philanthropic people and historians about his idea. Jewish scholars and philosophers were helping to create a proposal for a major memorial center.

"Miles wants the government here to help him with a museum," Jona reported to Anny. "Do you think he has a chance?"

"They weren't the criminals," Anny said.

"But the government could have moved faster. Now, we know they knew about the ovens. Perhaps they will help, this country is full of such richness and warmth to all peoples. Yet, Miles may be pleading in the wind."

Jona was sympathetic to his brother's mission and wished he was able to help him. Although he enjoyed a modest success, he was not on equal terms with the movers and shakers in American society.

As he spoke of Miles' idea, he found some curious reactions.

"Why should we remember that period, Jona?" one survivor of the camps asked him. "It was a horrible time for our people. Best to forget it. I don't want to be reminded."

"The memorial is not for you, my friend," Jona answered patiently. "It's for our children, and their children so they should never forget. The anti-Semites would like to say, it never happened. Shouldn't we have the documents, the tapes, the pictures, the testimonies for all to see?" Jona's friend was listening but his eyes were vacant.

"Soon we, who lived it, will be gone," Jona went on. "What then? Should this most horrendous act in mankind's history be an unspoken chapter."

The man rose and walked from the table where he had been seated to the foyer of the apartment. Jona followed to see if his friend was angry. He found the man holding his handkerchief to his face, sobbing.

Chapter 34

1973 — YET AGAIN!

Jona would not ordinarily turn on the television set on Yom Kippur, but early on the morning of October 6, 1973, without the need to make breakfast, he was fidgeting for something to do.

He began to read cables coming across the television screen. The news was from Jerusalem. Israel was under attack! Horrified, he ran to the radio. Broadcasters were describing an assault by both Egypt and Syria on Israel's territory.

"On Yom Kippur!" Jona said aloud, holding his head.

Skirmishes and gunfire between soldiers on either side of the Israeli-occupied Sinai border were a constant occurrence. But while U.N. observers were in place, the troops stationed on opposite sides of the Suez Canal fell into a friendly-enemies relationship. They hailed each other as they came on and off duty, and compared the fish they caught from opposite banks of the Canal.

On the Golan Heights, now occupied by Israel, Syrian fighters tangled almost daily with the Israelis guarding her border. Terrorists from bases in Lebanon attacked settlements, while along the Jordanian frontier with Israel, there were sporadic raids by terrorists that killed and maimed civilians.

But generally, the mood was, "This is the way we Israelis have to live until the Arabs will come to the table." Jona gritted his teeth. He thought of the three "nos" declared by the Egyptians and their Arab neighbor states—No to recognition of Israel; No to negotiating with her; No to making peace!

All along, their plan had been to build up their armies, and strike again, Jona thought.

"Where was Golda?" He called out.

Golda Meir, then Prime Minister, was aware of troop movements along her borders but anxious to avoid being the first to strike, she held back. Her advisors also believed these were ordinary maneuvers by Egypt and Syria designed to end October seventh.

Egypt was well armed in 1973. Now under the rule of President Anwar Sadat, his country was a major client of the Soviet Union. In the Cold War with the United States, the Soviets would fight their "hot" battle with America on the soil of the Middle East. Each nation supplied their clients with arms in response to the other.

The Soviets had shipped surface-to-air missiles, as well as fast fighter planes to Syria and Egypt, a wall of missiles, capable of reaching inside the Jewish state, was in place.

"On what day of the year would the Israelis be most vulnerable?" Jona asked rhetorically later that day.

"On Yom Kippur, the Day of Atonement, the holiest day on the Jewish calendar." Jona and friends were breaking the fast together in mournful silence as they sat in Jona and Anny's living room watching reports of the events in Israel on television. To them, an assault on this holy day was the saddest insult, particularly to those of Jona and Anny's acquaintance who were Holocaust survivors. Hitler had also chosen Jewish holidays to institute his vicious Aktions against Jews.

"The soldiers and airmen would be on home leave then," Jona noted to his American friends. "The religious would be in synagogue, their thoughts on a higher plane, and the rest of the population would be spending a quiet day at home because everything, everything is shut down on Yom Kippur in the Jewish state. Even the radio."

Ironically, the call-up of the defense forces was simple. Everyone was at home or in synagogue and could be quickly reached.

Although some Israeli generals had been pressing for mobilization, the Israeli cabinet was still discussing developments when the war started. Israeli radio crackled alive at 2:00 p.m. on Yom Kippur afternoon as the assaults began. IDF trucks streamed through streets, picking up soldiers on leave. Orthodox Jews in reserve units stowed away their tallit and kippas and ran home to change into uniform.

"But what happened to Israeli intelligence, always before so accurate?" Jona asked an Israeli, visiting in the United States to raise funds, some weeks later.

"There were plenty of signals, but we thought the Egyptians were having training exercises," the Israeli told him. "And they did a good job of deceiving us — the soldiers on the Canal bank wore no helmets and lounged about.

"Some of our regular army was mobilized," he related. "We just didn't listen to all the warnings; we were in denial, we wanted peace so bad, we thought we had a measure of it."

The Egyptians and Syrians had only one major objective. They had given up on the possibility of pushing the Israelis into the sea. Now all they wanted was to force the Israelis to give back the Sinai and the Golan Heights, and to do this without their having to recognize the Jewish state. By pushing back the borders, they hoped to achieve their goal.

But once again, after a week of heavy fighting in which 2,700 Israelis were killed, the Israelis began to control more territory,

President Nixon, and his new secretary of state, Henry Kissinger, air-lifted supplies to the Israelis once they realized that the Soviets were supplying the Arabs with planes and tanks.

The tide turned. Syria and Egypt feared they would lose more ground again. President Sadat asked Syria to agree to propose a cease-fire. Their grand gamble had failed.

The U.S. and the Soviets arranged the truce.

Once again, Jona and Anny were on the fund-raising trail. Israel Bonds ran an ad in the New York Times, which read— "Don't worry about Israel—do something." Americans bought bonds in great numbers.

In one night, the United Jewish Appeal raised thirty million dollars in New York for Israel. Jews and many non-Jews gathered in front of the United Nations buildings in New York to show Israel they were with her.

Nevertheless, American Jews felt torn. After fifteen years, the state still hung by a thread. The Arab states were cutting off their oil supplies to the West. The Israelis would be blamed as oil prices rose. It was an impossible tangle.

In Israel there was a hopelessness. Would the bloodletting never end? The next time they were attacked, they might not prevail. Weapons were becoming more sophisticated, and more expensive. Each side, armed to the teeth, could annihilate the other. What kind of life was that! Besides, this mad pursuit of arms was impoverishing the Israeli treasury. The oil-rich Arab states did not have this problem.

"Land for Peace," became the new slogan. The Israelis had given up the Sinai and Gaza once before, and got little for it but lip service to the Arab guarantees of safe borders. Now, Israel would not give an inch without firmer commitments from Arab states and recognition of her right to exist.

Jona had been in Israel in 1971 on a B'nai B'rith mission. He had seen, first-hand, the absorption centers for new immigrants, the need for care for the elderly, and the children. With peace, all things were possible.

At the final reception for the American mission that summer, David Ben Gurion came from the kibbutz in S'de Boker, where he lived in retirement, to address the group.

When Jona's turn came on the reception line, he shook the hand of the now elderly statesman and whispered in Hebrew "All the best."

Ben Gurion's eyes twinkled briefly, recognizing that this American businessman spoke Hebrew with a slightly Polish accent like his own. He pressed Jona's hand firmly and looked into his eyes, as only "landsmen" can. Jona moved along, so the statesman could greet the next in line.

Ben Gurion died in December of 1973, just weeks after the end of the Yom Kippur War.

The man, who had shepherded the yishuv's idea for a home-land from concept to reality, was reported to have said—"For a real peace, we should give up the occupied territories, but not Jerusalem or the Golan Heights."

Chapter 35

AT THE CROSSROADS

American Jews and Arabs watched with bated breath as their president, Jimmy Carter, attempted to bring Egyptians and Israelis together to talk peace.

In November 1977, President Sadat went to Israel to initiate peace talks. Prime Minister Menachem Begin went to Egypt on Christmas Day, 1977 and met with President Anwar Sadat. A good sign, to Jona and others watching the reports.

But Sadat found Begin "rigid," and other Arab states called it the "Treason Summit."

Then Carter went to Egypt in January. In March, Sadat came to Washington. Despite terrorist attacks from the Arabs, trying to interrupt negotiations, the talks continued.

The Zionists never wanted to rule another people. They had accepted partition, an Arab Palestine, and a Jewish Palestine in 1948. It was the Arab states that had fought it.

Now, the Israelis shrank from annexing Palestinian land for a very simple reason. The goal of the Zionists had been to become a majority in the one land in the whole wide world where this could be so. If they annexed the Palestinian territory they had won, the Jewish majority would disappear. In a democratic state, one in which each citizen had an equal vote, one day the Jews might be out-numbered and out-voted by their Arab countrymen.

"Land for Peace!" became the standing offer of the Israelis. So what was holding it up? Israel was wary of giving up land without guarantees. Finally, Prime Minister Begin agreed to abandon all of the Sinai, military bases, airfields, and settlements, but to keep control of the Gaza Strip.

For that, Anwar Sadat was willing to sign peace accords, agreeing to full diplomatic relations with Israel. Egypt needed the Sinai with its air bases and oil fields, and Sadat was statesman enough to move his country forward toward a peaceful and prosperous Middle East.

And, wonder of wonders, that militant Menachem Begin, inheritor of the philosophy of Vladimir Jabotinsky who wanted to push the British into the sea and the Arabs out of the land, that uncompromising warrior of the Irgun—Menachem Begin accepted!

The peace accords, hammered out with the help of President Carter, would be signed months later in Washington.

Jona was ecstatic!

"You realize what this means," he bellowed to Anny. "If one country like Egypt makes peace, the rest will follow!

"Call up our friends — order food. Ask the doorman to tell everyone to come here to celebrate!"

The Lermans had moved from New York City to a huge apartment house on the Jersey shore of the Hudson River—everyone in that vast building was invited.

Throughout the afternoon and evening, close to three hundred people came through Jona and Anny's door to hug and kiss and rejoice

When he calmed down, Jona wrote three letters congratulating each of the participants in the peace process. He received three replies. One from President Sadat, one from President Carter, and a short note from Menachem Begin signed in his own hand.

Now Jona felt comfortable about having a serious talk with Anny about returning to Israel to live.

His business had flourished. He had no difficulty dealing with the Hasidim he met in the jewelry center on New York's 47th Street. He fell back on his Yiddish, which was their language of choice.

As he greeted these Hasidim with their beards and dangling

earlocks, their black hats and coats, he felt like he was in a time warp. Wearing beepers, they stood three-deep at the few kosher lunch counters on the street, screaming their orders to the harried countermen. At one o'clock on Friday afternoon, they quit for Shabbat no matter what big deal was in progress.

For most, a handshake was good enough to make a deal. But a few took advantage. One man asked for an expensive necklace from Jona on consignment. Jona had to stop him to find out what happened to it some days later.

"I sold it," the jeweler said.

"So—how come you don't come in and pay for it?"

"I will— what are you worrying about, Jona. Count on me for a dollar a week."

"From now on, payment up front," Jona told Anny. And they stuck to it.

Now, Jona's idea of returning to Israel took Anny by surprise.

"First, the children and grandchildren. Izzy's Demian is so wonderful. And Yael's Drew, and Justin's only a baby. How could I leave all that. Then, business. You say you could do business from there. But, Jona, it's a new generation there now. You'd have to make contacts all over again. It's too late for us. Visit, spend months at a time, wonderful. But while we're still active, and the little ones can use us. Please let's stay here."

Soon after they were in Israel on a visit once again. Since they were not returning to live, and Anny's parents needed a smaller place to maintain, Jona sold their villa in B'nai B'rak.

It was one of their last visits with Jacob Lanel. The two friends lamented the new battles emerging on the border with Lebanon and the massacre of Sabra and Shatilla.

For security reasons, Israel has annexed the Golan Heights, abutting Syria and Lebanon. From those countries, Hizbollah fighters have staged raids into Israel and fired missiles into Israeli territory.

For historic reasons, and emotional ones, too, Israel's center has always been Jerusalem, with free access to the shrines of every faith in that city. But what is Jerusalem? The ultra-Orthodox community in Israel, and many others, maintain that the West Bank land surrounding Jerusalem is rightfully theirs.

In fact, the municipal boundaries of Jerusalem were expanded in 1967 when the city was reunified, after Jordan was beaten. Prior to that, the frontier of the State ran through the middle of the city, and bitterly, Jerusalemites remember how their synagogues in the Old City were wrecked by the Arabs in 1948, gravestones in the Jewish cemetery used to pave streets.

Once reunited, the frontier line, which ran through the city, was moved to the east, encompassing twenty-eight Arab villages. Some villages are comprised of only six or seven houses, but even in those small enclaves, some Arabs own land on which they wanted to build houses for their children. Arab plans have been subsumed by Israeli housing demands. Israelis have been moving to East Jerusalem and West Bank towns for practical reasons.

Thousands of Jews from the Arab states fled to Israel in the 1950s. In 1983, the persecuted and starving Jews of Ethiopia were airlifted out to join their brothers in the Jewish state. Thousands more arrived in 1984. Throughout the 1980s and 1990s, over 800,000 Jews from what is now the Former Soviet Union have entered Israel in a steady stream.

The Jewish population in Israel since 1948 has increased over seven fold, from 650,000 to over four million! New towns have sprouted on land purchased from the Arabs in the West Bank purely to accommodate these millions. Other land, has simply been taken by the government and forests chopped down to make room for housing.

In recent years, the Israeli court has mandated that housing be constructed for Arabs in the territories. Their numbers have grown, too. One million Arabs live in Israel.

In other West Bank towns, historically Judea and Samaria, the Orthodox Jews state that this area on the west bank of the

Jordan River belongs to their heritage and must be reclaimed in preparation for the return of the Messiah. The area available for giveback to the Arabs is thereby diminished. However, the Israelis claim the give–backs are one sided. They have not received the security they were promised in exchange.

Palestinian terrorists have retaliated with suicide bombings and barrages of stones. Israelis in West Bank towns must drive around with mesh grilles on their windows to protect them from youths flinging rocks at their cars. Israeli details stand guard, as did Haganah patrols, sixty years ago.

After incidents of murder and bombings, Israelis strike back. Arabs are kept from going to their jobs in Israel; their houses are demolished for infractions; suspect terrorists are jailed. Arabs threaten to kill fellow-Arabs who sell land to Jews.

In this tangle of claims and counter-claims, grave injustices on the part of both populations must occur, and do.

"It was Arab against Arab at Sabra and Shatilla, but we were not vigilant enough to see what might happen," Jona declared sadly.

"We had such provocation from the PLO, and riots in Gaza, and from Lebanon, we'll never get it right if we can't make peace," Jacob replied.

"The Arabs are their own worst enemy," Jona insisted.

"Once we were friends with the Arabs, we trusted them, they trusted us," Jona said. "We came to each other's simchas—weddings, remember."

Jacob, his thick hair grayed but his eyesight still keen, smiles.

"That Arab wedding feast when we were so hungry?" he teases Jona. "You carried on to the host how delicious the meat dish was 'til he sent for a bag of the roast for you to take home. Then we left the celebration tent and saw the remains of a camel roasting on the fire..." Jacob slaps his good knee and throws back his head, laughing.

"You asked the attendant—'Is this the meat we ate?'"

"He said yes!" Jona sputters. "I gagged all the way home.

Then a squadron of dogs began following us. I left them a feast to remember.

"Ah," he adds reflectively, "we got along then. Now there is so much bitterness."

"There is enough blame for injustices to go around the two populations" Jacob agreed. "If only we could look in each other's eyes, Jew and Arab, and see that the we both have suffered, perhaps we could begin a real dialogue."

In Jona's life in Israel and before, he saw so many parallels between Jew and Arab.

"The Arabs value education, as we do," Jacob nods in agreement.

"Do you know, Jona, that they have ten universities here training Arab students?"

"They could be the future of their own nations, if they're not just being indoctrinated in terrorism. They should understand that their history records great Arab contributions to the arts, to science, to medicine, as does ours," Jona adds.

"They have lived on this slim piece of land for centuries and love it. The thistles in the hills, the hot summer winds, the sand and sea, all of it. They love it as we do," Jacob asserted.

"We're not talking about the big-shots. Right, Jacob? We're speaking about the ordinary folk—like you and me. If the Arab leaders would leave their people alone, we'd be at peace already.

"The great task for our two peoples," Jona says bruskly, "is to learn to respect each other's dreams."

Chapter 36

PURIM II

In 1985, at the age of seventy-five, Jona decided to slow down. He and Anny had been in the jewelry trade for almost twenty years.

"It's enough!" Jona announced one day. "Time for chess, for

tennis, for sculpting, for our friends, and our grandchildren."

Jona would not be at a loss for what to do with extra time. As for Anny, she went from one activity to another, helping friends, minding children, no slowing down for her. In the winter, they spent months in their Florida apartment. In summer, they were often in Israel, but other countries were visited as well.

In 1989, Anny received an amazing invitation. There would be a fiftieth reunion in Israel of people who had been aboard the *Aghios Nicolaus* in 1939. The phone rang at the Garfields. Had George received an invitation? He had, and they were going.

"I was just a girl then, I don't know how many people I'll remember, but George will help. He remembers everyone," Anny laughed with enthusiasm. "Jona, may we go too?"

Over one hundred people from that difficult journey convened in Israel. A woman of fifty had been born on the voyage. They arrived from South Africa, Europe, America. One elderly woman grabbed Anny's hand.

"I remember your father, when I was sick. He helped the doctors. He cleaned up after them. He was such a gentle man."

Anny couldn't bring the woman's more youthful face to mind, but she was glad to speak to someone who remembered her parents, now gone. They spoke of their lives since those frightful days aboard the stranded vessel.

After the reunion in Haifa, the Lermans visited Jerusalem. They walked about the historic sites and bustling streets. Jona commented on the increase of Yiddish-speaking American Jews among the ultra-religious in the Israeli population.

"Some of my former customers no doubt, fed up with the struggle for a living in America," Jona joked to Anny.

Inspired by the concept that they are "guardians of Jerusalem" these young people, strings of little children in tow, seem as fervent as the Zionists of old. But there was a difference, Jona thought. While the Zionists protected the religious community in the yishuv, the present religious contingent was hostile to secular Jews, or any Jew who followed more liberal religious practices.

When the Lermans returned home, they had stunning news awaiting them!

The United States government had designated a site on the Mall in the nation's capital for a holocaust museum! Miles and his band of professors and philanthropists had succeeded beyond their most fervent dreams.

Some time before, The President's Commission on the Holocaust had set up a Memorial Council. Elie Wiesel, the survivor who, through his writings, had vividly brought the horrors of the Holocaust to public consciousness, was designated its chair by President Carter. His idea, and that of the council members, was to create a teaching museum, rather than simply a monument.

Miles was named to the council in 1979. His tasks were obtaining archives for the museum, and also raising the funds to finance its construction.

"A huge responsibility for my brother and his friends," Jona said thoughtfully. "So many expectations to satisfy."

In the next years, Miles would travel the country, speaking before corporate boards, fraternal organizations, meeting with Jewish and Christian sympathizers, speaking to congregations of both faiths.

Miles never rested during those long years of fund-raising. He was constantly on the road, going from one engagement to another. Jona hardly saw him.

"I read about my brother in the newspaper," Jona said proudly.

As contributors to the project, Anny and Jona received updates from the Council. Finally, it was announced that the funding was in place. James Ingo Freed was engaged as the architect.

What design would he create that could do justice to the grand concept of education and memory, and still make it compelling enough to attract visitors?

Anny reminded Jona that the building would also have to fit

in with other government architecture surrounding it. She wondered if the museum would be too sterile, too grim.

Jona worried about his brother's long hours on the road, but he knew hard work was Miles' meat. He wished he could be of help to Miles.

With all their granchildren off to school, Yael's eldest already in college, the Lermans decided to give up their Jersey home. Like many of their friends, they chose to live full-time in Florida. They purchased an apartment along the ocean in Palm Beach County. George and Suzi Garfield were nearby. So was Miles. New Jersey, where their children lived, was less than three hours away by plane. The granchildren could visit on vacations, and Anny and Jona would go north for holidays and special occasions.

In Florida they found a multitude of organizations interested in charitable work and Israel. There were thirty-one synagogues in Palm Beach County, two Jewish community centers, and several colleges. All offered adult education courses, discussion groups and interesting speakers. The Lermans fit right in.

Involvement was lively among the retirees, many of whom had held leadership roles in Jewish communal life. When war in the Persian Gulf seemed likely in 1990, there was consternation among the seniors about Israel's location if a war should erupt.

Saddam Hussein, ruler of Iraq, was moving in on Kuwait, which it claimed was stealing Iraqi oil from an underground natural reservoir. President George Bush had enlisted the support of Arab states in the region to oppose Hussein's aggression. Jordan refused to join with the others, but the U.N. was mounting a force to attack Iraq if its deadline for withdrawal from Kuwait was not met.

Iraq threatened to attack Israel if she were bombed. Israel was asked to have its military stand down. To let the U.N. handle any engagements.

Jona was listening closely to an argument among his neighbors.

"Israel is like the net on the tennis court," one man said. "The missiles will fly over it like balls over the net. Our Patriot missiles will shoot them down."

"But those balls will fall on Israel, not on a net!" another declared angrily. "Israel should not be put in that position!"

"We must give the U.N. force the right to control the enemy. It will go well for Israel if she cooperates. These other Arab states may look with favor on Israel, afterward," a former economist offered. "But they would never join America if Israel were involved."

"Saddam says we encouraged him to go after Kuwait," one woman ventured. "Maybe we should try talking to him again."

"Talk cannot work with a dictator," Jona chimed in. "Saddam won't listen to reason until he's hit. With a democracy, you can deal. Does the U.S. agree with Mexico and Canada all the time? No. But do they shoot at each other? No. They sit together. They talk. They work it out. With dictators there's no option. I, myself am going to Israel, to be with the Israelis if they're in harm's way."

"You, Jona?" one friend asked. Anny looked sternly at him.

"Yes. I will go. As an American, I must show my support of Israel. As an Israeli, I must show my support of America."

"What can you do there, Jona?" his friends challenged him. "You're eighty years old. Stay home. It's a danger zone."

Anny said later, "Jona, did you mean what you said?"

"I do, Anny. I make my plane reservations tonight. This is important to me."

She sighed. There was no way to argue with such a person. But as the day for his departure neared, she tried.

"Just because you said you'd go doesn't mean you have to. Explain that you're not a hundred percent in the health department," she timidly offered.

"I am a hundred percent! Don't fight me on this Anny!" Jona retorted.

Despite Jona's bravado, as the deadline for war got closer, he made a tape, putting down his thoughts and his plea for peace. Anny heard him speaking into the recorder at four o'clock one morning.

She went to him.

"Jona, my heart's delight, please stay home," she begged.

He kissed her shining face, and wiped away her tears.

"Go back to sleep, Anny," he said gently. "I'll come back to you, you'll see."

He returned to his recording task.

As if speaking directly to Hamas and Yasser Arafat, the Palestine Liberation Organization and all the foes surrounding Israel, he declared on the tape —

"You murder a hundred, five hundred will come to take their places. You'll never win by terror. On the other hand, we can work together and help each other. When will you see that!" He also taped messages to his grandchildren. After all, who knew what could happen in a war zone?

The whole family was concerned about Jona's trip. His grandson, Justin, even wrote a poem, which revealed the youngster's worries as well as his admiration for "Grandpa."

At the airport in Miami, there was another scene. Anny fell to weeping, as Jona shouldered his bag to enter the plane.

"Did you see the people coming off—from Israel! Why must you be one of the few to go?"

"I'm not one of the few. The B'nai B'rith president, Kent Schiner, is going—and with his wife. And thousands of others. Anny, that's it. Don't let me leave you like this."

Anny touched his face, and tried a smile. He left the gate and disappeared into the jetway. She went to her car, steaming.

The most stubborn man in the world! She told herself. Stubborn when his father sent him money. Stubborn when he wouldn't compromise with the union. Stubborn to go on this journey! She turned on classical music, to blot out her thoughts, as she drove home alone.

Jona was in Tel Aviv when the first Scuds fell, lobbed by Iraq into the heart of the city. Hotel guests were herded into "safe rooms," windows and doors taped shut against possible germ warfare. Gas masks were put on.

Jona ventured out during the day to see friends. He found the house of an old comrade-in-arms, only to discover the man had died some months before. His widow sat in her darkened room, alone and afraid. Jona went food shopping for her and stayed with her most of the day.

"Jona, you're a prayer answered. I thought I was forgotten," she said as she hugged him goodbye.

Jona spoke with Uri Pe'er in Haifa. His brother Yonatan was still in the military, married to a woman who was a top officer in the parachute battalions. The air force stood ready to spring into action if the bombing continued and escalated.

A representative of the Jewish Agency came to call on him. The man wondered if he'd brought a large contribution.

"I just brought myself," Jona admitted. "To show Israelis that just because I live abroad, I haven't forgotten what the homeland means."

The young Agency man shook his hand and left shaking his head. Jona imagined him laughing and saying back at the office—"These old guys, idealists to the core; they're something else."

Many people left Tel Aviv for safety in Jerusalem. The holy city would not be harmed because of the many shrines there. Jona stayed put in Tel Aviv, except for one day when he went to Jerusalem because a friend insisted that he come. On that day, the outskirts of the city took its only hit.

In the end thirty-nine Scuds fell on Tel Aviv, Haifa and the countryside. Buildings were destroyed, houses wrecked, and three people in Tel Aviv died of heart attacks related to the bombing, one died from falling debris.

Israel took the blows.

The 100-hour Desert Storm ground assault against Iraq, turned the tide. Saddam Hussein began his withdrawal from Kuwait.

The U.N. objective had been achieved. U.S. President George Bush and the U.N. declared Operation Desert Storm ended.

It was Purim, February 28, 1991. Israel was out of harm's way. Tel Aviv erupted in joyous celebration. Jona stepped out, hugging and kissing all he met. There was dancing in the streets, singing, shouting. He returned to his room to call Anny on the overseas line.

"It's just as wonderful as my first Purim in Tel Aviv, Anny." he bubbled. "Now, I'm coming home."

Chapter 37

REVELATION

For twelve years, Miles Lerman traveled the country raising funds for his dream. If he felt a pain, he ignored it. If he was tired, he roused himself. He kept going until the job was done.

The United States Holocaust Memorial Museum began to rise from the ashes of Yachad Lerman, Esther, her husband and children, and the six million Jews and other millions of innocent peoples destroyed by the Nazi reign of terror.

Then Miles gave in to his pains. He required a serious operation. He and his wife went to their Florida winter home to recuperate. Jona lived just minutes from Miles.

Jona came to visit Miles every day, to talk with his brother, to keep him company. When Miles was stronger, he encouraged him to walk in the hallway outside his apartment, later on the path that bordered the lake near their apartment homes.

"He nursed me," Miles said later of his older brother. "He encouraged me. He was always my hero."

During their time together, the brothers began filling in each other about the many years they had spent apart after Jona left for Palestine.

One day, Miles, in speaking of the year before their father died, said—"Of course, if he had built the mill in Palestine, things might have been different for us."

Jona looked at him.

"What mill in Palestine?" he asked, his temples pulsing.

Then Miles told him a story he imagined Jona knew.

Jona, breathless, listened.

Srulke was worried that Jona was suffering in Palestine in 1937 along with the other settlers enmeshed in the depression there. Jona's bravado in sending back his father's money did not convince Srulke that Jona was well off.

For the moment, Srulke would put aside the religious issue in favor of simply helping Jews in trouble.

He did the paper and pencil work of figuring out how to build a flourmill in Eretz Yisroel! The mill would add an industry to the few at present in the yishuv. Britain would approve. Men would be put to work, women could buy flour for less if it was ground locally. Srulke had the funds, the know-how, all he needed was permission from his Rebbe.

But the Rebbe went by the Book.

"No, Srulke-Lerman. You may not send funds to Palestine for such a purpose," the Rebbe said firmly. "Not until the Messiah comes may we try to re-establish our homeland. To be buried there, yes. To go there to study, yes. But to build in the country beforehand? No! It is forbidden!"

Srulke had based his whole life on the teachings of the master. To go against the ruling of the Hasidic leader was impossible for Srulke. He and his family had followed the doctrines as long as anyone remembered.

Perhaps Srulke sensed what might happen to the Jews of Poland, and was torn apart between reason and faith. Faith won. Not long after, Srulke had the stroke that killed him.

Jona put his hand through his hair, sighing deeply. He himself was torn in sympathy for his father and in anger anew at the Rebbe

Krisha came in with a lunch tray for Miles and Jona. The two brothers ate silently, each with his thoughts.

"Now that the museum is finished, Jona, you'll come," Miles said at last.

Jona nodded. What else was there to say.

Chapter 38

MUSEUM ON THE MALL

Early on a spring morning in 1995, Jona and Anny left their hotel room in Washington, D.C. to meet Miles at the United States Holocaust Memorial Museum at 100 Raoul Wallenberg Place.

A handsome classic edifice greeted them on the outside. But the sharp gravel border along the plaza, like a railroad track bed, set the tone for what they would find inside.

A long staircase faced them, set off by sheer brick walls and open steel beams. Not the usual look for a place devoted to the Muses. This museum had a different purpose.

The architect, James Ingo Freed's concept was austere but powerful. Visitors would embark on no sentimental journey inside, but one that would remain with them, and would deepen their understanding. Its design received universal acclaim when the doors opened in 1993.

Miles was strong again after his illness. He took Anny and Jona to the permanent exhibit floor of the museum. There were General Eisenhower's prophetic words over the doorway.

After he saw the horror of a concentration camp on Victory Day in 1945, he said:

"... I made this visit deliberately in order to be in a position to give first hand evidence of the things if ever, into the future, there developed a tendency to charge these allegations merely to propaganda."

Anny and Jona were silent as they toured the exhibit.

While telling the tragic story of the Holocaust, the walls of documents point out how things might have been different. Letters from government officials denying refuge to desperate Jews are there for everyone to see.

"What could have been the mental conditioning of human beings who could pile up thousands of pairs of children's shoes, of people's eyeglasses and hair, and go on with the slaughter?" Anny murmured to Jona.

They noticed a group of high school students, who had entered the museum with them in a jovial spirit, now wore intense expressions, some with tears in their eyes.

Miles, appointed by President Clinton, was now chairman of the Memorial Council. He explained that he had to prepare for the ceremony about to take place on the outdoor plaza. Jona's seats were reserved downstairs, he reminded them.

"Miles, this is remarkable," Jona said with admiration as Miles left.

Jona and Anny stared at the photographs that surrounded them on the soaring walls of a passageway representing the final records of communities in Poland that once were renowned for Jewish learning and culture. Only these brown-edged photos of the families, who lived in them, remain.

They toured "Daniel's Story," a presentation for youngsters, for which no ticket is needed.

Children walk into Daniel's room in his home in Germany. They see his bicycle, books and toys. He writes in his diary how the world closes down on him because he is a Jew.

Reading his words as they walk along, children can connect to those years, that start out like their own but end so differently. When they exit, they may write postcards to Daniel about their impressions.

Jona read some of these cards which are posted on a wall.

"I didn't know about this. I'm glad I found out. Never again!" one child wrote.

"I love you, Daniel," wrote another. "Forgive us for what happened."

Jona shook his head and sighed. He thought of his friend, the survivor, whose pain was so great that he could not bear to remember. Would he not agree that these children should know what happened in those years?

In the computer rooms of the museum are stored the archives of families of the Holocaust on video tape, to be retrieved by scholars and other people, for years to come.

Anny Lerman's story of her escape from Czechoslovakia, aboard the *Aghios Nicolaos*, is now part of these filmed archives. Steven Speilberg, the film executive, has created Survivors of the Shoah Visual History Foundation to film the testimony of survivors who have bravely recounted their memories of their years in the camps, their nights and days on the run or in hiding. The museum, and other locations, will have copies of these testimonies. Enter "Anny Lerman" on the computer, and her face and her witness will appear.

But on that April morning in 1995, Miles' determination to set straight the record of Jewish resistance was about to be realized.

Anny and Jona took seats near Krisha, and turned to listen to the speakers on the podium, a roster of Washington leaders and historians.

The museum trustees that day inaugurated the Miles Lerman Center for the Study of Jewish Resistance. It was Miles' dream to make clear to the world that even in death camps, Treblinka and Sobibor, Jews rose in rebellion, and escaped.

Yet, it was not so simple to resist, as Miles tells in the supplement to the Museum's newsletter later that year. His story reveals the heart-breaking choices, which had to be made.

"In 1941," he writes, "I was arrested and deported to a slave labor camp not far from Lvov. When we came to realize the true purpose of the camp, we prepared for escape. Our camp consisted of 450 men of various ages. As the news spread among the prisoners that a small group was preparing to break out, the Jewish elders of the camp summoned our leadership to a secret meeting. They asked us, 'Who gives you—the young and the healthy — the moral right to buy your freedom at the price of the lives of those who will not be able to escape with you?'

"After pondering the question, we could not go through the our plans. Had thirty or forty of us succeeded in escaping, those left behind in the camp would have been liquidated the following day."

Later, he and other young men were taken from a slave labor camp to work in a quarry.

"When we were somewhat apart from the others, I, and two others, over-powered our guard and ran for the forest," Miles relates. The men formed a partisan unit, fighting from hiding places in the forest for the remainder of the war

The mission of the Miles Lerman Center for the Study of Jewish Resistance is to prove that despite being hunted, starved and shackled, Jewish men, women and even children fought back, often with nothing but their bare hands.

At the inaugural ceremonies, Jona and Anny stood and applauded Miles along with the distinguished audience present at the museum. From the podium, Miles raised his hand when he caught Jona's eye, to salute him. Grinning, Jona held his hand above his head to salute Miles.

Here were two brothers — Srulke and Yachad Lerman's boys—who had, each in his own way, done so much for their people.

"Jona was my hero when I was small," says Miles, smiling, some time later. "He paved the way for me to go on to study in the gymnasium. He was brave enough to follow his dream of a homeland for the Jewish people. He is my hero, today."

Chapter 39

ONE OF THOUSANDS

Jona was living in Israel when Prime Minister Ben Gurion negotiated a payment of a billion dollars from West Germany.

Jona had a hard time understanding how his country could take anything from the Germans. Then he realized that the infant state was desperate to build the infrastructure that would create jobs, housing and health care for the thousands of survivors who had entered the country and needed services.

Nevertheless, Jona felt Ben Gurion was compromised. Now, many years later, he realizes that the Prime Minister showed concern for the living, the ones in need, and for the Germans who earnestly sought some way to compensate those they devastated.

Yet Jona finds he still cannot forgive, even more than fifty years later.

This is particularly true when it comes to Poland. Miles has been back to Tomaszov on more than one mission. He has asked Jona to accompany him, but Jona has, as yet, refused.

Miles has negotiated with officials in Poland for a memorial at the Belzec death camp. Poland leaders have more recently been responsive to the need for some acknowledgment of their responsibility for the annihilation of nearly the entire Jewish population of their country. Of the three million Jews in Poland in 1939, half fled to the eastern sector when it was taken over by the Soviet Union. Of the remaining 1.5 million, only 250,000 were alive at the end of the war.

Jona has remained in touch with Uri Pe'er, son of his friend Frieda Stuhl Pe'er. Uri also has been to Tomaszov on several trips, accompanied by his students. Israel wants younger people to understand the desperate condition of Jews before the state was established. Israeli youngsters like young people everywhere, take for granted the benefits so hard fought for by their parents and grandparents.

As assistant principal of a school near Haifa, Uri has worked with the principal of a school in Tomaszov. The high school's principal hosted the Israeli students recently. He arranged a reception at which eighty-five of his students and their parents came together with the visiting youngsters. Addresses were exchanged and Polish students sounded enthusiastic about visiting Israel some day.

The mayor of Tomaszov has agreed that Kiryat Hayim, Uri's town, and Tomaszov, where his mother was born, should become Sister Cities.

"I was stunned," says Anny. "I'm sure there are good Poles, but where were they? Sister Cities? It's good for tourism," is her cynical response.

Jona is silent, mulling over Uri's news, trying to reconcile the past with the present.

"Listen," he says, "Miles is trying to build relations with the Croats, the Hungarians and Germans, all three had citizens who cooperated willingly with the Nazis. Perhaps this approach is right. It is better if those who would have destroyed us — try to understand. It's too hard for us.

"It must be meaningful for Uri and his town, or he wouldn't do it."

"Uri's right, of course, I know it in my head," Anny adds. "It's just in my heart that I have trouble."

Jona smiled inwardly. Those were his mother's last words to him so long ago.

In the summer of 1996, Anny and Jona made their regular pilgrimage to Israel. But this time, they were in for a new adventure, one achieved by many lives and the courage of a king.

In 1994, King Hussein, a Bedouin of the Hashimite kingdom, became the second ruler to lead an Arab country to the peace table. Land on both sides of the Jordan River had been part of the Palestine Mandate when the British took over. Then the Brits appointed an Arabian, Abdullah, emir of Trans-Jordan. His successor King Hussein had rejected the Egyptian peace treaty with Israel in 1974. Now a new age was dawning.

"Too bad it took forty-six years for Jordan to come to the table, but later is better than never," Jona remarked as their tour bus crossed the Jordan River and sped on to Amman.

Their destination was the excavated city of Petra with its amazing earthen buildings hugging the hillsides. Hikers from Israel had tried to look upon the city before the treaty, only to be shot or imprisoned. Now, the Israelis were welcomed warmly by the Jordanians. The tourists, who come from afar to marvel at the beauty of the ancient site, are a new and welcome source of revenue.

Later in the capital city, Anny and Jona walked around the streets lined with shops, returning greetings to Jordanian Arabs who beam back at them, especially when Jona returns the greeting in their own tongue.

"See, was that so terrible that we had to wait years to make peace," Jona announces to the busload of tourists as they return to Jerusalem. "We could all work together, enrich ourselves, instead of killing our children."

"Hush, Jona, enjoy the sights," Anny chides.

Back in Tel Aviv, they visit old friend Rivkah Goldstein, who Jona started in the chicken business. Moshe, her husband, became a successful builder, putting up a series of small condominium apartments in Bat Yam.

Rivkah was able to give up poultry farming, and after she raised their two daughters, she turned to philanthropy on a one-to-one basis. Rivele, as she was known, never forgot her harsh years in Siberia, where the Russians sent her family during the war. She and her sister were forced to chop wood in the forests in winter, dressed in thin clothing with potato sack strips wrapped around their shoes for protection as they stood in the snow.

She felt the plight of the new immigrants in her bones. They needed housing, furniture, and clothing. She embraced the Ethiopian Jews, bringing toys to the children, brow-beating landlords to rent apartment for less to them and to Russian families. She found jobs for the newcomers, bought them furniture and new clothes, always making it seem that they were doing her a favor.

"Wherever she sees a need, she tries to fill it," Jona boasts, proud to talk about the child he knew in Tomaszov who became a beacon for other survivors.

Walking with her one day, Jona found he was talking to himself. Rivkah had disappeared.

"Where are you, dear lady?" he called. She waved to him from behind a tree. There she was, stooping over a beggar on a bench, giving him money for a meal.

Jona and Anny visited Jona's first neighborhood in Tel Aviv.

" I lived here, and Ben Gurion's house was the last house on this street," Jona points out to Anny. "Now it's in the beginning of the city."

Shacks and small houses that had lined the beaches have given way to the Tayelet, a broad colorful promenade that stretches for three-and-one-half miles along the Mediterranean shore from Tel Aviv to Jaffa. Strollers, joggers and in-line skaters whisk past.

Jona looks toward Jaffa where he had his feed warehouse. He doubts that the Arab owner ever returned. There is talk of making restitution to Arabs for property they abandoned when they fled. This seems fair to Jona.

They stroll along the crowded Dizengoff which was once the only popular thoroughfare for shops and cafes. Now there are countless shopping avenues, and lively Sheinken Street boasting antique shops and cafes, art galleries and workshops.

Skyscrapers, their glass windows reflecting the broad Mediterranean Sea and each other, rise above what used to be a collection of uninspired plaster buildings. "Some of them I helped plaster," Jona laughs.

The Lermans take the growth in stride. Of course the city would develop. It is now the business center of the Middle East.

But these changes are as nothing, compared to the changes in

Israeli society.

Israel is still a place where any law-abiding Jew who wished, could find a home. In seven years, 800,000 Jews from the Former Soviet Union have emigrated to Israel. Earlier there were the Ethiopian Jews, and before that in the 1950s the Jews of North Africa. All were welcomed, and most have come to realize a better life than they had before.

But he is dismayed at the divisions he sees in Israeli society.

Civil Law prevails in the government of Israel, with the exception of personal matters such as marriage, divorce and conversion. These affairs are the domain of the Orthodox establishment which makes the rules and receives state funds for their activities.

Increasingly, the arguments between Israel's secular Jews and religious Jews are at the boiling point, over land, over who shall govern, and over activities forbidden on the Sabbath according to the ultra-Orthodox. The Ultras force the question—Is Israel to be a state of Jews or a Jewish state? A democracy or a theocracy?

"It is a nation like any other," Jona declares, "with one exception—any Jew shall have the right to live there."

Even more disturbing to Jona is the sight of Jewish fanatics praising Yigal Amir before his prison gate. One woman was screaming—"Yigal, I want to have your baby!" The Lermans were mortified.

The rabid zealot, Amir, murdered Prime Minister Yitzhak Rabin in 1995 because, under the Oslo Accords, he was working to return to Palestinians West Bank land for peace. These Jews claim Jewish soil is never to be shared. Like Jabotinsky before them they cry—"We were here first—it is ours by right!"

Jona stands up for the pioneers' point of view.

"We never wanted to take land, we wanted to purchase it and we did. We came with shovels, not with rifles. We wanted to build along with the Arabs."

Jona has harsh words for the Ultras who are determined that

only their understanding is the correct one.

"You can brainwash people just so long, though," he smirks. "In New York, the Hasidim hold their kids close because they know all you need is a subway token and a shave, and you can leave. And some are leaving. Here, the government pays to support thousands of 'students' who don't serve in the military and live on the dole. The Israeli taxpayer is waking up to the rip-offs. I know this from Israel's press which highlights some of these inequalities, and from talking to Israelis." He has these answers ready for people who are concerned with these issues in America.

Among the ultra-Orthodox, one of their most divisive convictions is the one that holds that Reform and Conservative Jews are "enemies of Judaism." They call ordained rabbis of these streams of Judaism, "Mister" to their faces. A day school building in Israel, sponsored by a non-Orthodox movement, was destroyed the day before it was to open to its students. Fanatics of the right are believed responsible.

"Fanatics, on either side, are our greatest danger," Jona says to Anny, shaking his head. "Murder over who has rights to occupy land! Hamas suicide bombings of children to make point! Khomeini tactics!"

Anny wonders if Jona has too much emotional baggage for him to visit modern Israel.

But there are positive moments too.

That night, they are in high spirits as they prepare to go to the theater in Jaffa.

They are to see a play performed in Hebrew by actors who not so long ago came to Israel from Russia. At first, the Gesher troupe spoke Hebrew, learned by rote. Now they are fluent in the language, and the company is lauded as one of the best in Israel.

Anny and Jona arrive early at the Gesher's newly acquired theater. They sit at a table in the lobby area sipping coffee. In years past, people would stop to greet them.

"Ach," says Anny, "people pass us by. It's like we didn't live here at all. They should be proud to greet you."

"What should they do, Anny? They must build for their future. I was no one special. We all had a dream then—and were willing to give our lives to achieve it. I am one of the lucky ones, here to see a dream come true."

"I wish our grandchildren were here with us," Anny says, wistfully. Izzy has had three more children with his caring second wife Linda, two boys and a lovely daughter, Nadine. Yael and Robbie have three sons.

But Jona's heart is full. He is here with his dear wife Anny who understands his thoughts.

"Look what we accomplished, Ima," he smiles, using the Hebrew word for mother.

"I wish that my dear friends who gave their lives and limbs, Amos, and Jacob, and so many others, could be sitting next to us now. They would feast their eyes on this crowd. There are people from so many lands—living in a free country. It was worth all the perils, the fevers, the sunstroke, and the hunger.

"I'm so proud of all those pioneers who endured so much, and enjoyed so much," Jona says, his eyes smiling. "The hora dances, planting and harvesting, reaching up to take an orange from the tree.

"We, the Jewish people, who were called every name to denigrate us, are as productive a people as any other on earth."

He pauses, and turns somber suddenly.

"The picture of the Belzer Rebbe is in front of my eyes. I see my mother and me standing before him, listening to his words— 'Only the Messiah will bring the Jewish people to the Holy Land, and that will be when all the Jewish people will be observant and righteous!'

"Well, you know what happened. Four out of five Hasidim who listened to their Rebbes perished. My mother and sister among them. But the Rebbe was saved, and spent the rest of his life here.

"The thousands of us who couldn't wait, made it possible for all of us to be here tonight in this cherished land. If there were no Israel, I'd like to know where the Algerian Jews, the Syrians Jews, Jews of Tunis, of Ethiopia, of Russia, of Yemen would be today!"

"The Belzer Rebbe Aharon established yeshivot throughout Israel. His name is very much revered. And the present Rebbe, his nephew, has said he is open to all Jews," Anny reminds him.

The foyer lights flicker. It's time to take their seats. They join the throng moving into the auditorium. Jona waxes philosophical.

"In a way, Anny, these young people have just as many tough problems to solve as we did. We solved our problems, and they will do it too."

. . .

It is 1998. The Motion Picture Academy Award for Best Documentary Film has just been won by the Simon Wiesenthal Center film, "The Long Way Home." The documentary tells the story of the plight of the survivors of the Shoah who were kept from entering Palestine during the years just after the end of World War II.

On this March day, the film is being shown at Temple Emanu–El in Palm Beach, courtesy of member Pearl Resnick whose foundation sponsored the film's production.

After the showing, a speaker presents a pamphlet to members of the audience. In it are pictures of maps that hang on Yasser Arafat's wall and in other offical places in territory under Palestinian control. The maps show the entire area of pre-state Palestine, without labeling any part of the map "Israel." Children's schoolbooks do not mention Israel. It is as if, on this fiftieth anniversary of the State of Israel, the country did not exist!

The speaker says, "The PLO's objective of obliterating Israel remains unchanged. There can be no peace in the Middle East as long as the Palestinians teach, preach and work for the destruction of Israel!"

People begin to grumble in chagrin. Another speaker rises to agree that the Arabs still believe they can "wipe us out."

From the back of the room, a man raises his hand.

"May I speak for a moment?" he asks in his Israeli accent, warmed by its Yiddish influence.

The Rabbi in charge says, "Of course."

People turn to see a rather short man, with bushy white hair, his collar open at the neck, standing erect, his jaw firm.

"It is true that these maps are disturbing," he begins. "But I know the Arabs. I was in Palestine from 1934. For fourteen years I was in the Haganah. I've been listening to them for sixty-four years. This is their bluff to their people.

"I ask you to remember Stalin—he said he would rule the world! Remember Krushchev banging his shoe yelling—'We'll bury you!' Remember Saddam who promised—'Your rivers will run with blood.' Where are they now, I ask you?

"We must keep striving for peace—and not be deterred by the bluffers!"

The auditorium bursts into applause.

Afterwards, a crowd assembles about the white haired man.

"I always wanted to meet someone from the Haganah to thank you for all you did," an elderly woman gushes, holding out her hand. "May I learn your name, sir? You are one who made the State of Israel possible."

"Thank you very much," the smiling octogenarian answers. "Nice to meet you. But I didn't do it alone, to create a homeland for the Jewish people took generations from the whole world. I'm Jona Lerman, just one of the thousands."

Jona Lerman, 1931,
a recruit in the
Polish army

Left: Yitzhak Blank and Jona
Right: Jona painting houses in
Tel Aviv, 1934

Jona's family posed for this photo, taken in Tomaszov, Lubelski, in 1936 to send to Jona in Tel Aviv, Palestine.

Top Row: L-R, Shmuel (Miles) Lerman, Esther Lerman Fuchs Steinberg (d. Belzec, 1942), Moshe Strazberg (Jona Feldzon's brother-in-law), Shmuel (Samuel) Lerman, (Shlomo's son, d. Siberia, 1943).

2nd Row: L-R, Edza Lerman (daughter of Shlomo), Shlomo Lerman, Jona's older brother, (d. Munich, 1981) holding daughter Salla, Pesha Lerman Glanzer (d. Israel, 1994), Israel (Srulke) Lerman (d. Tomaszov, 1938), Yachad Feldzon Lerman (d. Belzec, 1942), Jona Feldzon, Polish recruit.

3rd Row: L-R, Oskar Glanzer (Pesha and Hershel's son), Hershel Steinberg (Esther's son, d. Belzec, 1942).

4th Row: L-R, David Fuchs and Yitzhak Steinberg (Esther's sons, d. Belzec, 1942).

Bottom Row: L-R, Ruza Lerman (Shlomo's youngest daughter), Rosa and Rachel Glanzer (Pesha's daughters).

Miles Lerman with Mother Yachad Lerman, in Lemberg (Lvov) USSR, 1941

A Haganah group visiting the grave of the poet Chaim Nachman Bialek. Jona is third from left.

Jona, right, wearing the uniform of an auxiliary policemen, 1938.

Jona on a donkey in an Arab headdress. With a Haganah comrade.

Wedding photo of Anny (Hannah Ulmer) Lerman and
Jona Lerman, Tel Aviv, Palestine, 1945

Israel (Izzy) and Linda Lerman
with children Austin, Seth and Nadine

Robert and Yael Lerman Morris

Jona and Anny pose with grandchildren at Justin Morris' Bar Mitzvah, 1991. Top row left: Justin Morris and Demian Lerman. Second row: Austin Lerman, Jona, Drew Morris holding Seth Lerman. Seated: Keith Morris, Anny and Nadine Lerman

ADDENDUM

Personalities in "The Stone Pillow"

JONA'S FAMILY
Aaron Feldzon, grandfather
Yachad Feldzon Lerman, mother
Israel (Srulke) Lerman, father
Shlomo Lerman, older brother
Mattel Teicher Lerman, Shlomo's wife
Esther Lerman Fuchs Steinberg, eldest sister
Yoshe Steinberg, Esther's second husband
Pesha Lerman Glanzer, older sister
Hershel Glanzer, Pesha's husband
Shmuel (Miles) Lerman, younger brother
Krisha Lachs Lerman, his wife
David and Jeanette Lerman, their children
Anny (Hannah) Ulmer Lerman, Jona's wife
Yael Lerman Morris, Jona and Anny's daughter
Robert Morris, Yael's husband
Drew, Justin, Keith, their children
Israel (Izzy) Lerman, Jona and Anny's son
Rose Lerman, Israel's first wife
Demian, their son
Linda Lerman, second wife
Seth, Austin, Nadine, Izzy and Linda's children
Herz Feldzon, uncle
Feiga Feldzon, aunt
Jona Feldzon, their son
Oscar and Genia Ulmer, Anny's parents
Haya Ulmer, Anny's aunt
Bayla, maid in Yachad's home
Rachel, tutor to Jona's sisters
Idele, cook in Yachad's home
Malka, Idele's sister

JONA'S FRIENDS

Abdul, co-worker and fishing buddy, Jaffa

Zosia Adler, girlfriend in Tomaszov

Amos, a carpenter who stands guard with Jona

Asher, a non-believer

Yitzhak Blank, younger member of Tomaszov sports club, roommate in Tel Aviv, Colonel in the IDF*

George Garfield, friend from N.Y.C., B'nai B'rith president*

Susi, his wife

Rivka Arbesfeld Goldstein, neighbor from Tomaszov, chicken farmer in Israel*

Isaac, poor baker in mill town

Yosel Krellenbaum, young Polish man for whom the sports club raises money, later mayor of Haifa

Jacob (Yaakov) Lanel, schoolmate, roommate in Tel Aviv*

Max, owner of embroidery business in N.Y.C.

Jack, Max's son

Mordecai, soldier in the Polish army

Natan, leader of Halutz Hazair in Tomaszov

Frieda Stuhl Pe'er, friend from Tomaszov*

Monyu Pe'er, Frieda's husband

Uri and Yonatan, their sons

Joel Sheftelowitz, argonomist from Tel Aviv

Tovah, girlfriend in the Palestine kibbutz

Shulamit, girlfriend in Tel Aviv

Yossie, roommate in the Warsaw kibbutz

* Please see page XII for biographical tributes

GLOSSARY

Bar Mitzvah — literally in Aramaic, son of the Commandments. The age, usually thirteen when a male Jew joins the team, so to speak, and takes on the obligations of full religious observance. He then can be counted upon to make up a minyon. A girl may be Bat Mitzvah at age twelve. Her religious obligations are different under the Orthodox tradition.

Hasidism — a religious movement that began about 1736 by its leader Israel Ba'al Shem Tov. The Hasidic philosophy focused on an individual's one-to-one relationship with God and to joyful observance. It evolved into the fervent study of the Talmud and closeness of the community.

Histadrut — the general federation of Jewish Labor in Palestine formed in 1920.

Irgun — known historically as IZL. The Revisionists' military organization.

Jewish Agency — recognized by the British Mandate in Palestine as representing Jewish and Zionist interests in Palestine.

Jewish Agency Executive — a coalition of members of the Zionist executive, and other non-Zionist persons representing organizations interested in the development of the yishuv.

Kashrut — A system aimed at making us aware of the food we consume through rules that label animals and fish that are scavengers as not kosher. Kosher animals are generally herbivorous. The animal must be slaughtered in a way so as not to cause it unnecessary pain. An animal acquired through hunting is not considered kosher, even if it meets other criteria. Blood must be drained from the animal before cooking. One, who is kosher, will not mix meat and dairy products. He will have separate dishes and utensils for meat and milk. Vegetables and fruits are considered neutral and may be used with both meat and milk foods. The word "Pareve" found on some packaging indicates the foods are neutral, that is they are prepared without either milk or meat products.

Maccabees — When Jona tells his father "We are Maccabees, not goats" (to be led to the slaughter) he is referring to the band of fighters in the revolt against Syrian oppression in 167 B.C.E. Three years after the rebellion, the Maccabees were victorious against the Syrians.

Magid — one who traveled from village to village in Russia and Poland, preaching and telling wondrous stories of holy men and mystical happenings.

Melamed — teacher of Hebrew and Bible at the elementary level.

The Messiah — represents the hope of eventual redemption when a leader of the people will find a just and loving world in a just and Holy Land.

Minyon — (minyan) traditionally, ten Jewish men needed to conduct prayer as a community. Minyons (minyonim in Hebrew) are required for those remembering the anniversary of the death of a dear one, so it is an obligation to provide a community to assist the grieving person. The requirement of a minyon to make valid certain prayers serves as a reminder of the importance of people to one another.

Oral Law — work-of-mouth traditions are also taken into account in creating the explanations of the Torah. The discussions were eventually printed in large book called the Talmud, according to subject matter. One subject is "Damages," civil and criminal law, which Jona and Jacob were studying with the elders. It is covered by ten tractates, each containing many chapters.

Orthodox — the ultra-Orthodox traditional stream of Judaism holds that the Torah is the word of God and its 613 commandments must be followed as closely to the letter as possible. These more extreme Orthodox view as insincere and dangerous those Jews who do not observe strict doctrine and take liberties with kashrut, the separation of men and women at prayers, and who inter-marry. The Modern Orthodox stream, in contrast, permits its members to relate to the wider community, and views other streams of Judaism as partners in maintaining Jewish life, while disagreeing with many of its practices.

The Patriarchs — the founding fathers of the Jewish religion —Abraham, Isaac and Jacob. Jacob became "Israel" after his struggle with the angel. "Israel" literally means "he who struggles with God." Jacob bore twelve sons who became leaders of the twelve tribes known collectively as the people Israel.

Rabbi — a person qualified to give decisions on Jewish law.

Rav — a person with extensive familiarity with Jewish law but without ordination. One who assists in synagogue ritual. Also a form of address for a Rabbi.

Reb — a term of honor bestowed by custom on a learned religious person.

Rebbe — reserved for a rabbi who is a Hasidic leader. The leadership role is passed from father to son or to a son-in-law or nephew believed worthy of carrying on the dynasty.

Sabbath — Shabbat in Hebrew. Begins before dusk on Friday and ends when three stars are visible on Saturday night. Traditional Jews will do no work between these times, nor will they employ mechanical devices which they must set in motion. It is a time for prayer in the synagogue with one's neighbors and family, for rest and reflection at home, a time to re-create oneself. Based on words in the first book in the Bible, "Creation," — "and on the seventh day God rested from his labors."

Seven days of mourning — in Hebrew, shivah means seven. The time immediately after a burial, when the family of a person who has died remains at home receiving friends and family who come to comfort the mourners. The family does not observe mourning rituals during the Sabbath.

Talmud — a record of study and discussions by scholars over a period of eight hundred years. Its purpose was to expand understanding of the 613 commandments or mitzvot in the Torah as these commandments relate to every-day life.

Talmud Torah — a school for young people studying Hebrew, the Torah, and Talmud

Tiffilin — leather straps that hold boxes containing four paragraphs from the Bible. Men above Bar Mitzvah age, in the Orthodox and Conservative tradition, wrap these straps on the arm and forehead for morning prayers in fulfillment of the mandate to keep the Torah always before one.

The Torah — the first five books of Hebrew Scripture that form the basis upon which Jews are required to act. These include being just, having mercy, and seeking truth. Religious rituals include observing the Sabbath, remembering one's forefathers, and thanking God each day for His miracles as well as for order in nature, and our own well-being. The Biblical personalities mirror people of all times and places, with faults and virtues. The Torah points the way to overcome our animal nature and to fulfill the Jewish mission of mending the world. The Hebrew Bible contains not only the Torah, but also two other sections: the Prophets, and writings, which encompass Psalms and Proverbs among others.

Yishuv — the Jewish community of Palestine, mainly Zionist. The term was no longer used once Israel became a state.

Zionism — a belief in a return to the land in which the early Hebrews resided and ruled. Such a belief did not rule out working alongside other people in the same land, nor did it mandate only one strand of the earth's peoples, since anyone who wishes to become a Jew, regardless of color, previous creed or country of origin, after proper instruction, may do so.

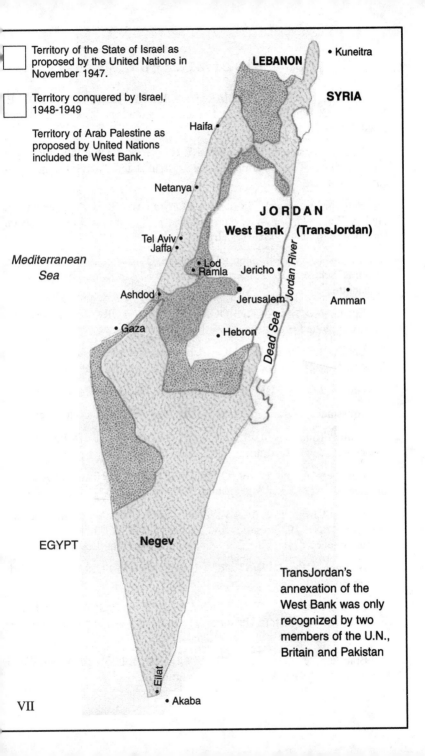

Territory of the State of Israel as proposed by the United Nations in November 1947.

Territory conquered by Israel, 1948-1949

Territory of Arab Palestine as proposed by United Nations included the West Bank.

• Kuneitra

LEBANON

SYRIA

Haifa •

Netanya •

J O R D A N

West Bank (TransJordan)

Tel Aviv •
Jaffa •

Mediterranean Sea

• Lod
Ramla

Jericho •

Ashdod •

Jerusalem

Jordan River

Dead Sea

• Amman

• Gaza

• Hebron

Negev

EGYPT

TransJordan's annexation of the West Bank was only recognized by two members of the U.N., Britain and Pakistan

Eilat

• Akaba

VII

BIBLIOGRAPHY

Ausabel, Nathan, PICTORIAL HISTORY OF THE JEWISH PEOPLE. New York: Crown, 1962; photos of Trumpeldor, tower and stockade, "Burma Road."

Begin, Menachem, THE REVOLT. New York: Nash Publishing, 1977 revised; views of Ben Gurion, Altalena Affair, stated "natural right to our entire homeland."

Ben-Gurion, David, ISRAEL: A PERSONAL HISTORY. New York: Funk & Wagnalls; Tel Aviv: Sabra Books, 1971; views and documents on Haganah, Beit Susin villages, Latrun, *Altalena.*

Collins, Larry and Lapierre, Dominique, O, JERUSALEM. New York: Simon & Schuster, 1972; Latrun, "Burma Road; *Altalena*; *Exodus*; Count Bernadotte.

Eban, Abba, AN AUTOBIOGRAPHY, NEW YORK: Random House, 1977; U.N. vote for partition.

ENCYCLOPEDIA JUDAICA, Jerusalem: Keter Publishing, 1972; Articles on Tomaszov, Lubelski Poland, and Rebbes of Belz, Poland.

Gilbert, Martin, THE HOLOCAUST, San Francisco: Collins, 1986.

Grossman, David, YELLOW WIND, New York: Delacorte, 1989

Gruber, Ruth, RAQUELA. New York: Geoghegan, 1978 Polish army service for a Jewish doctor.

Hertzberg, Arthur, Editor, THE ZIONIST IDEA, A Historical Analysis and Reader. New York: Antheneum, 1977.

Herzog, Chaim, THE ARAB-ISRAELI WARS. New York: Vintage Press/ Random House, 1982; battles and background of War of Independence, Latrun, Sinai campaign, Six Day War, Yom Kippur War, Lebanon.

Hourani, Albert, A HISTORY OF THE ARAB PEOPLES, New York Warner Books, 1991, Nationalism, Partition.

Katz, Steven T., THE HOLOCAUST IN HISTORICAL CONTEXT, Vol. 1. New York: Oxford University Press, 1994; pre- and post war populations.

Branstern, Thomas R., Editor, MEMOIRS OF BEN GURION, NY, World Publishing Co. 1970, Altalena Affair; Latrun.

Lewis, Bernard, THE SHAPING OF THE MODERN MIDDLE EAST, New York:Scribner, 1995; reasons British wanted mandate; and wanted to end it.

McDowall, David; PALESTINE AND ISRAEL, The Uprising and Beyond. Los Angeles: University of California Press,1990 Arab viewpoint and history.

Meir, Golda, MY LIFE. New York: Putnam, 1975; Arab riots, 1936; quote, page 157; declaration of the State of Israel.

Pogonowski, Iwo Cyprian, JEWS IN POLAND, a Documentary History, The Rise of Jews as a Nation from Congressus Judaicus in Poland to the Knesset in Israel.

Rabin, Leah, RABIN, Our Life and Legacy, New York: G. P. Putnam, 1997; bombing of Tel Aviv.

Richmond, Theo, KONIN. New York: Pantheon Books, 1995; views of Poland pre-and post war.

Rosten, Leo, THE JOYS OF YIDDISH. New York: McGraw Hill, 1961, spelling of certain Yiddish words.

Scheimann, Dr. Ladislav, AGHIOS NICOLAOS, unpublished memoir of a passenger on the ill-fate ship.

Shipler, David E., ARAB AND JEW, Wounded Spirits in the Promised Land. New York: Times Books, 1986; how Arab and Jew view each other differently.

Telushkin, Rabbi Joseph, JEWISH LITERACY. New York: William Morrow, 1991; quote of Ben Gurion on Golan Heights and Jerusalem overheard by Knesset member, page 281; general information and dates.

Teveth, Shabtai, BEN-GURION, The Burning Ground, 1886-1948.Boston: Houghten Mifflin, 1987; Arab disturbances, *Aghios Nicolaos*, *Exodus*.

United States Holocaust Memorial Council, THE LIBERATION OF THE NAZI CONCENTRATION CAMPS. Washington, D.C.: U.S.H.M. Press, 1987; eye-witness accounts of liberators, Belzec.

MAGAZINE AND NEWSPAPER ARTICLES

Associated Press, ROBERT DANIELL, Liberator. West Palm Beach, Florida, Palm Beach Post, December 1997 obituary; British officer quoted on entering Bergen-Belsen Camp.

Associated Press, DECLASSIFIED PAPERS INDICATE BRITISH KNEW OF HOLOCAUST, West Palm Beach, FL: Palm Beach Post, May 20, 1997.

Central Rabbinic Congress of the U.S.A. and Canada, A CLARIFICATION OF TORAH DOCTRINE. New York: Advertisement in the New York Times. "Any sovereignty over the Holy Land before the Messianic Epock is sinful and sure to lead to tragedy."

Hertzberg, Arthur, ARMED PROPHETS, Baltimore, Md.: Baltimore Jewish Times; fanatics are prolonging conflict.

Lerman, Miles, JEWISH RESISTANCE. Washington, D.C.: United States Holocaust Memorial Museum "Update" Supplement, Lerman Center, Spring, 1997. Quoted material on resistance with permission from Mr. Lerman.

Lurie, Jesse Zel, ISRAEL'S FRONTIERS, Facts vs Misconceptions, Deerfield Beach, FL.: Jewish Journal, May 13, 1997; parameters of Jerusalem, lack of housing for Arabs.

May 14-30, 1948, NEW YORK TIMES, Declaration of the state and confict that follows.

Milgrom, Jacob, SHIFTING BORDERS, The Whole Land of Israel. Washington, D.C.: Moment (magazine) August, 1996; Maps of ancient Israel according to the Bible.

Shiff, Yehuda, Danny Dor, Editors–in–Chief, ISRAEL 50, Israel, Alfa Communication Ltd., 1977, Contemporary news accounts and photos from Israel sources, 1948–1998.

Shtein, Gershon, THE ALIYAH BET, History of Illegal Immigration, 1934-1948, Haifa, Israel, Am Ovet Publishing; pamphlet with photo and story of the freighter *Farita*, in Hebrew.

Toameh, Heled Abu, FROM CRADLE TO GRAVE, Jerusalem, Israel: Jerusalem Post, Sept. 4, 1997, background on Hamas.

United States Holocaust Memorial Museum, ARCHITECTURE AND ART OF THE U.S. HOLOCAUST MEMORIAL MUSEUM. Washington, D.C.: U.S.H.M. Press; pamphlet with photos.

FILMS AND VIDEOS

Goskind, Yitzhak & Shaul, POLAND IN 1939, Jerusalem: Hebrew University, Steven Spielberg Archive, ERGO Media, Teaneck, N.J. 1988; film clips of Jewish institutions in major cities.

Khlief, Michael, Director, WEDDING IN GALILEE. Belgium, France: Marissa Films,1987; Arab fields are mined, farmers can't plant, hard to congregate.

Moriah Films, THE LONG WAY HOME, Los Angeles: Simon Wiesenthal Center, 1997; DPs difficulties trying to enter Palestine.

INTERVIEWS & LECTURES

Jona Lerman 1995 - 1998

Anny Lerman 1996 - 1998

Miles Lerman 1997

Abba Eban, interview, Temple Beth El, West Palm Beach, Florida, 1983. Dilemmas for Israel in the Occupied Territories.

Professors Zev Mankowitz, Yael Isakovich, Melton Center, Hebrew University, Jerusalem, Israel, visiting lecturers, Temple Israel, West Palm Beach, Florida, 1998. Current concerns of religious groups in Israel, polarity of Jewish society; Are we Jews or Israelis?

Professor David Engel, History and Politics in Contemporary Israeli-Palestine Relations. Lecture, October 11, 1998, College of Arts and Science, New York University. Scholars have found no evidence of an organized policy to remove Arabs from Israel during 1948-49.

TRIBUTES TO MY FRIENDS

By Jona Lerman

REMEMBERING A DEAR FRIEND,
FRIEDA PE'ER STUHL

Frieda was called Fredle in Tomaszov when she was born. Her parents, like mine, were followers of the Belzer Rebbe and therefore she was brought up in a strictly Orthodox way. As did many young people, she rebelled and joined Halutz Hatzair, the Zionist pioneer organization.

She made aliya in 1933. Upon her arrival in Palestine, she lived in the Beit HaHalutzot, which is similar to a Jewish "Y" in the States, a place where women could stay until they found permanent quarters. Fredle, now called Frieda, settled in Haifa. She worked as a waitress and studied Hebrew in night school. A friend introduced her to Monyu Pe'er and they were married in 1936.

They struggled to make a living during this period of economic depression. Their son, Uri, was born in 1937. They decided to join the Kibbutz Tel Yosef where many of Frieda's friends from home belonged. Just then, their baby came down with an infectious lung disease. They needed special medical care for Uri, which was not available at the remote area of the kibbutz. They settled in a suburb of Haifa. Uri recovered and was the apple of their eyes.

Monyu worked in a flourmill. He and Frieda, like other pioneers, joined the Haganah. After a hard day's work you could see Monyu riding about on his motorcycle, always with a girl perched behind him. If it weren't Frieda, it would be another Haganah member. It looked like they were on a joyride, but it was far from that. Monyu was a courier for the Haganah; the girls were a ruse to avoid suspicion.

Frieda also patrolled the watchtower, looking for Arab bands that tried to sneak into the settlement during the night. Arabs had raped women or stabbed people on the road.

Besides tending to little Uri, Frieda joined a group of women whose task it was to integrate new immigrants, especially the ones from Yemen who lacked knowledge of a sanitary life-style. She taught them how to improve and learn modern ways of living.

Frieda and Monyu always had room for a newcomer to stay with them, until he or she found a permanent place. It seemed that the little house was made of rubber.

In the year 1939, Frieda saved up the sum needed for a ship ticket. She wanted to see her family and bring little Uri with her for them to enjoy. The trip was not to be for them. Frieda's father wrote back, after receiving a letter about her plans, expressing his fear in these words: "Something smells fishy. Dear daughter, please don't come now." Frieda never saw her family again. Hitler did his job!

Even during the most difficult times, Frieda and Monyu had a very full social life. They tended their little garden in a rented small house. They grew vegetables and raised some chickens. You never knew how difficult life was for Frieda. She displayed a soft and lovely smile and had the calmest disposition.

Yonatan, their second son, was born in 1944. As a bachelor, I visited Frieda and her family whenever I could manage to get to Haifa. Once, I even rode my bike the 65-mile stretch one way.

The only place I was not ashamed to say that I am hungry was at Frieda's. Otherwise, I always lied. When invited for a meal, I said I had just eaten. I was too proud to admit that I had fallen on real hard times.

Not at Frieda's. There I felt like it was my home. Frieda made all her friends feel that she had everything in abundance. Frieda was the most devoted friend you could imagine.

Hannah, my wife, became very fond of her as well. When our daughter, Yael, was born, Frieda left Uri, the ten-year-old, with his dad, and came with Yonatan, the little fella, to help us with our new-born. She was like family to us.

Eventually, things got better economically. Frieda and Monyu bought a small house in Kiriyat Chayim, a suburb of Haifa. Monyu built a shed on the premises where he did every repair imaginable. He was a very talented man working with his hands.

As the children grew, Frieda joined the Magen David Adom, the Israeli ambulance service. Frieda suffered in silence from severe back problems. She wore a heavy back brace and slept in a cast at night, but she continued her life of giving. She lost her partner and best friend, Monyu, in 1976.

Frieda lived ten more years. She enjoyed her wonderful family. Uri the oldest married a lovely girl, Shoshana. They had three children and two grandchildren. Uri is a vice-principal.

Yonatan, the younger son, is married to Drora whom he met while both served in the IDF. Drora was a parachutist. Both husband and wife made their careers in the military. Yonatan retired from the IDF and was hired by a major corporation as head of human resources, while Drora is still serving. She is the highest-ranking woman in the IDF. They have four children: Tomer, a young lawyer; Oren, just out of the IDF and traveling in the U.S.A.; Hadas, a soldier; and Gal, now five years old.

As for Uri's daughter, Segall, her son, Tal, works as a business administrator. Elad, the youngest, is a member of Kibbutz Malkiah. He is a true idealist. Uri said that he is from another generation, like years ago from his grandmother's time.

The Department of Education in Israel encourages schools to arrange trips for students to visit former concentration camps and villages, shtetls. In Tomaszov, as well as in other towns, there are no Jews today. Uri, acting vice-principal of a school, accompanied a group of students on such a trip. He wanted to take them to his mother's birthplace, Tomaszov.

Mr. Moshe Vertman, a member of the Israeli parliament, as well as Mr. Pincas Milch, an active member of the Tomaszov Society, were very helpful. They contacted the officials in Tomaszov and made the arrangements.

In 1995, Uri, 85 students, and with his brother, Yonatan, and their sons, arrived in Tomaszov. They were very doubtful as to the outcome of this visit. In the past, Jewish visitors in many Polish places were booed and even spat on by Polish youngsters. The hatred to Jews was transferred from their grandparents who were collaborators with the Nazis, turning over Jews who were deported to the gas chambers.

Uri hoped to make a difference by introducing Israeli kids to the Polish ones. Surprisingly, they were well received. They visited the Jewish cemetery, which was restored with funds sent by the Tomaszov Society of Israel and the U.S.A. With great emotion, they walked on a street paved with tombstones from the cemetery.

Since most of the buildings in the Jewish quarter were destroyed during the bombing by the Germans, they did not see any remains of the once thriving Jewish culture nor was there anything on the spot where the big and small synagogues stood. With sadness in their hearts, they prayed for the six million Jews murdered.

Uri went to see the house where his mother was born. The heavy hearts turned into a ray of hope for the future, however. The children of both schools interacted and made a solid connection. They correspond with each other. The Polish students are very interested in visiting Israel. At this point, they have not the means to carry out such a plan. It is a great step of improved relations, and maybe, in the future, we will have less anti-Semitism. Young people are the world.

I have purposely listed the descendants of Frieda in much detail. Here is a wonderful family which sprouted from two pioneers who Hitler defined as vermin, unworthy of living. They and their descendants are a living example of how distorted a mind the Germans had.

Dear Frieda, I am proud that I was your friend.

(YITZHAK) YITZCHAK BLANK

Yitzchak was born in my hometown, Tomoszov, in the year 1913, which made him three years my junior. He was the only son, and had a younger sister. His parents were one of the more progressive Zionistically oriented Orthodox families. From early childhood, Yitzchak excelled in studies as well as in all sports. He was a true child of brain and brawn.

Yitzchak and I went to the same heder. I remember him telling me about confrontations with the gentile students. The Jewish children were taunted and beaten for many reasons. When they entered public school, their command of Polish was poor or almost nil. They wore their earlocks pushed behind their ears, but the curls were still noticeable. They were frail looking because they hardly did any outdoor activities. They were forced to be bareheaded while in class.

Since public school was mandatory, every child had to be enrolled. They had no choice but to go by the rules. Here in the States, the government recognizes any parochial school as an acceptable substitute for the public school, but this was not true in Poland at that time.

As the children grew older, a remarkable change occurred. When Yitzchak was twelve and I fifteen, I spoke to the youngsters and they joined Zionistically oriented groups. I saw in Yitzchak a prize kid, which he indeed turned out to be.

The children in the organization were coached in sports activities and therefore became strong and more confident. They fought back when attacked. Yitzchak emerged as a terrific organizer and excelled in soccer, ping pong, track and any sport. Several times a week, he was out, at dawn, running. One time his soccer team, Hapoel, was playing against Polish students, children of army officers. The Jewish team won. All excited, their fans poured onto the field, hugging and kissing each other. In no time, the gentiles arrived with clubs and wildly assaulted the Jews, swinging away and chasing them. They wounded many.

How could a Jew, a Jyid, win? They could not bear this insult. But it was a great victory, a mental elation for the Jews.

All these sport activities had one main purpose, to raise material for future immigration to Palestine. The kibbutzim that were organized in areas in Poland, and some other European countries, served as training ground to acquire working skills that would be useful to the emigrating pioneers. Yitzchak was fortunate to have parents who had the same ideals as he had, while I had to fight constantly with my whole family.

At age eighteen, Yitzchak joined a kibbutz in Bialystock. His skills and dedication were recognized, and he was sent to organize a charter kibbutz elsewhere.

Needless to say, young women too were in the kibbutzim. While the fellas were working on cutting down trees, or on farms, the girls had jobs in housekeeping.

In 1935, Yitzchak's dream materialized and he made aliyah to Eretz Yisroel. He joined a kibbutz but left due to differences among its members. He came to Tel Aviv and we lived together for a year, working on plastering. He also became a member of the Haganah. He got a job selling tickets for those who wished to rent beach chairs at the municipal beach of Tel Aviv. He then joined the police force to become a Gafir, an auxiliary policeman. While serving on a collective farm near Haifa, he married Tova, whom he had known while both were in the kibbutz in Poland. One night, in 1938, Arabs attacked their kibbutz. Tova, hearing shots and knowing that Yitzchak was on post, went out to look for him. She received a bullet, and died on the spot. Yitzchak lost his young beloved partner.

He transferred to the Kibbutz Ramat Yochanan whose members recognized his capabilities. In 1942, he married Miriam, a widow whose husband, Amazia Cohen, had been killed during one of the Arab assaults on the kibbutz. Miriam and Yitzchak had a son, David. David and his wife, Yardena, are both successful architects in Haifa.

At the kibbutz, Yitzchak was assigned to work in the stables. He also was commander of the Haganah in the Z'vulun region where Ramat Yochana is located. In 1948, he became a soldier in the Israeli army of the State of Israel. He carried the rank of colonel. Whenever Yitzchak was in Tel Aviv, he would drop in to see us. These visits were always surprises, as we had no telephone. Very few households did, as there was a shortage of available lines. The few lines went to doctors and businesses. We finally were given a line in 1951, I believe.

It was always wonderful when Yitzchak stood at the door. Anny and Yael were very fond of him. Yael was examining his uniform with all its stripes, and immediately perched herself on his lap. He knew how to captivate the three-year-old with stories while enjoying the snack that Anny set before him.

At the culmination of the War of Independence, Yitzchak resumed his duties in the kibbutz. He was sent to accounting school. He held many administrative jobs in the kibbutz, treasurer, workforce organizer, delegate to the agricultural co-op of kibbutzim, and also served as vice-president of the council of the Z'vulun region. Even though he held very responsible jobs, he worked at the stable and other similar jobs when he didn't have to travel on various assignments.

We had the pleasure of spending time with him while he visited the States. Every time we visited Israel, we made sure we saw Yitzchak. He was an inspiration to us and many others. Yitzchak was a unique human being; his life dedicated to his country. He passed away after a long illness, in his late seventies. I miss him greatly. His memory will be with me as long as I live.

REMEMBERING A DEAR FRIEND,
GEORGE GARFIELD

 During the period when I owned the C & R Embroidery factory, I met George Garfield. It was a one-in-a-million chance! I was meeting many production managers of various garment manufacturers in order to obtain work. George was working for a large lingerie firm. When I came to see him, I noticed that George too had a foreign accent. One word led to another, and to our great surprise, we found out that George was on the same freighter as Anny and her parents on their illegal journey to Palestine. They both were very excited to meet. George knew Anny's parents from the ship and Anny as well. Anny however, then a child, did not remember him. Nevertheless, it was an emotional reunion. A friendship was established with George and his wife Susi, whom he had married in Palestine.

George was an active member in B'nai B'rith Lodge, #15, the Jordan Manhattan lodge, one of the oldest in B'nai B'rith. I joined and was eventually elected president. Amazing as it sounds, I with my poor diction, my strong Polish accent, had a very successful term. I noticed that monthly meetings were down to a handful of members, even though the lodge had a membership of several hundred. Members supported the organization money-wise, but there was little interest in attending meetings. This changed when the wives, who were members of the women's chapter, became involved.

We started to organize combined socials. The meetings came to be well attended, lively gatherings. When George completed his term, I was installed as his successor.

At the installation, several members presented a skit, "This is Your Life, George."

It was a great surprise to him, especially when Anny, as part of the skit, rendered the story of the Exodus-type freighter that brought both of them to Palestine. Naturally, she mentioned the way I met

George in New York.

While living in Palestine George joined the Haganah. He was on many dangerous missions. One of his tasks was to fill hand grenades with explosives. This was done in a secluded part of an orchard and always alone, so as not to lose two people in case of a mishap. When the State of Israel was established, George served as bodyguard to David Ben Gurion. He also drove cars or trucks loaded with ammunition to needed sites. This was done during the night, without headlights on, so as not to be detected by the British or the Arabs. These assignments were also one-man missions. In 1956, George and Susi moved to the United States.

George was very well liked. His polite manner, his uniquely clean humor and his dedication were admired and greatly appreciated by everyone who knew him.

The Lermans and the Garfields have been friends for many years. The Garfields moved to Florida and there we visited often. George passed away in 1995. He is greatly missed by many. Susi continues the tradition of our friendship.

(JACOB) YAAKOV LANEL, A FRIEND, A HERO

Yaakov Lanel was born a year before me in Tomaszov. He was the son of a melamed, a teacher who taught in the heder for Jewish children. Yaakov was one of four boys. The family occupied a single room. During daytime, this room was the kitchen and classroom. When evening arrived, and it was time to sleep, the benches were laid out to turn into sleeping cots. This family was very poor, but rich in knowledge and love.

Yaakov's older brother, Shimon, was a genius. He could make music by filling tea glasses to different levels with water. Using a metal object, he would tap the glasses creating a melody. He taught himself Spanish from a book and then taught the daughter of a Polish nobleman the language.

Yaakov, though not as gifted as his older brother, was very studious and well read. Yaakov arrived in Palestine about a year after I did. He joined a kibbutz but left. Not every person is made for commune living. He worked for some time in Hedera, located halfway between Tel Aviv and Haifa. When his job in an orange grove ended, and there was no other work available, Yaakov decided to come to Tel Aviv. He stayed with me and since I was working at the time as a painter, I took him along. The depression made it harder and harder to find work, and Yaakov moved to Haifa.

He found a room with a young couple, and soon they were a family. Yaakov was unemployed, as were so many other pioneers. He was taking in laundry, washing it and pressing it. His landlord had a job at the Shemen factory where oil and margarine, soap and other items were produced. It was the only manufacturer of these products in Palestine at that time. Yitzhak, the landlord, was able to get Yaakov a job there. In 1939, Yaakov decided to visit his family in Poland. He barely escaped the Holocaust, as Poland was occupied by the Germans in September 1939. Yaakov fled through neighboring countries to Romania and made it to a ship to Palestine. Back home, he resumed his job at the factory and continued his service in the Haganah.

In 1944, he enlisted in the Jewish Brigade, a division of the British Army. The Jewish soldiers were the most dedicated soldiers. Yaakov was fighting as a canonist in Italy and took part in the occupation of Bologna. When the war ended, he was stationed in Italy. In 1945, I received a letter from Yaakov who wrote that his brigade was assigned to remain in Italy. After some time, he was sent to France, Holland, Belgium, Germany and Austria. They were part of a so-called peacekeeping force, to retain some order in the chaotic post-war situation. While in Austria, Yaakov took part in taking survivors from Austria into Italy, via the Alps. Once over the mountains, they boarded illegal transports destined for Palestine. He was discharged in August 1946. He served over two years and received the "Italy Star" and an exemplary military conduct discharge.

Yaakov was in the Haganah before he enlisted, and as soon as he returned, continued his duties. He got his job back at the factory. Yaakov was a skilled marksman. The Arabs started the war in 1948. Yaakov was a troop leader, defending a post in downtown Haifa. The British withdrew, but gave the Arabs ammunition and strategic advantages. It was believed that the British shot at some Jewish posts. One bullet pierced Yaakov's main artery on his upper leg. There was no electricity in Haifa. The doctors could not operate. Later, they were unable to save his leg, as gangrene had set in. His leg had to be amputated.

Yaakov was an avid hiker. Whenever he had spare time, he would set out on hikes in different parts of the land. He was a member of a group called Nature Lovers. The loss of his leg was devastating for Yaakov. Anny was devastated too, as she had become very fond of Yaakov.

After several operations, Yaakov was transferred to a rehab center in Jaffa, where he was fitted with a prosthesis. He was in a depressed state. He went back to work as a bookkeeper at the Shemen factory. His love for nature did not diminish. You could not have asked for a better guide. Whenever a visitor arrived in Israel, whether a friend from his hometown, who was living now in the U.S.A., or a relative or even a friend of a friend, they looked forward to having Yaakov show them the countryside in his specially equipped Volvo.

Whenever Anny, the children and I visited, it was a great treat to have Yaakov take us on a day trip. He was unique in transferring his love for the country to his guests. He knew how to make it so very interesting, and he was so knowledgeable.

He married very late in life, and passed away in1987. He was a very special person, and an inspiration to many. He is talked about and thought about frequently, but especially he is missed by all his admirers whenever they visit Israel.

Yaakov was very disciplined and honorable. He was serious yet had a great sense of humor. He could tell great jokes, making one laugh.

Whenever Anny and I visit, we see Rachel, his wife, her son David, and his family

Not a week goes by without my mentioning friend Yaakov.

RIVKAH ARBESFELD GOLDSTEIN

Rivele, as she was called in Tomaszov, led quite an eventful life. She was one of five children born to an observant Jewish couple the Arbesfelds, who were our neighbors. Her parents were Orthodox but not Hasidic. She mingled with the Polish gentile children at public school. She did not experience much anti-Semitism because she spoke Polish and dressed like the gentile girls. It was different for boys; they looked different with their earlocks and special caps. They studied after school at the Yeshiva and spoke only Yiddish. They were slower to pick up Polish. Rivele was barely a teenager when I left for Palestine and I befriended her only later in life.

At the onset of the war, after Tomaszov was bombed by the Germans, the Arbesfelds moved to Lvov. The city went from German occupation to Russian and then back to German. Once, the Germans caught her grandfather and cut off his beard, including part of his chin. During the Russian occupation of Lvov, the Arbesfelds were asked where they would like to relocate. They said they wished to go back to Tomaszov. It was a big mistake. Their request was looked upon as disloyalty to Russia and they were punished for it.

The Arbesfelds and one grandfather were put on a train and traveled several weeks under harsh conditions, arriving finally in Siberia. It was one of many labor camps located in the northwestern part of the country, stretching down from the Arctic Circle.

The weather is treacherous with long cold winters. No one could escape from such a place, as there was nowhere to go.

The Arbesfelds were assigned to a barracks that they shared with two families. In order to get food rations, everybody had to work. The work was felling trees and chopping the logs into pieces. If one wants to eat, one learns fast. Rivele and her sister learned how to use the big saw with a handle on each end.

When the family arrived in Siberia, it was summer. They were greeted by blood-sucking flies, millions of them, getting into everything. When winter came, the family was unprepared.

They had no winter clothing. They wrapped their shoes with strips of potato sacks, and wore sacks over their clothing. The grandfather was too frail to work and received no rations. Even though they gave him of their rations, he could not withstand the harsh conditions and he died.

Finally, after fourteen months, they were transferred to Bisk, another Siberian city, where conditions were much better. Everyone found work. There were doctors for the sick. With the end of the war, they were sent to a displaced persons camp in Germany, set up by the Allied forces. She met Monue Goldstein, a young man from Tomaszov, and they tied the knot in 1946. Three years later, they arrived in Israel with their little daughter, Galila.

Israel was in its infancy in 1949, trying to absorb the influx of Holocaust survivors. Food was rationed; unemployment was at its peak. I had just started the feed business and mentioned to the Goldsteins that they might get started with some chickens which required only a small investment. The government provided an abandoned Arab house on the outskirts of Jaffa. They worked extremely hard there, but Rivele said this was paradise compared to the labor camp. Everything was bearable because they were home. Their second child was born, and named Tova (good in Hebrew).

Monue was an enterprising fellow, and once the chickens were on a routine, he began building small apartment condominiums. Gradually, he developed a big business, and became one of the respected builders in Bat Yam.

Once her girls were in school, Rivele had time to do the work which suited her most. She was a specialist in finding anyone in need. Her house was open. She advised and gave monetary help to many new immigrants. She became president of a chapter of B'nai B'rith Women, (now Jewish Women International) and then gave her time to Ilan, the organization working for polio victims.

She gave of herself, besides donating money. She visited schools, rehab centers and hospitals. When the Russian immigrants came, she convinced a neighbor to rent a vacant apartment for a very low rent to a Russian family. She spoke Russian and could help besides giving money. She always made it look like she was the one to benefit, and not the immigrant.

When the Ethiopians arrived, she visited a class that she sort of adopted. She collected clothing for the children and their families, and bought them craft supplies. When we visited Israel, we always enjoyed hearing about the various accomplishments of the organizations she worked for.

I recall walking with her on busy Allenby Street, engrossed in conversation. Suddenly I realized I was talking to myself. I noticed that she stopped at every beggar, handing out some money. Then she sprints across a street, and what do I see? Another beggar. It seems she knew them all. Without a big fanfare, she does her good deeds.

The Goldsteins were a happy family, enjoying their four lovely grandchildren when tragedy struck. They lost a grandchild in an auto accident. It was shock to all of us, but for them it was devastating.

While I write these lines, Monue has passed away, but getting on in years does not hinder my dear Rivele, called Rivkah in Israel. She was not a pioneer, but her love for her country is not less than anyone's. Rivele, keep up your good work. Wherever you are, you'll find somebody who is in need of attention.

Grandpa

Violence and fear filled your life,
not being able to stay in one place,
going from Poland to Israel,
and still having to run,

Losing most of your family,
to Hitler's nasty clan,
fighting in war,
Protecting your Israel,
only to see your best friend killed,
and your son in a wheelchair,

You built up your courage,
during those years,
Never letting anyone break you down,
You've endured enough pain,
to last 10 lifetimes,

Now Hussein was terrifying Israel,
And you had to go back,
Back to Tel Aviv to watch the scuds,
and see your Israel,
the way you used to.

Justin Morris, Age 12